Classic Family Portraits

Lighting, Posing, and Composition for Location and Studio Photography

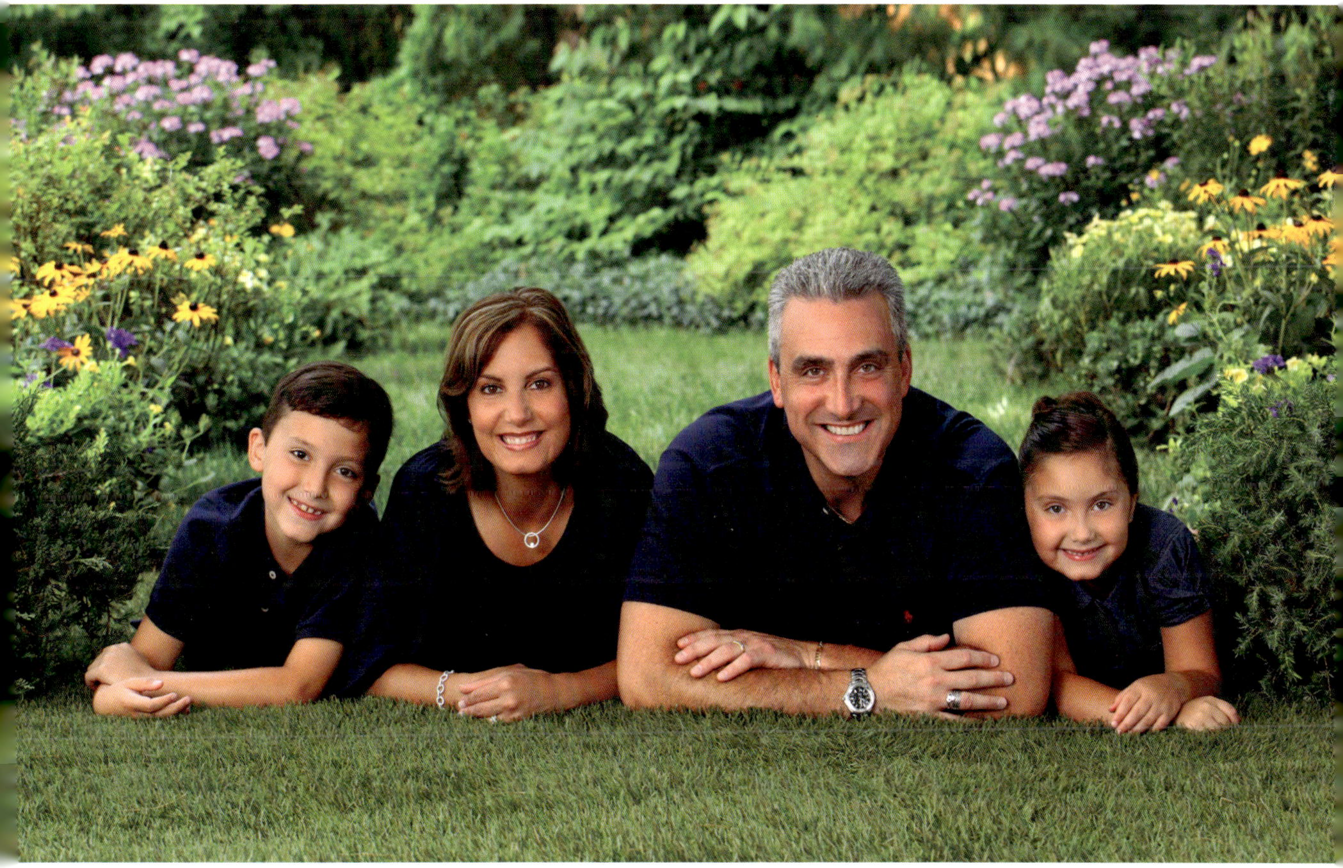

Ed Pedi
M.Photog.Cr.

Amherst Media, Inc. ■ Buffalo, NY

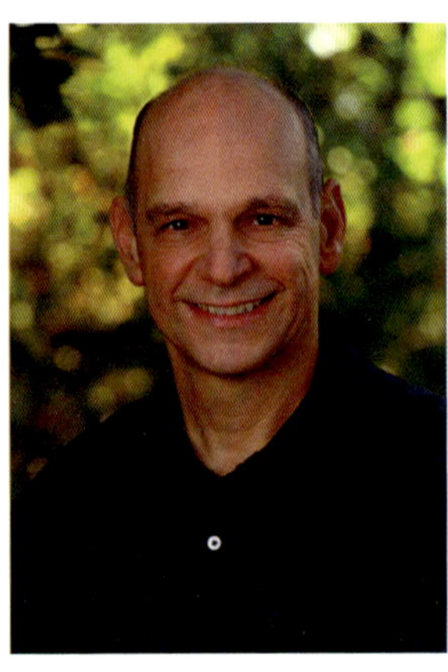

About the Author

Ed Pedi, M.Photog.Cr., CPP,is an award-winning photographic portrait artist who creates beautiful storytelling-images. He works exclusively in photographing family and children because he believes that family heritage is at the foundation of our very being.He is the recipient of numerous national awards such as Professional Photographer of America's Photographer of the Year award, four Kodak Gallery Awards; six FUJI Masterpiece Awards; three Court of Honor Awards, and many Judges Choice Awards. His images have been displayed at the Kodak Exhibit at Disney's Epcot Center and he has images published in *Professional Photographer Magazine*. His portraits can be viewed on his web-site: www.edpediphoto.com.

Copyright © 2014 by Ed Pedi
All rights reserved.
All photographs by the author unless otherwise noted.

Published by:
Amherst Media, Inc.
P.O. Box 586
Buffalo, N.Y. 14226
Fax: 716-874-4508
www.AmherstMedia.com

Publisher: Craig Alesse
Senior Editor/Production Manager: Michelle Perkins
Associate Editor: Barbara A. Lynch-Johnt
Associate Publisher: Kate Neaverth
Associate Editor: Beth Alesse
Editor: Harvey Goldstein
Editorial Assistance from: Sally Jarzab, John S. Loder, Carey A. Miller
Business Manager: Adam Richards
Warehouse and Fulfillment Manager: Roger Singo

ISBN-13: 978-1-60895-701-9
Library of Congress Control Number: 2013952499
Printed in The United States of America.
10 9 8 7 6 5 4 3 2 1

No part of this publication may be reproduced, stored, or transmitted in any form or by any means, electronic, mechanical, photocopied, recorded or otherwise, without prior written consent from the publisher.

Notice of Disclaimer: The information contained in this book is based on the author's experience and opinions. The author and publisher will not be held liable for the use or misuse of the information in this book.

Check out Amherst Media's blogs at: http://portrait-photographer.blogspot.com/
http://weddingphotographer-amherstmedia.blogspot.com/

Table of Contents

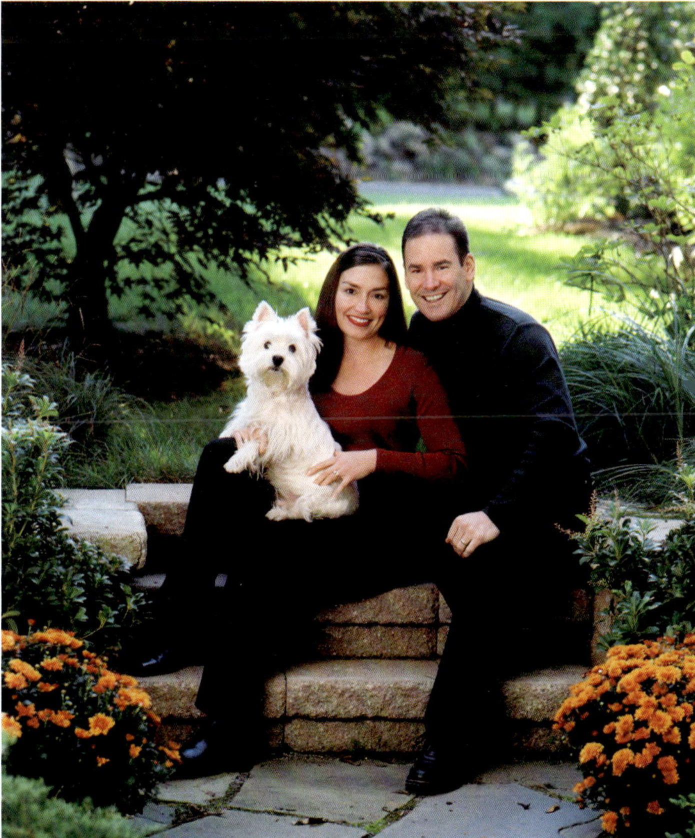

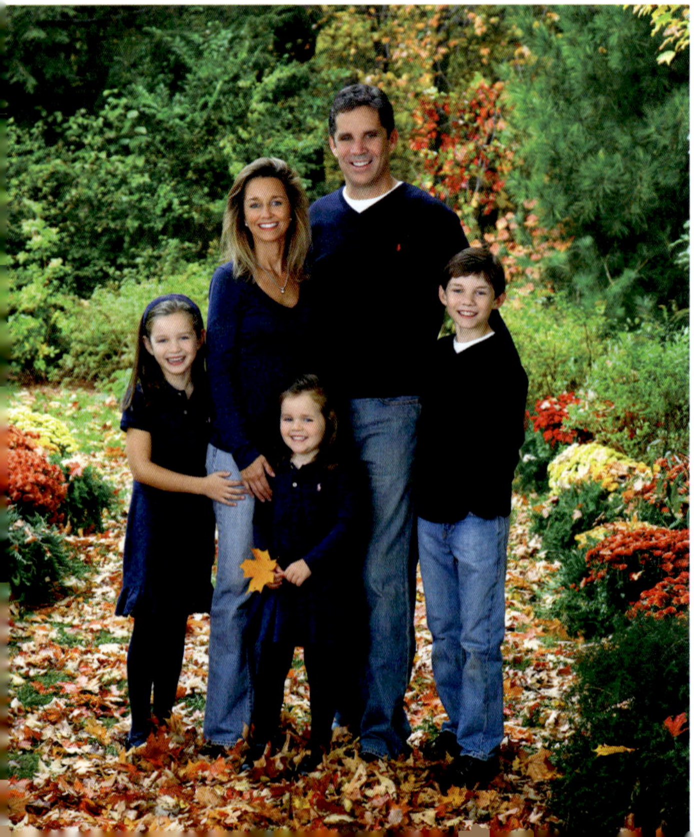

Introduction

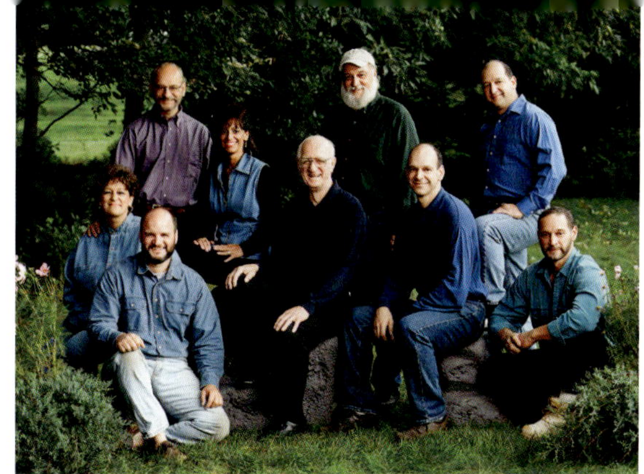

It is my pleasure to introduce Ed Pedi, M.Photog. Cr., CPP, to photographers beyond New England where he is known and highly regarded by other professional photographers. When Amherst Media approached me to collaborate with photographers on a series of books, each with sixty world-class images by a single photographer, Ed Pedi and his family portraits was the first name and subject that came to my mind.

Ed's passion for family portraits was evident in our six-hours of interviews. He excitedly spoke of his love and the importance of family portraits and explained many of the challenges he faced with portraits in this book, including weather for some of the outdoor sessions and tight working spaces at some of the indoor locations. He was always ready for whatever he faced; he always expected the unexpected and he was prepared for it. It is interesting to note that most of Ed's clients call him for updated family portraits every few years; as their families continue to grow, their need for new portraits are important to them. A perfect example is the family we watch grow in *Waiting for Child #3*; *On a Cold, Cold Day in the Snow*; *Another New Addition;* and *All Grown Up.*

Ed's book, *Classic Family Portraits*, holds nothing back as he describes his lighting, posing and composition for location and studio portraits. He has even created his own set of posing rocks to help in the composition of family portraits on location.

Classic Family Portraits is an important tool for those who wish to create beautiful portraits. The information Ed shares is just as important for portraits of individuals as it is with families; it is all about knowing how to pose and light a subject, as well as the composition of groups and incorporating the background to compliment, and not overpower, the subject.

Harv Goldstein, Cr.Photog.

Dedication

- In memory of Len Levy (aka: Mr. NEIPP). Len was a master at working with people and one of the great patriarchs of portrait photography. For 38 years, Len faithfully taught the week-long Basic Photography class at NEIPP and was responsible for launching the careers of so many New England photographers.
- To all photographers who teach. By sharing your knowledge of photography and your business experience, you are contributing to the success of your peers.
- Last but not least, to my wife and best friend Linda who has stood behind me for over 30 years and was the only person who encouraged me to leave my first career and pursue my dream of becoming a full time photographer. Your love means the world to me.

Acknowledgement

A special note of thanks to my friend, Harvey Goldstein for encouraging me. Your guidance and patience during many hours of dictation, transcribing and editing is greatly appreciated.

1 From Ireland with Love

Assignment

This session came about as a result of previous portrait assignments of the family's children's First Communion portraits. The father, who was originally from Ireland, wanted the portrait to be made in back of his house.

Lighting and Exposure

Due to the very sunny conditions, I had to improvise and find shade. With the sun behind the house on the right, I placed the family in the shadow of the house. I use the Photogenic 750 mono flash, which was aimed into a 42-inch umbrella to the left of the camera, raised up on the light stand. I skimmed the light across the faces to illuminate their eyes.

Posing the Family

In posing the family, my premise was that because our culture reads left to right, I was going to have the lines in the portrait also read left to right. I began with the diagonal line from the boy's right foot (extreme left as we view the portrait), to Mom, the big sister, and finally up to the Dad's face.

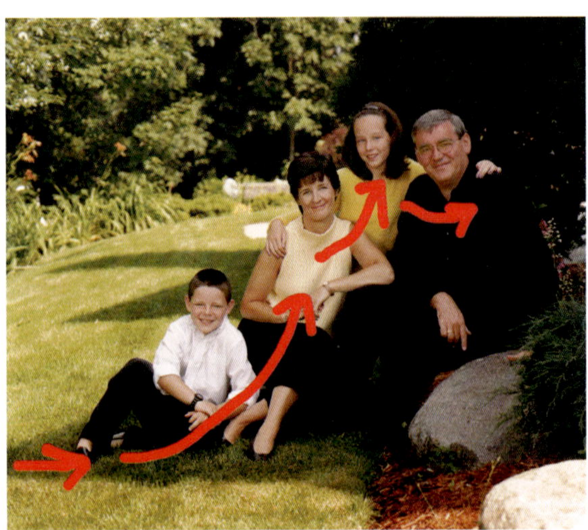

TECH SPECS > I photographed with 400 speed film using a Mamiya RZ67 and 150mm lens. The exposure was f/8, 1/60 second, and 400 ISO.

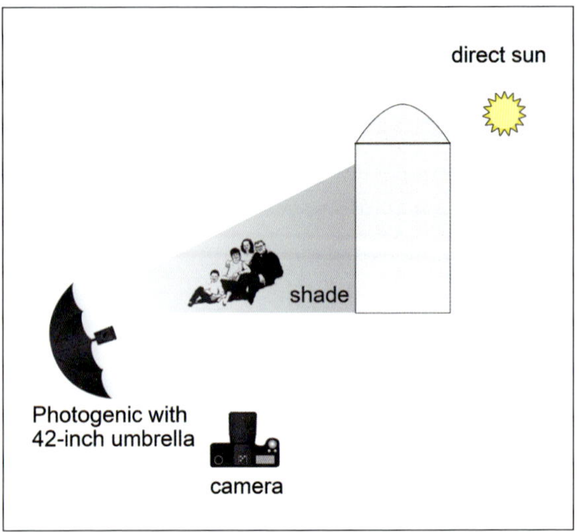

Photographing on Location. Photographing on location will not always be a perfect scenario. Actually, it is rarely a perfect scenario. If the light is terrible, as a professional photographer, you have to look to remedy the situation. I used that little piece of their yard, which made them very happy, and as long as the client is happy, everyone is happy. The key to photographing family portraits on location is to overcome obstacles and build relationships.

The key to photographing family portraits on location is to overcome obstacles and build relationships.

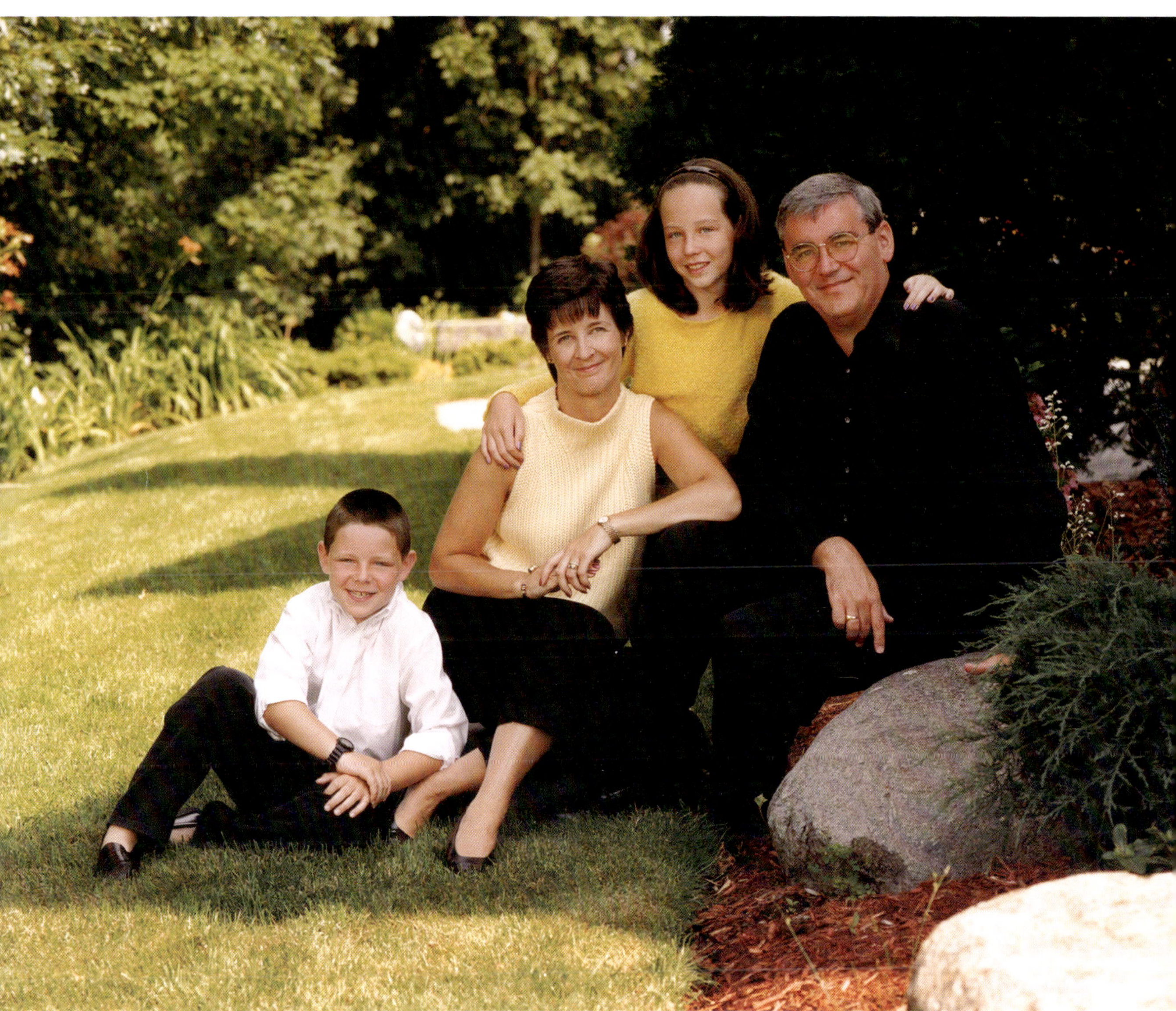

2 A Christmas Portrait

Purpose

This photo may be fifteen years old, but it is still relevant and it still works today. I photographed the three generations at Christmas time, as can be noted by the decorations above the fireplace. The mom and dad on the right requested this family portrait because the grandfather in the center had cancer. He passed away shortly after this was made.

Posing

To make this portrait work, my assistant and I rearranged the furniture, with the family's permission, to give the photo a nice flow. The furniture was moved to an angle so I did not have to photograph them head on, which would have given me a lot of glare on the walls and in the window. Because we read left to right, you are first brought to the man on the floor, then to the grandfather and grandmother, next to their other son and his wife holding the baby, and finally to the little girl on the couch.

Lighting

I balanced my flash with the window light so that when you look at the portrait, the people are lit evenly and the outside is properly exposed as well. I placed the plant on the left to fill the void so that there was no dead space. This helped to balance the composition.

For even lighting, I placed my Photogenic 750 flash unit with a 42-inch umbrella to the left of the camera, feathering the light across the subjects for an even exposure across the whole group. The light needed to be high to avoid the flash reflecting into their eyeglasses.

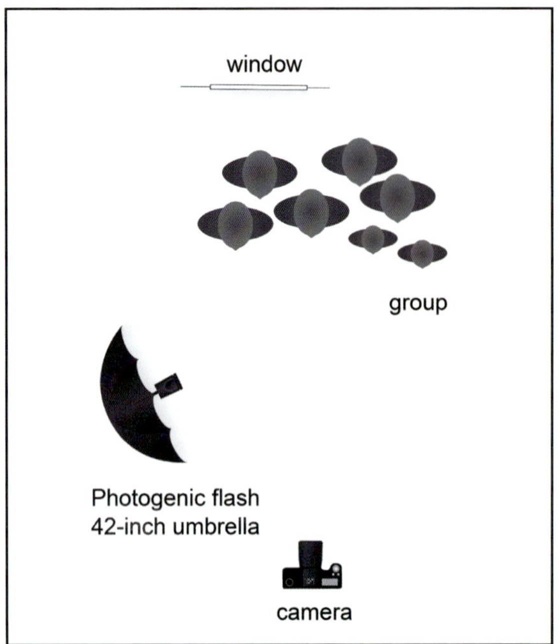

TECH SPECS > I used a Mamiya RZ67 with an 80mm lens. The exposure was f/8 at 1/60 second with Kodak Portra 400 film.

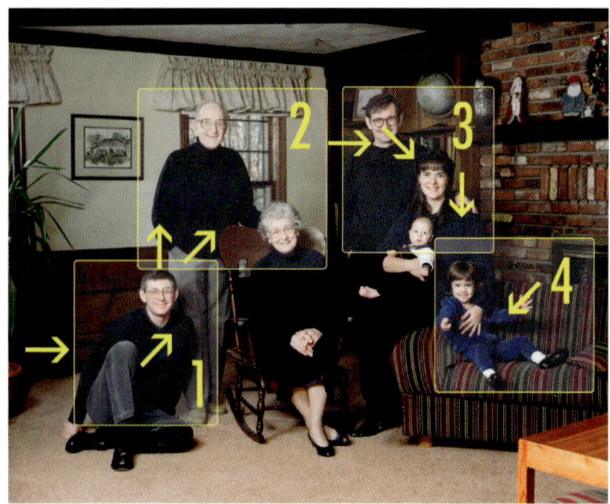

The light needed to be high to avoid the flash reflecting into their eyeglasses.

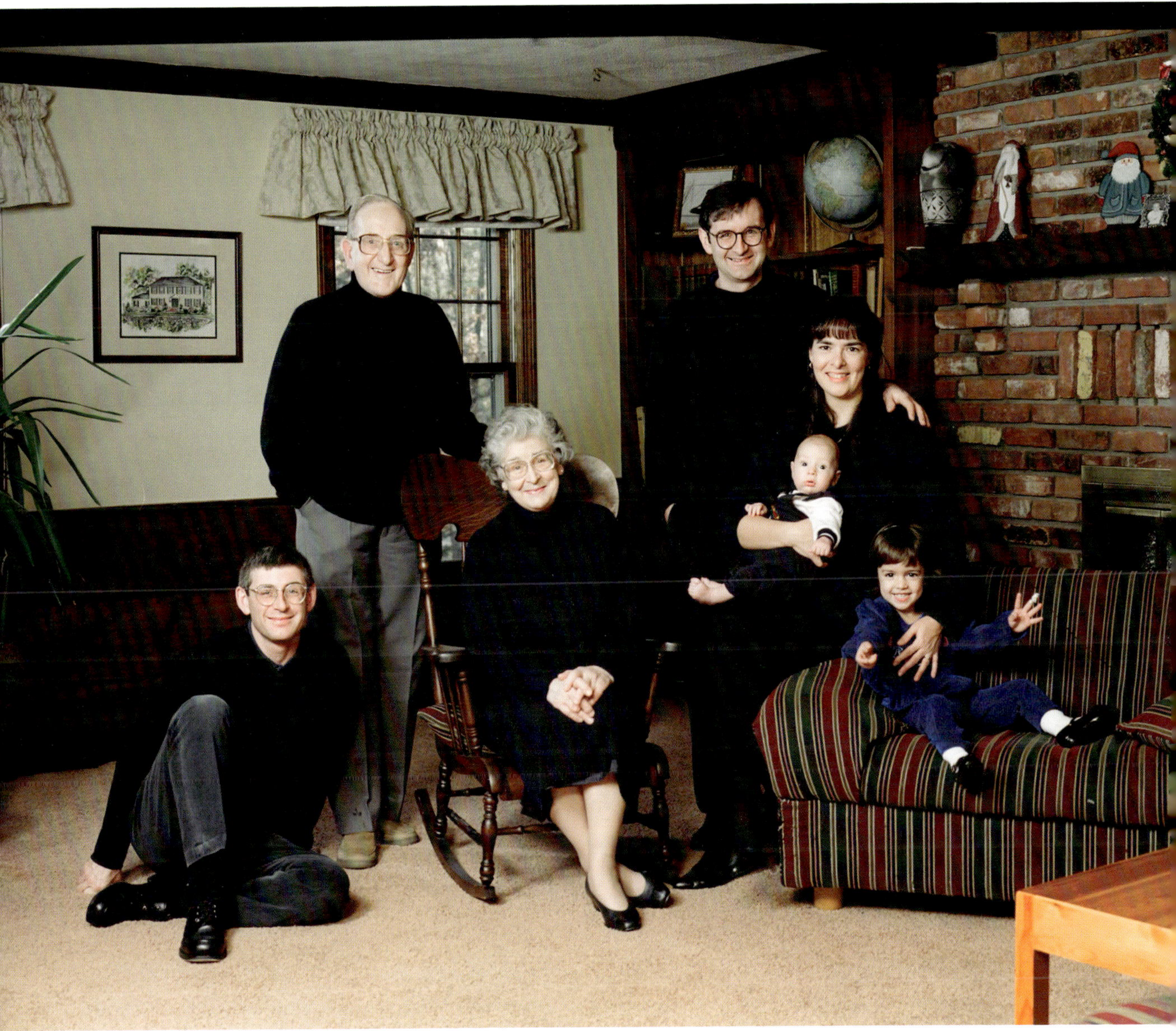

3 Photographing in the Rain

Overcoming Obstacles

One of the brothers was visiting from out of the area and the portrait had to be done that day; they wanted an outdoor portrait even though it was pouring rain. I photographed them in my outdoor studio with a 9x9x9-foot awning (see page 40) above their heads to keep them from getting wet. I used a 4x6-foot softbox on the left skimming across the group with a white 6-foot square panel on the right side to fill in the shadows, so you still get a direction of light. I also used a large patio umbrella that protected me from the rain. The challenge is to please the client. They wanted an outdoor portrait and it was raining; I had to find a way to accommodate their wishes and to produce what the client wanted when they wanted it.

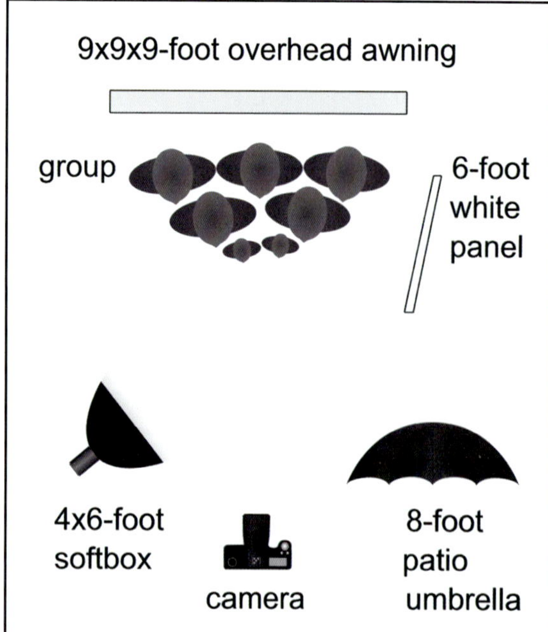

Exposure

I exposed my camera for the light on the background and added flash on the people under the awning to raise the intensity of the light on them and match the light of the background. The 4x6-foot softbox gave me a lot of light, so the light on the subjects was very believable. You would not know how dark and rainy it really was. This proves that you can photograph in the pouring rain and still get a good image.

Breakaways and Sales

I also photographed the children in "breakaways." The family portrait session is not complete until I have photographed every possible combination. In addition to the entire group, I also photograph each family and the children separately, increasing my options for greater sales. Using this approach allows me to sell not just one wall portrait, but multiple wall and gift portraits.

TECH SPECS > This was photographed with my Canon 5D Mark II, using my 24–105mm lens set at 100mm. My exposure was f/7.1, 1/30 second and ISO 800.

The session is not complete until I have photographed every possible combination.

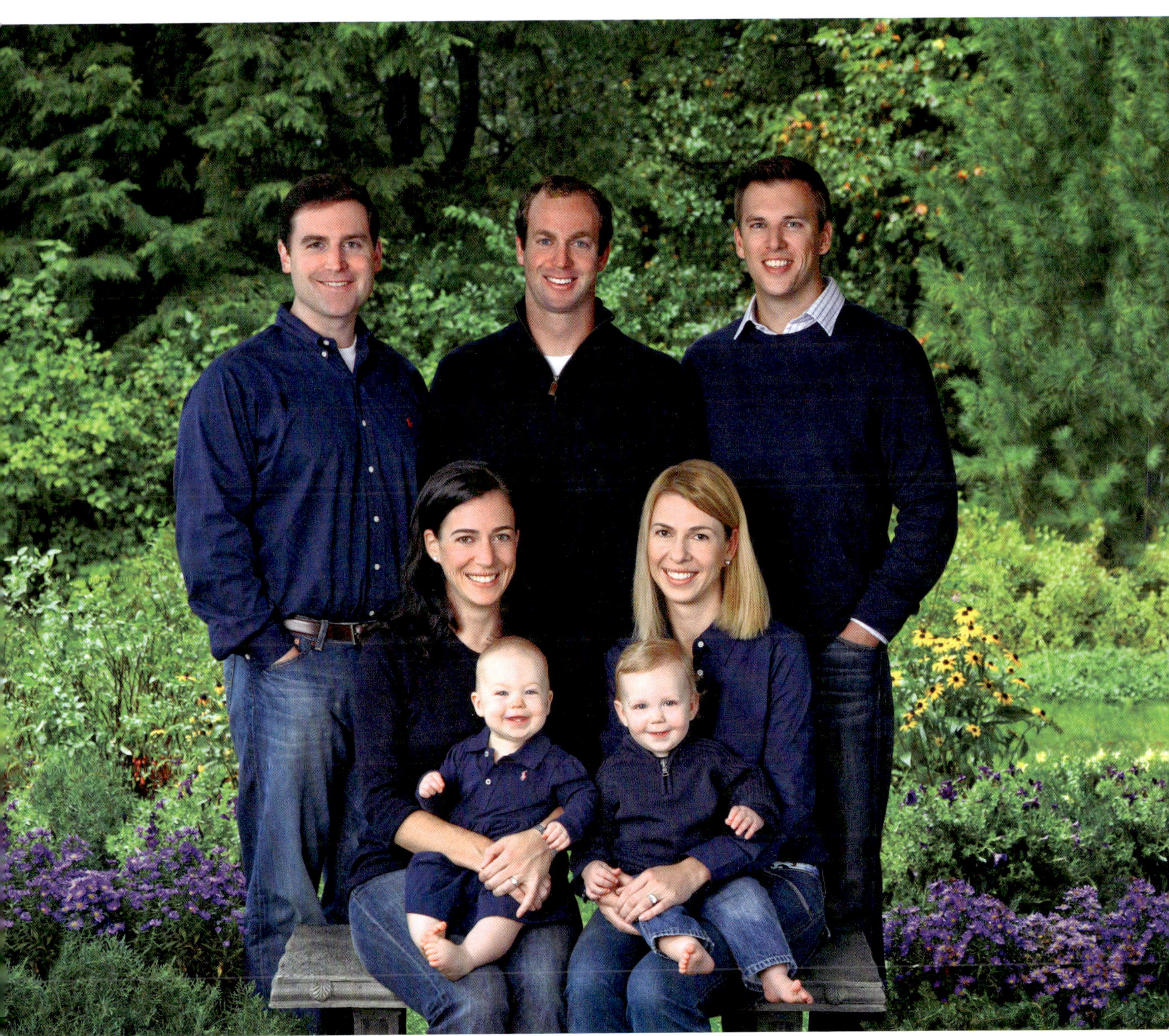

Studio Portrait #1

Purpose

This family has been coming to me for years; I had photographed the two older children's high-school senior portraits. They had recently adopted the little boy on the left, thus the need for a new family portrait. This portrait was created in my studio (see below) using a David Maheu background.

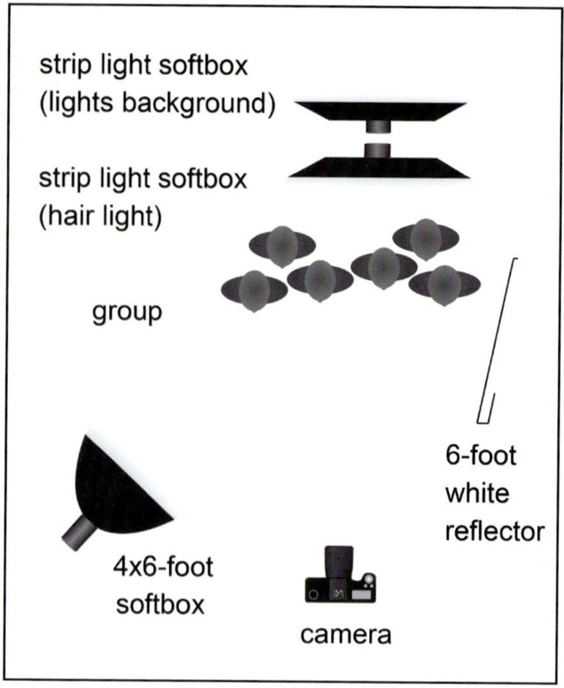

Lighting

My main light was a 4x6-foot softbox set at f/8 placed to the left of the camera, skimming across the group to the right. I used a Photogenic 750 light in a 12x36-inch strip softbox which was attached to the rail system on the ceiling, lighting the background at f/5.6. A 10x36-inch Photogenic in a Larson strip softbox, also at f/5.6 and on the ceiling, served as a hair light and separation light. There was a 6-foot white panel on the right side as a reflector to fill in the shadows.

Clothing Choice

Even though we always discuss clothing in advance, Dad wanted the boys to wear ties but not suits, hence the white shirts. I would have preferred everyone in darker colors, but despite the white shirts, I felt that the portrait was a success. We talk to our clients about darker tones in advance and ask them to check out our web site to see other families, but this is what they wanted to wear and I am fine with it. My objective is to create the best possible portrait when they are with me, and I accomplished that with this portrait.

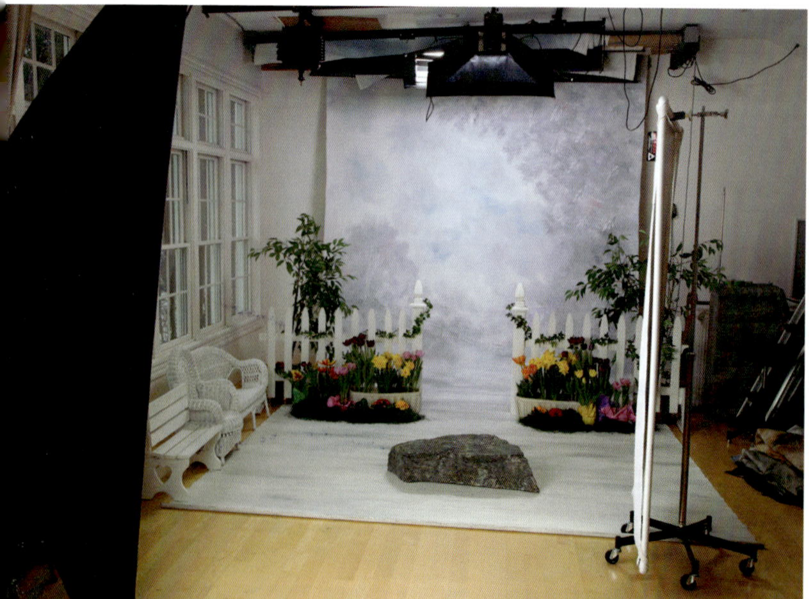

TECH SPECS > I photographed them with a Canon 5D Mark II with a 70–200mm lens at 70mm. The exposure was f/7.1 at 1/125 second and ISO 100.

My objective is to create the best-possible portrait when they are with me.

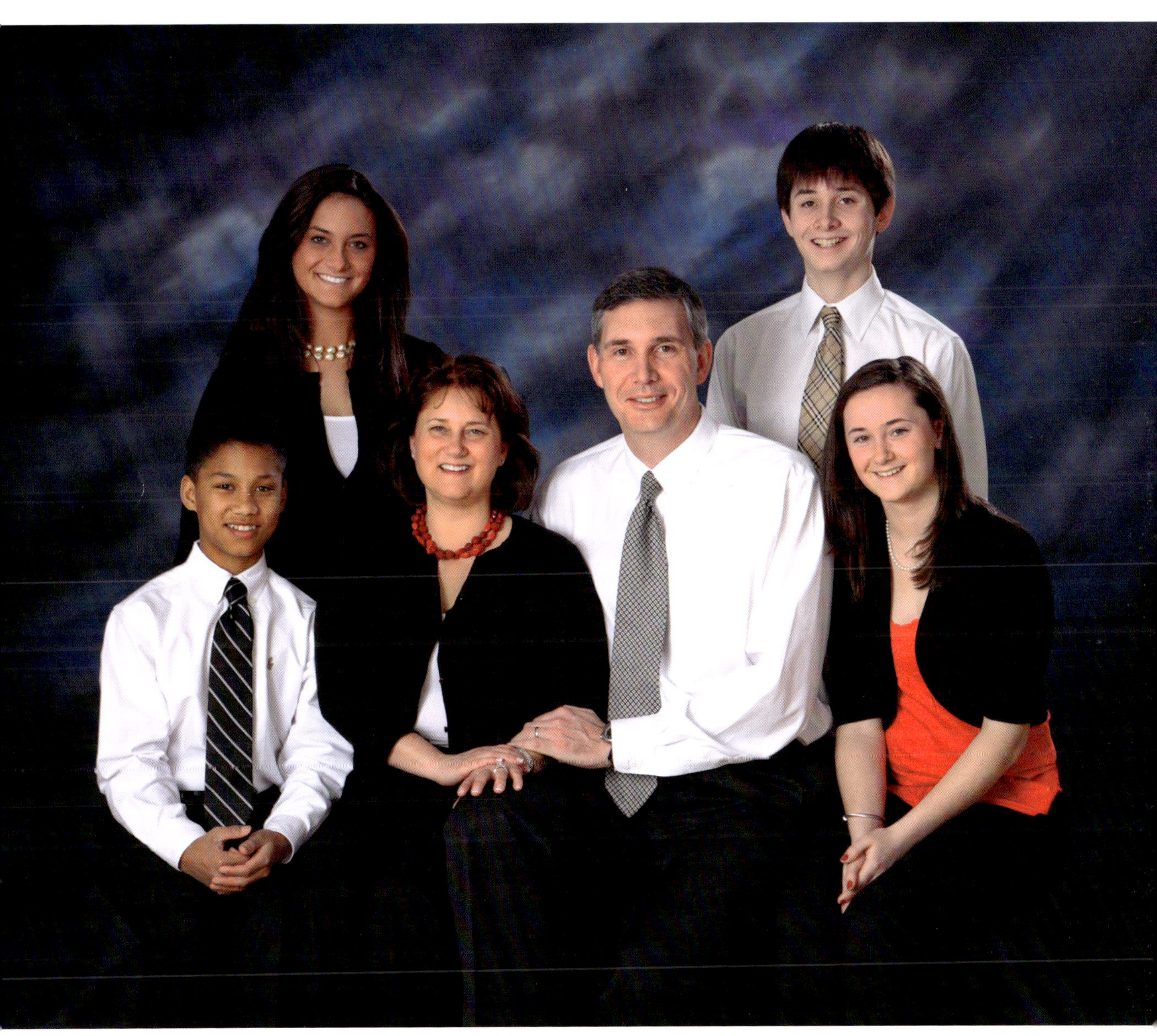

5 One Family, Twenty-Eight People

Purpose

This was a special birthday portrait for the grandfather, seated in the middle of the group. In addition to the portrait of the entire family, I also photographed thirteen breakdowns of the different families and the kids from each family.

Posing

I placed a bench in the middle for the grandparents and one of the daughters. I had three people sitting in chairs and two on my posing rocks. I gave those sitting on the "grass" in the front a square piece of black plastic; it is not visible in the photo but it prevents a wet bottom. I asked for a family tree (a list of names, ages and relationships) a few days in advance. This gave me the opportunity to design the pose of the group before they arrived. By doing this I was able to pose them in just a few minutes. I did not want them to arrive and then have to figure where I would have someone sit or stand.

I metered and balanced my lights before they arrived and set my exposure so when they arrived we could begin the session immediately.

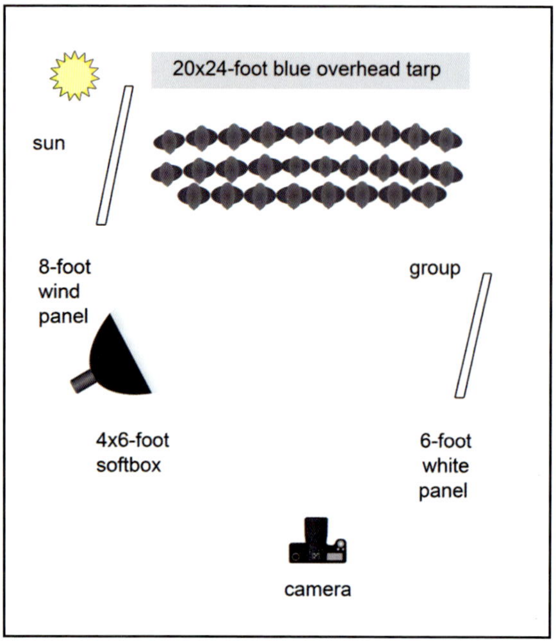

20x24-foot blue overhead tarp
sun
group
8-foot wind panel
4x6-foot softbox
6-foot white panel
camera

Setup

I strung a 20x24-foot blue tarp from a tree on the right to my porch about 15 feet above them. I had a 13-foot stand on the left and tied the tarp to it, extending it to my porch on the left. This was done to block the down-light so they would not have dark circles under their eyes. The tarp was slightly in front of them keeping them in the shade while allowing the sunlight behind them to light the tops of their heads and the trees in the background.

Lighting

The flash was set at f/11, and I used one 4x6-foot softbox, raised up high right next to the camera on the left aimed across the group to those on the right side. By feathering the light I was able to light all of the faces evenly. I used my 6-foot square panel on the right to kick back some light so we did not get green shadows on the faces and my 8-foot wind panel (a scrim with slits in it) on the left to block some of the sun.

TECH SPECS > I used my Canon 5D Mark II with a 24–105mm lens set at 60mm. My exposure was f/11, 1/60 second at 800 ISO.

By feathering the light I am able to light all of the faces evenly.

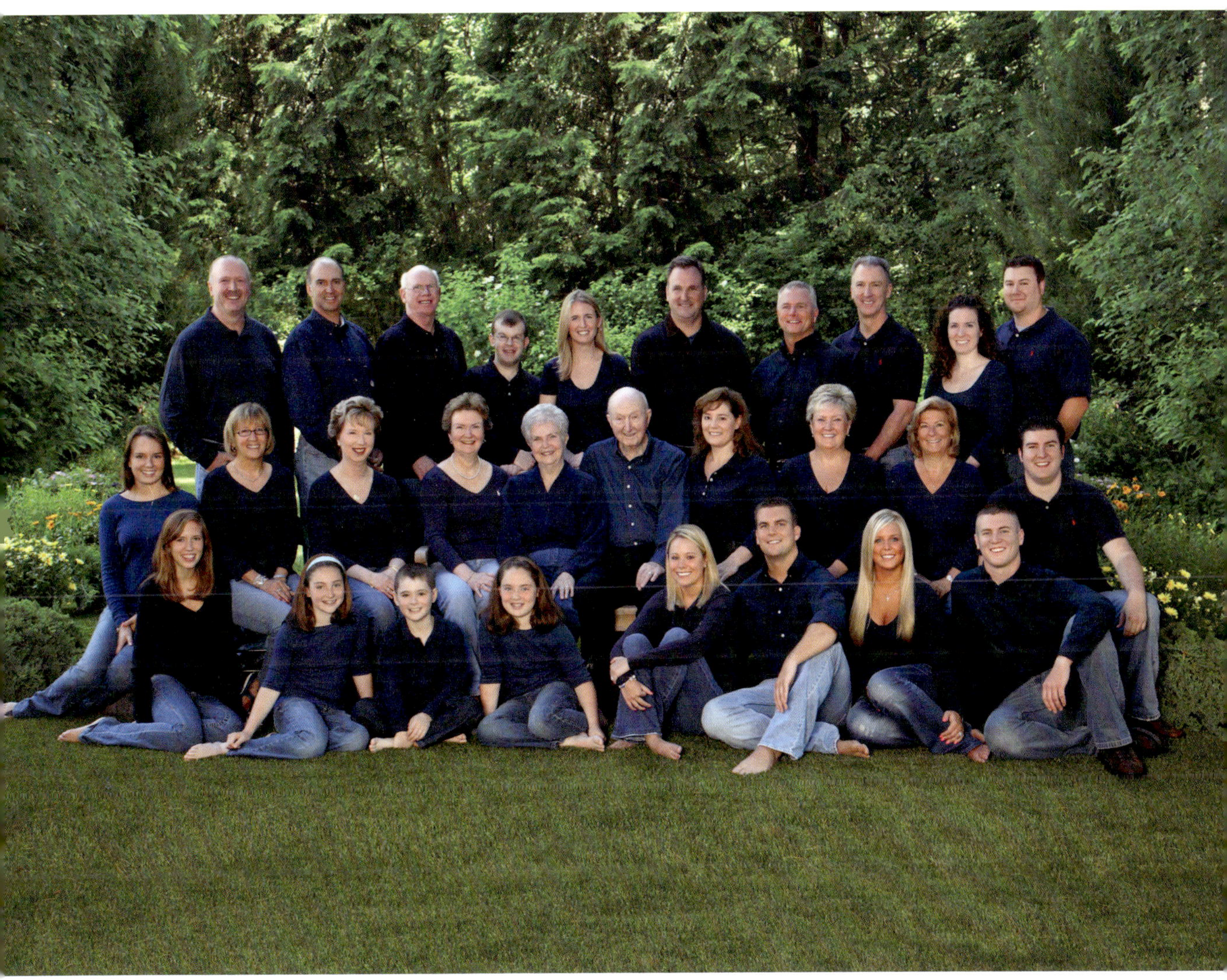

6 Breakaway: From the Group of Twenty-Eight

Purpose

This family portrait is one of the many "breakaways" I did from the group of twenty-eight. The family loved this portrait because the young man with special needs looks great; the mom and dad said that he usually does not look where he needs to look, and I was able to capture the moment.

Posing

The son on the left and the daughter on the right leaned in towards their parents so that there was no space between them. I had them sitting in such a way so that the parents were higher than the kids and Dad was the tallest in the photo. I was also working very fast because I had twenty-four other people around me and I had many more breakaways to do.

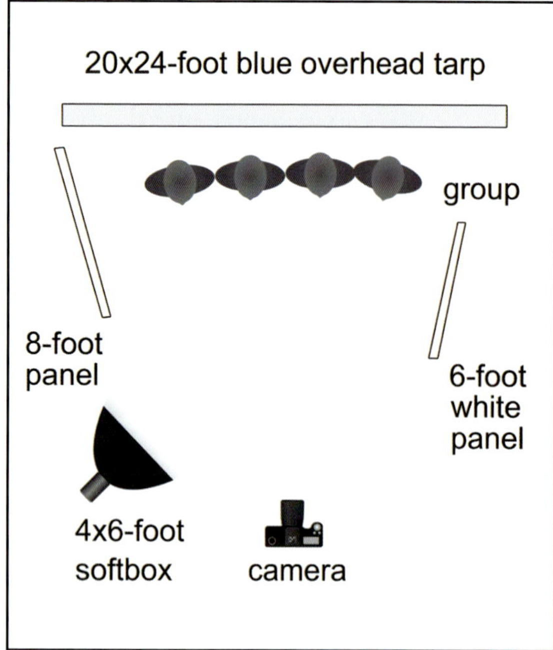

Arranging the Breakaways

When I photograph a large group, I set everything up for that photograph. When I do the breakaways, I leave most of it the same, including the 20x24-foot blue overhead tarp. After I do the larger groups, I ask them for a few moments and start bringing the plants in closer for the smaller groups. I bring the main light in closer and place it more to the side than it was for the large group.

Camera and Lighting

Because it was such a sunny day, I set my ISO for 500 for this portrait as my base exposure. My 4x6-foot softbox was just to the left of the camera. An 8-foot panel to the left of the softbox blocked the ambient light and reflect the directed light onto the subjects. A 6-foot square white panel was placed on the right to reflect light back onto the faces.

Posing Guide. Arrange the family so that the top of the parents' heads are higher than their children even, if they are fully grown. Have the dad as the tallest in the family group. This can be accomplished subtly and artfully by having seats of different heights.

TECH SPECS > This was photographed with Canon 5D Mark II with the 70–200mm lens set at 150mm. My exposure was f/7.1, 1/60 second with 500 ISO and plenty of light in the background.

I was working very fast because I had many more breakaways to do.

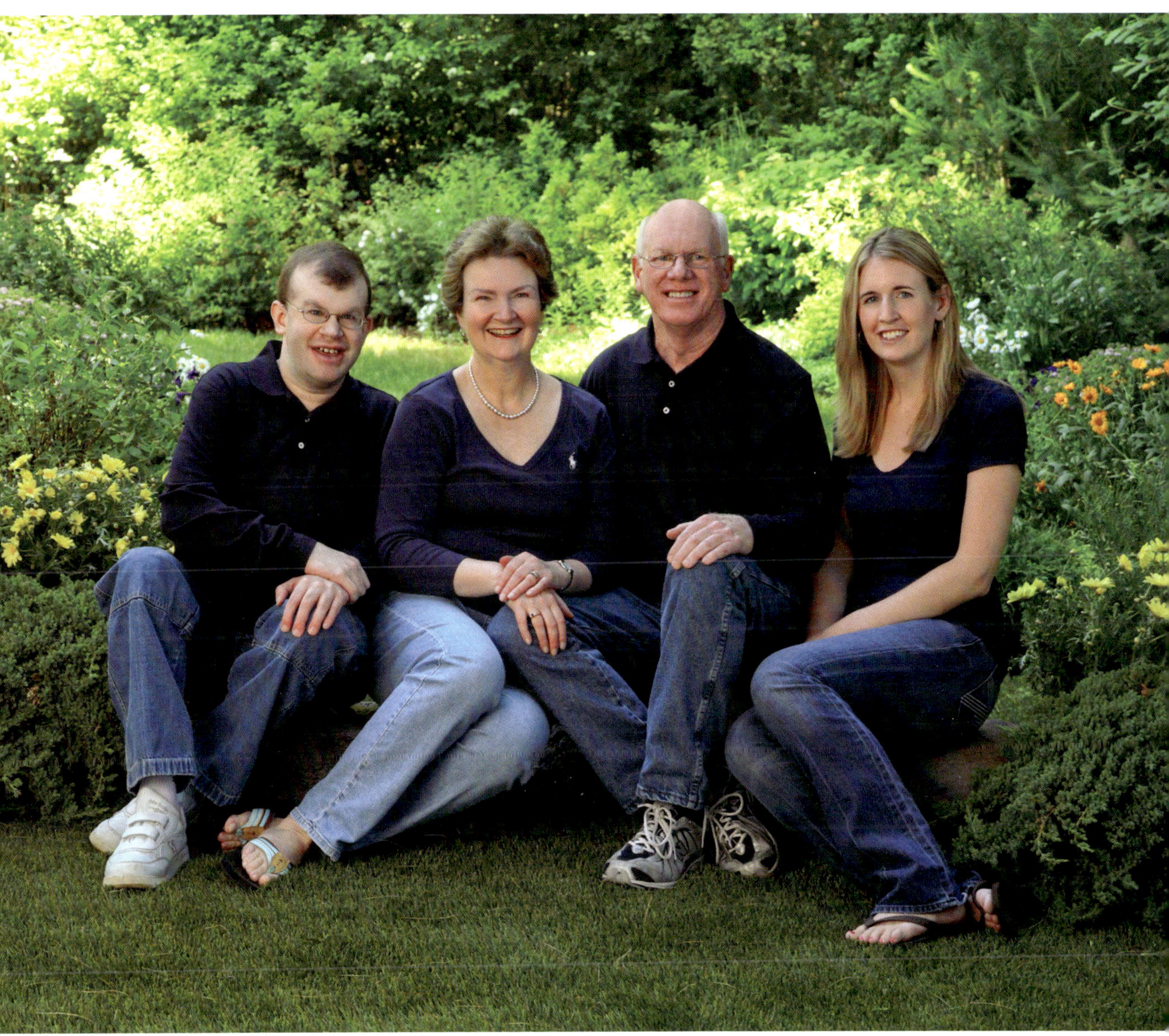

7 Breakaway: Grandparents

Purpose

This is the patriarch and matriarch of the family of twenty-eight and it was a special day for the grandfather. This large portrait session was a celebratory occasion because they had created this wonderful family (see page 15).

Posing and Setup

I used a 4-foot bench to pose them. I would have liked to have positioned them a little lower, but they are not as flexible as the younger people, and this was the best we could do. They were very pleased with this photograph because they look so happy.

Clothing Guide. Dark clothing draws the viewer right to the faces. This works well with small, medium, and large groups.

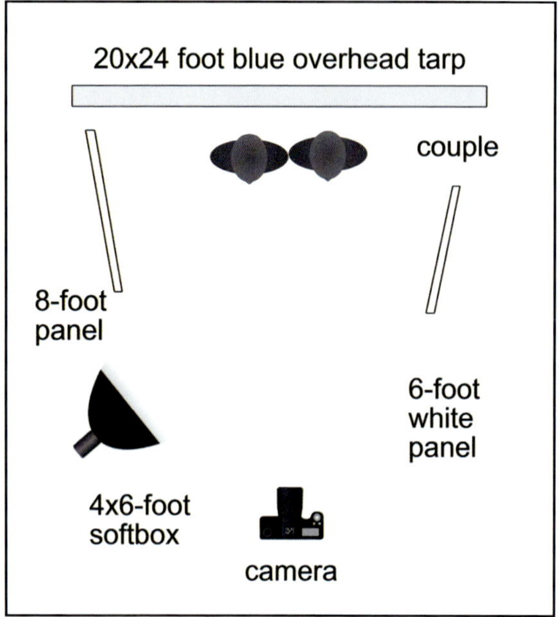

I moved the flowers and plants in on the left and right to fill in the area; it looks so much better than if it were just grass. I moved the flower pots right up to the bench, again filling in the area rather than having a space on either side of the bench. As it got to be around noon, the sun ate up the background with light; they didn't mind it, but I did. However, there was not much I could do about it. This is normally the time I would move to another part of the property, but with such a large group, I stayed and worked with the situation.

Lighting

My ISO remained at 500 for this portrait to set my base exposure for the background, and I brought up the intensity of my flash to balance the people under the awning to the background. My 20x24-foot blue overhead tarp still above them. My 4x6-foot softbox and the 8-foot panel used to block out the sun were on the left. A 6-foot square white panel was on the right, reflecting light back into their faces.

TECH SPECS > This was photographed with a Canon 5D Mark II with the 70–200mm lens set at 180mm. My exposure was f/7.1, 1/60 second with ISO 500 and plenty of light in the background.

My ISO remained at 500 for this portrait to set my base exposure for the background.

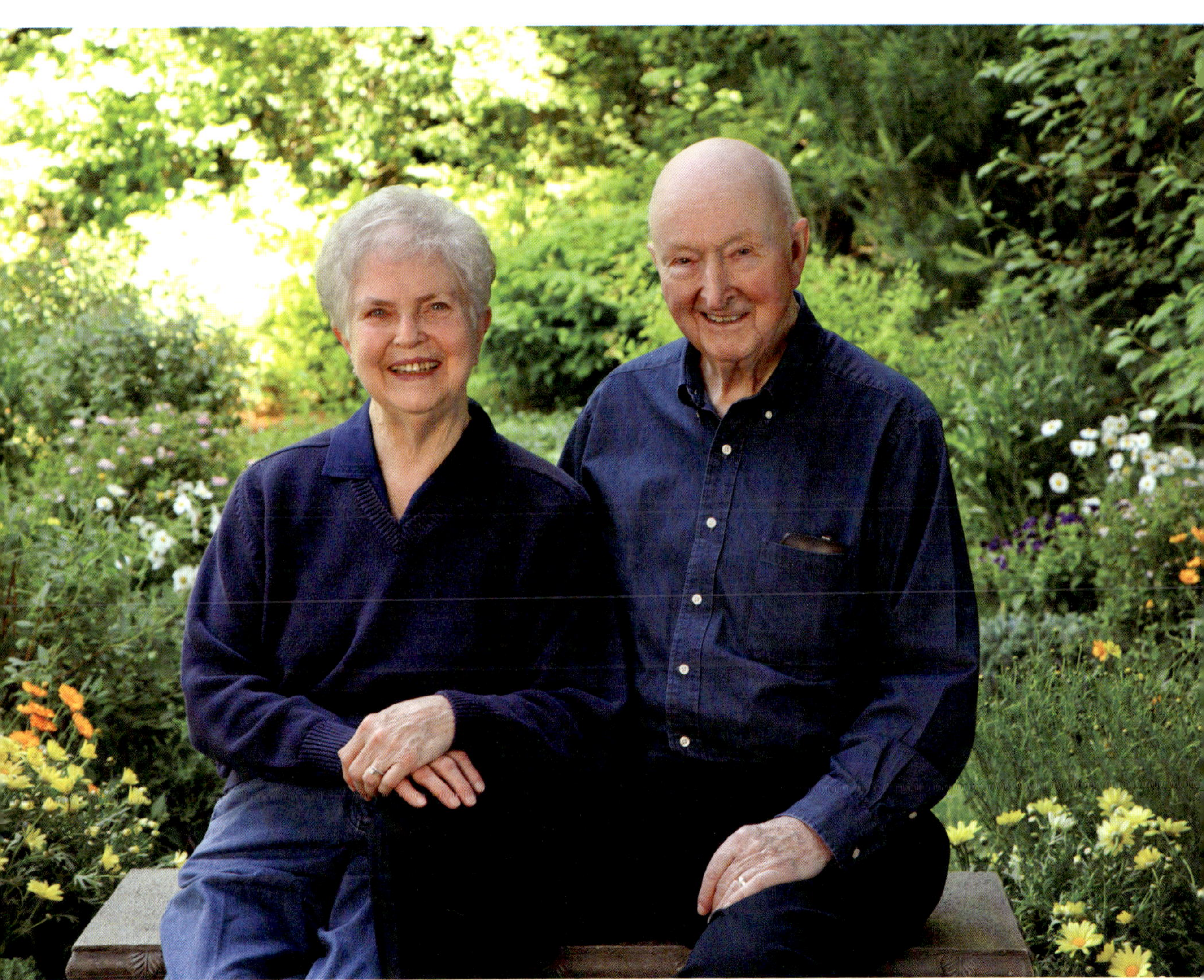

8 Waiting for Child #3

Purpose

This is the first of a series of portraits of the same family that I made over a period of a few years. Mom wanted to have a portrait made of her current family while she was nine months pregnant with the next child and before their family changed. In this first photo made in their backyard garden, she was almost ready to deliver child number three.

Posing Guide. Keep the pose from being too static. Make sure everyone in the group is not on the same level. Use key features, such as eyes, mouth, chin, and the top of heads, to help vary the alignment of elements within the photograph.

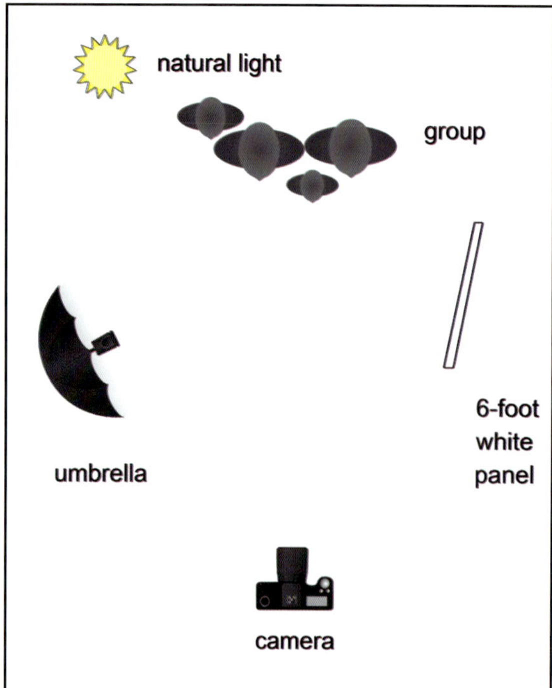

Execution

I photographed them with a Mamiya RZ67 with an 80mm lens. My exposure as set at f/8, 1/125 second, and ISO 400 with natural light from above and light coming from the left from my large umbrella with a 6-foot white panel fill reflector on the right. I posed Mom and Dad sitting on my rocks and had the little boy rest his hand on Dad while the little girl was nestled in the middle on Dad's leg, touching both Mom and Dad. Again, my family portraits are all about relationships.

Posing

Not wanting everyone to be on the same height level, I made sure that Mom's eyes were at the same level as Dad's mouth; the boy's mouth was on the same level as Dad's eyes. I consider this a posing guide to keep the pose from being too static.

TECH SPECS > I photographed them with film using a Mamiya RZ67 with an 80mm lens. The exposure was f/8, 1/125 second, and ISO 400.

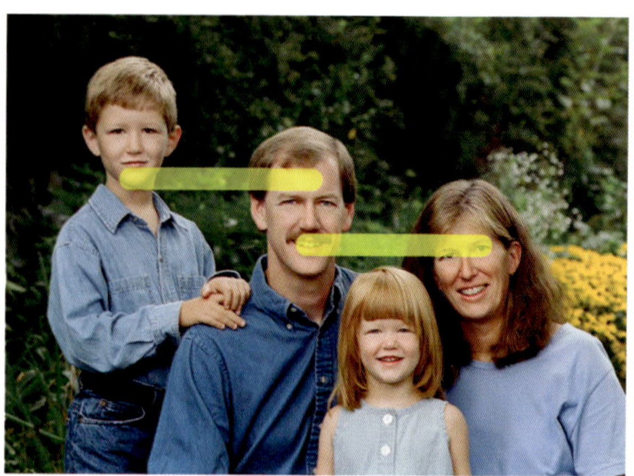

My family portraits are all about relationships.

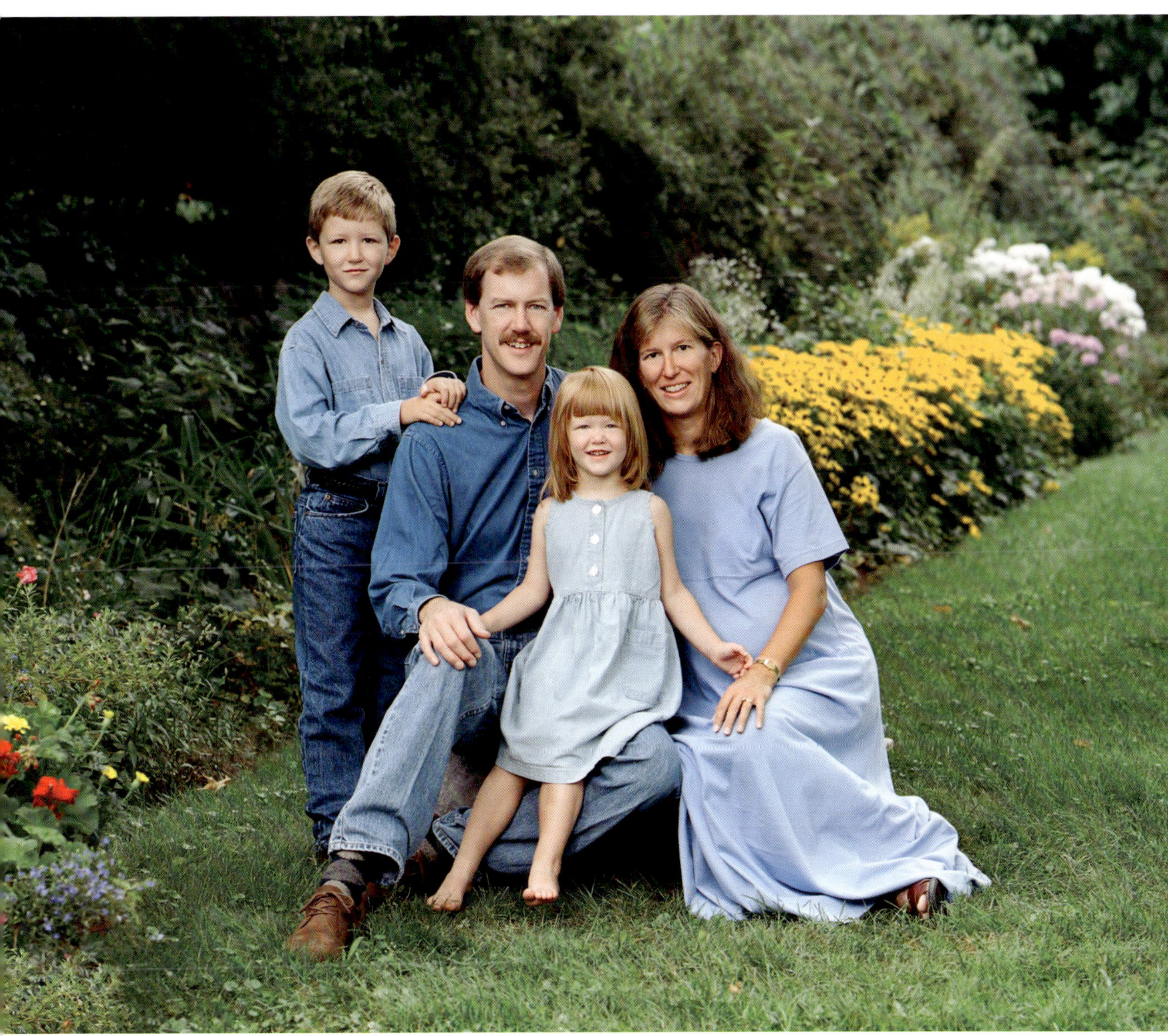

9 On a Cold, Cold Day in the Snow

Objective

This portrait was made a few years after *Waiting for Child #3* when Mom was nine months pregnant with her fourth child. They wanted something different and opted to have their portrait created in their yard.

Setup

It was a *cold* ten degrees when we did this session in the snow. We would do a few exposures, go into the house to warm up, and then return outside for a few more exposures. We did this until the session was complete; we just couldn't stay outside for an extended period of time.

The sweaters that the subjects wore were made by the grandmother, but Mom's sweater wouldn't fit her because she was nine months pregnant. She contacted her father in Wisconsin the day before our appointment, and he overnight-mailed his sweater to her so they could all be dressed alike.

The snowman in the photo was actually made in another part of the yard, but I liked it so much that the dad and I dug it up and moved it to this location.

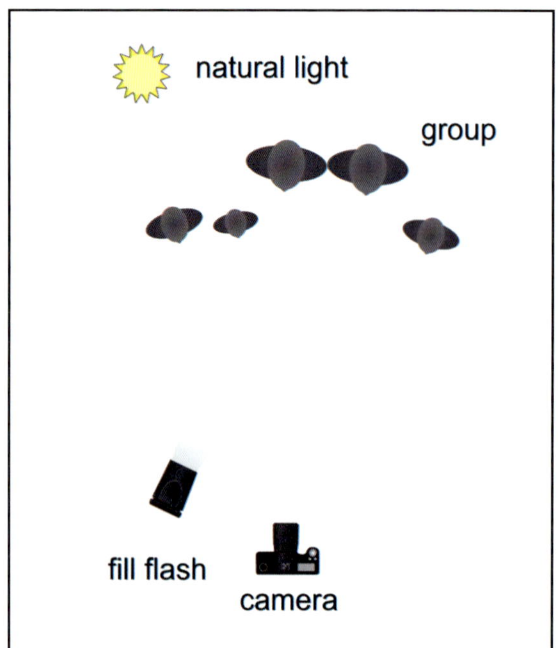

Composition

I am always looking for angles, and I liked the way the fence was positioned in the background. I wanted to photograph them from a higher level rather than straight on, so I brought my step stool. The only problem was that every time I got up on the step stool, it sunk down into the snow.

Lighting

I used an incident light meter and metered for all of the snow. I added a little fill flash to create nice catchlights in their eyes. I was looking for good skin tones and exposing for that; I metered from the people back to the camera. I put my hand above the meter so that I was not picking up the light from the sky which would have influenced my exposure reading.

TECH SPECS > This was photographed with a Mamiya RZ67 using Kodak Portra 100 film with an 80mm lens set at f/8, 1/125 second.

I am always looking for angles, and I liked the way the fence was positioned in the background.

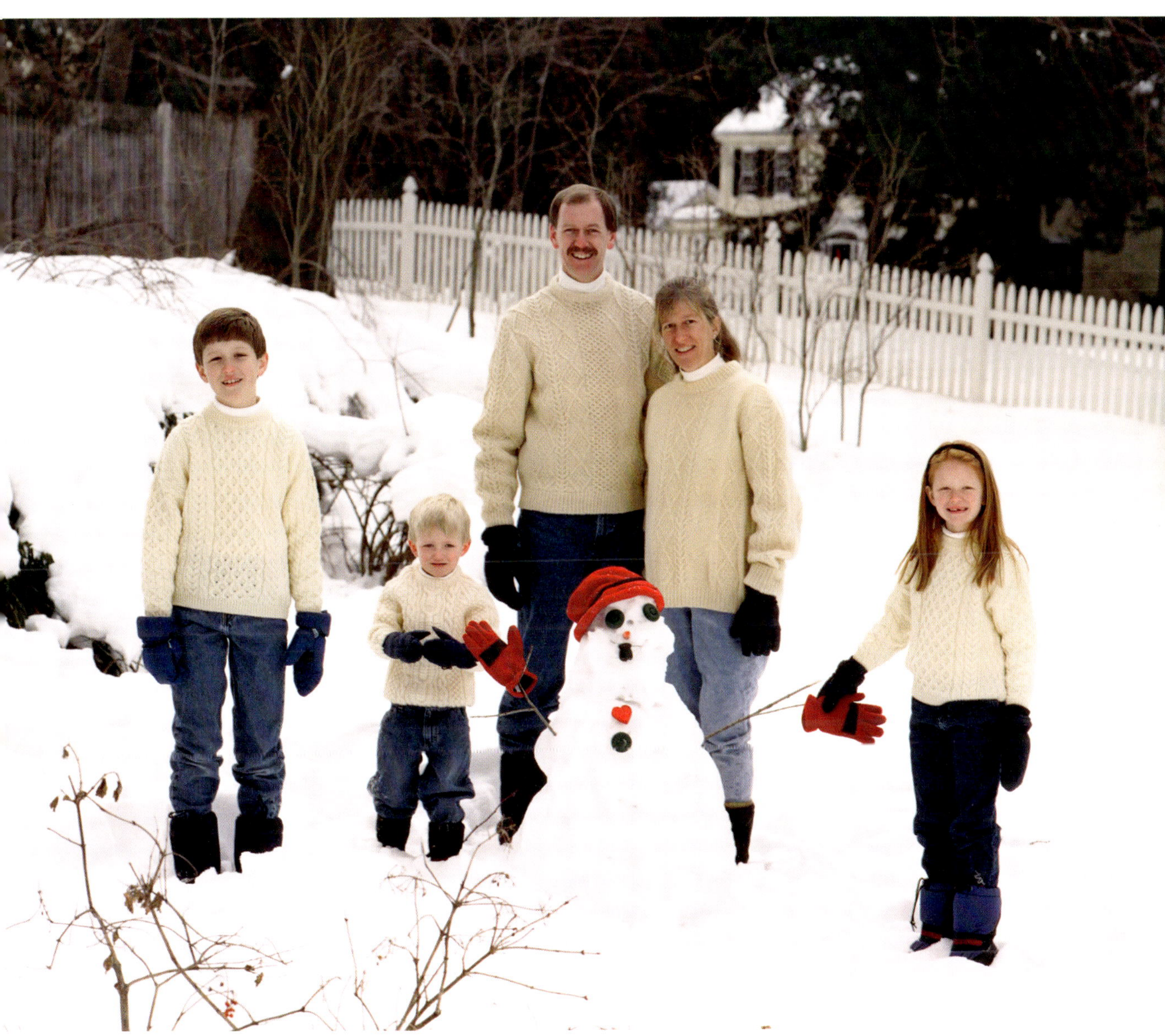

10 Another New Addition

Purpose

The third in the series of the same family is a portrait of them in their home with the family complete. The new addition is this room.

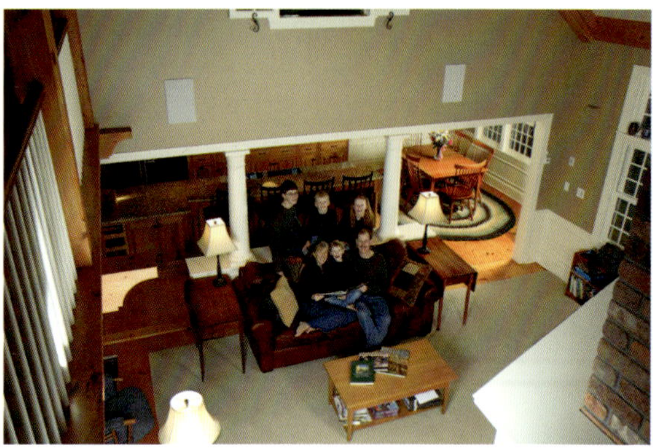

Setup

It was a tight fit; I was standing beside the camera, which was on a tripod up against the fireplace. I brought the table closer to them and asked if they had anything we could place on the table that shows what they like to do as a family. Because they enjoy hiking the national parks in Maine, these magazines worked. I posed the three oldest kids on the back of the sofa and the parents sitting in the front with the youngest child between them.

I had to be sure that the camera was straight; if I had tilted the camera down or up, the columns in the background would have begun to converge. This family loved this pose and purchased a 24x30-inch canvas for their home.

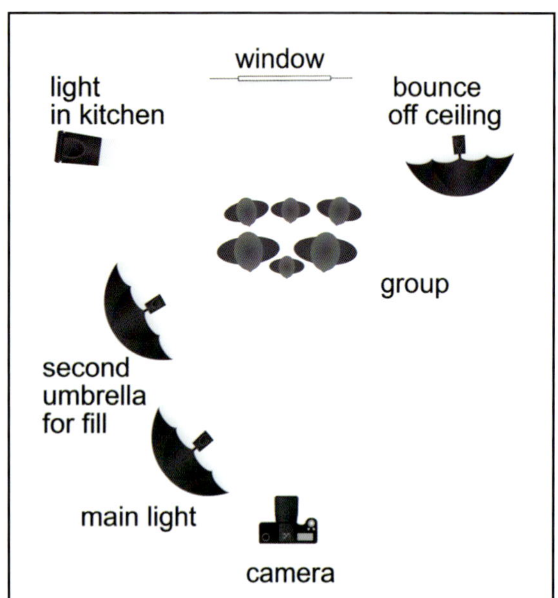

Lighting

The first thing I did was bring my meter to the window and get a reading of the light outside. My camera setting became f/11, 1/30 second with an ISO of 400. Once I had the outside exposure, I set my umbrella on the left to light the family. I set the flash at f/11 and shot at 1/30 second, essentially dragging the shutter to show the ambient light in the room to keep the exposure the same as outside. I used a second umbrella to the left of my main light for fill.

I had a flash in the kitchen skimming across the left side of the room and a flash in an umbrella on the right bouncing off the ceiling for light on the right side of the room. The lights in the kitchen on the left and right were set at a half-stop lower (f/8.5) than my main light (f/11) which was lighting the family.

TECH SPECS > This was photographed with a Canon 5D Mark II with the 24–105mm lens set at 50mm. The exposure was at f/11, 1/30 second, and ISO 400.

If I had tilted the camera down or up, the columns in the background would have begun to converge.

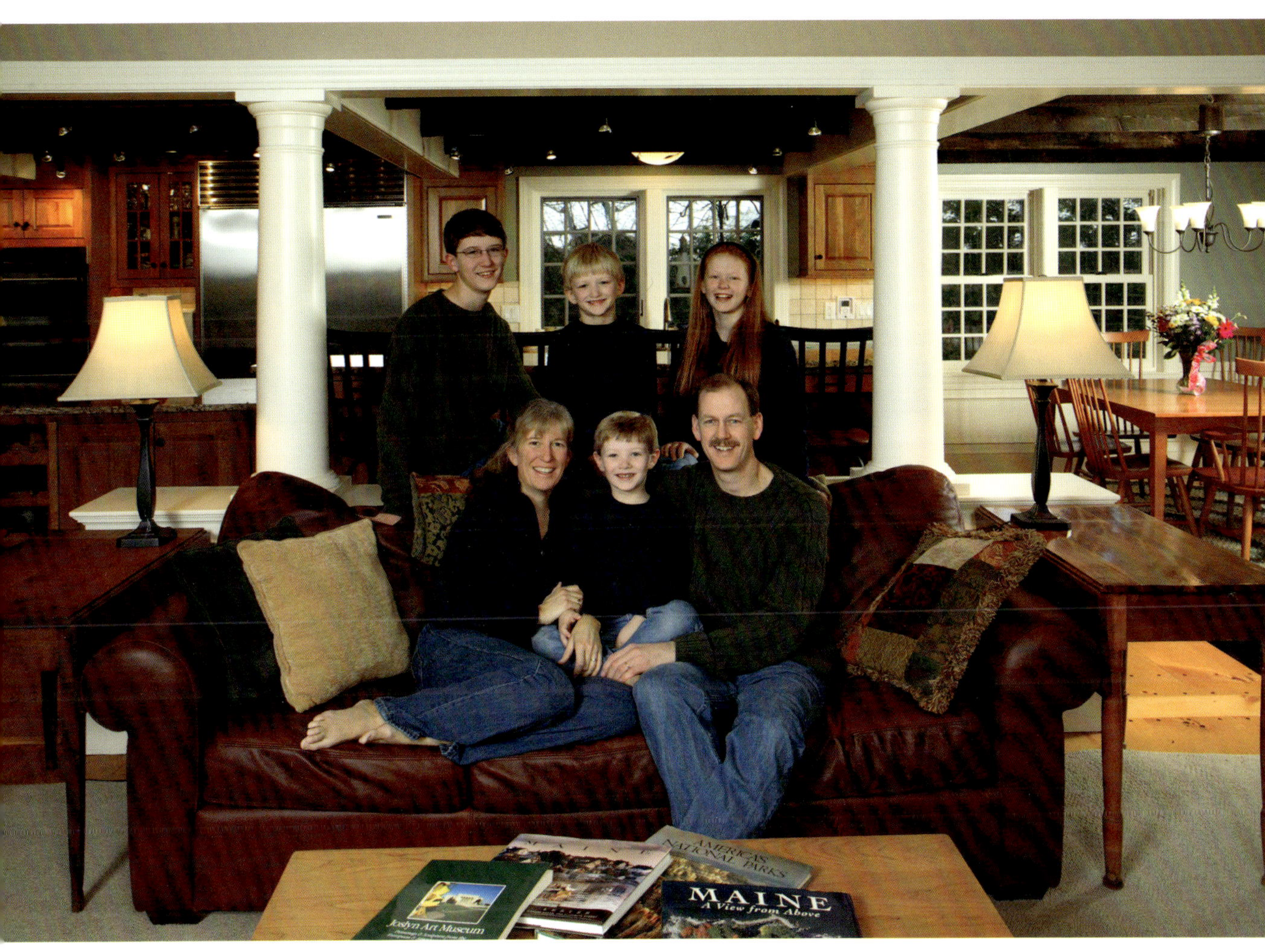

11 All Grown Up

Purpose

This is the most recent portrait of the family shown in the previous three photographs. While some may say that this is not the most exciting portrait, my purpose is to demonstrate that if your clients appreciate your image quality and professionalism, they will return to have new portraits made on a regular basis. They may not come annually, but they will call you every three to five years, depending on what is happening in their lives. All clients are wonderful and certainly appreciated, but there is something special about repeat clients.

Lighting

The main light was a 4x6-foot softbox on the left of the camera set at f/8. I skimmed light across the group with a 6-foot panel on the right side to soften the shadows. I used a Photogenic set at f/5.6 in a Larson 10x36-inch strip softbox attached to the rail system on the ceiling as a hair light. A Photogenic 750 light in a 12x36-inch strip softbox was also attached to the rail system on the ceiling, lighting the background at f/5.6.

strip light softbox
(lights background)
strip light softbox
(hair light)
group
4x6-foot
softbox
camera
6-foot
white
panel

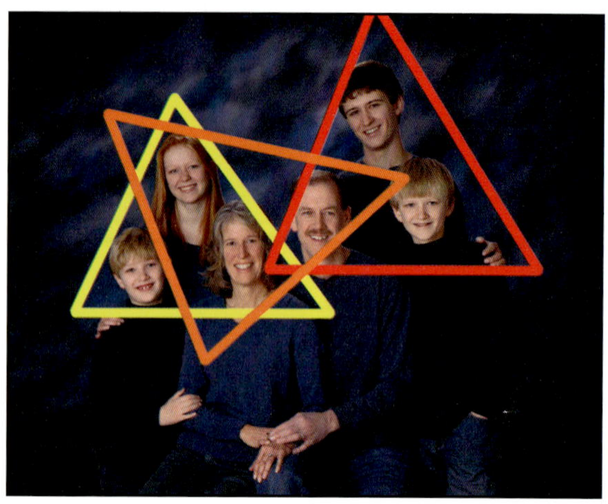

Composition

Their clothing of jeans and dark tops was perfect for drawing the viewer right to their faces. I created triangles with my posing, reading left to right. My first triangle is the youngest child with his sister and mom; the second triangle is inverted with the sister, mom, and dad; and the final triangle is dad and the two older sons. It is a simple yet effective, pose for a family.

TECH SPECS > This was photographed with Canon 5D Mark II and my 70–200mm lens set at 70mm. My exposure was f/8, 1/100 second at ISO 100

I skimmed light across the group with 6-foot panel on the right side to soften the shadows.

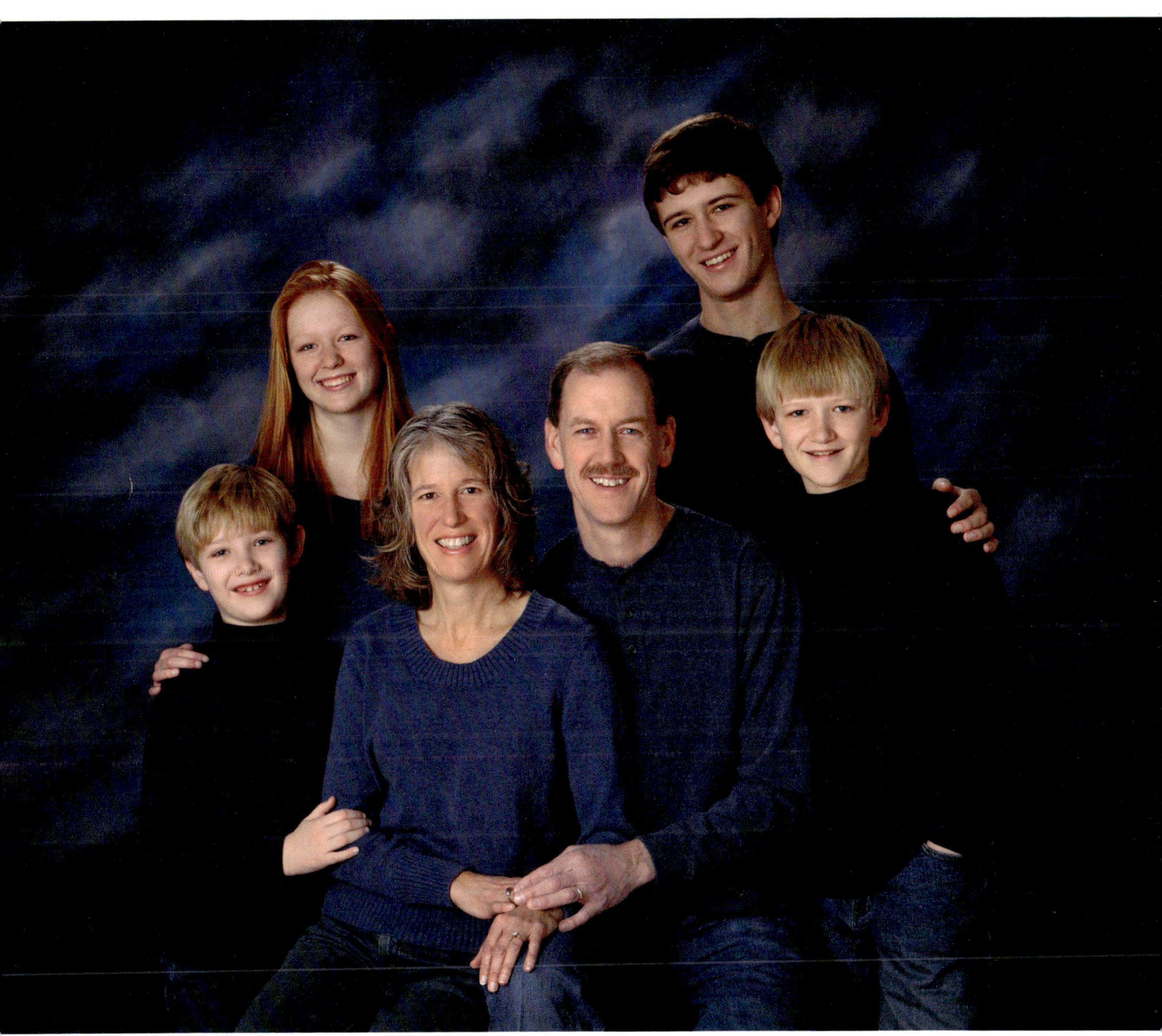

12 Family Reunion

Large Group Composition

When working with a large groups, it is important to move the group in from the left and right. If you do not bring them to the center, people's arms—and perhaps even entire individuals—would be cut out in an 8x10-inch print. For this image, I climbed up on a 15-foot ladder to compose the group. From that elevated position, I was able to prompt people to move a little to the left or right so I could clearly see every face.

Lighting

Natural light was the main light for this portrait. To ensure everyone in the group was evenly illuminated, my assistant held the fill light—a Quantum flash in a parabolic on a 13-foot pole—at camera left. I hand-held the camera at the top of the ladder and focused about 1/3 of the way into the group.

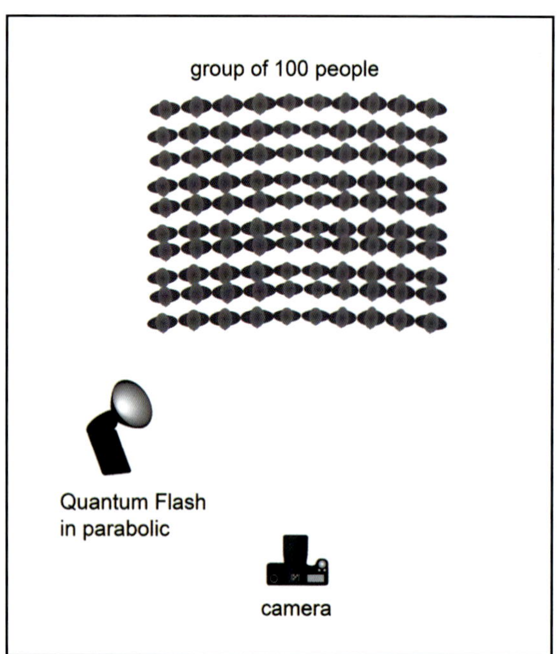

I always make a few text shots just to be sure my exposure is good. In the days of film, I would take a Polaroid test first, but in the world of digital photograph, you see the results right away.

Reunion Photographs

I offer reunion photographs at a discounted price so that each family can purchase an 8x10-inch print. I try to price this type of assignment to make it profitable for me and worth my time and effort, yet still be able to offer discounted prices for small-sized photographs.

The trick to reunion photography is to work quickly or you will lose the crowd. You need to be fast and efficient. Once you are ready to begin, get their attention and act as silly as you can, balancing on top of a tall ladder to get them to look at you and smile.

- Arrange the group into a rectangle.
- Camera is high on a 15-foot ladder.
- Take test shots for good exposure.
- Work quickly.
- Get their attention any way you can and get them to smile.

TECH SPECS > This was photographed with a Mamiya RZ67 and 50mm lens. The exposure was f/16, 1/125 second, and ISO 100.

You do not want the group elongated in the center because that would not work for a standard 8x10-inch print composition.

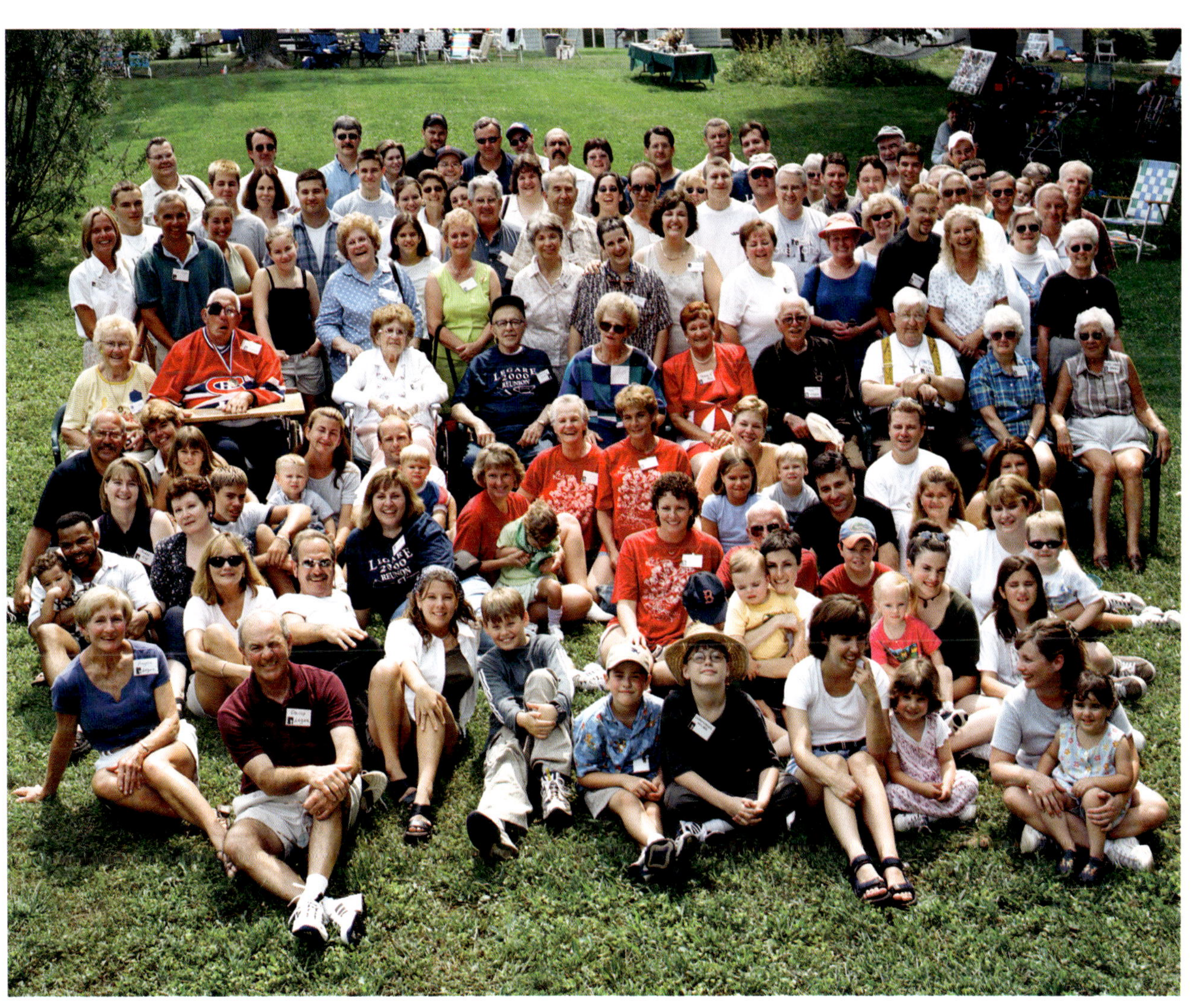

13 A Family of Five, and Even the Dog Looks Good

Purpose

Mom and Dad wanted a family portrait with their home in the background. The little boy on the left and the little girl on the right are twins that I have been photographing since they were babies.

Equipment

My Photogenic light and umbrella was just to the left of the camera, skimming the light across the group. One assistant was holding an 8-foot panel on the left side to keep the sun from washing out the family and allowing me to photograph them in the shade, and a second assistant is holding a 6-foot square white panel on the right to throw light back into their faces.

Posing

The challenge was to keep the kids looking like they are interested and to keep the dog's attention as well. I instructed the parents to watch me and not be concerned with their children. They instinctively wanted to look down and see how the kids and the dog are doing, and invariably, I would get photographs of the tops of their heads. I used loud, squeaky noises to get the dog to look at me at the right time.

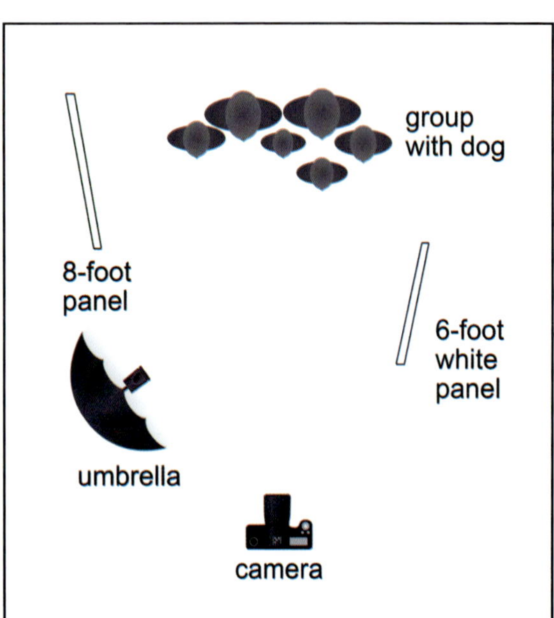

Composition

This was taken in the fall as indicated by the chrysanthemums and the pumpkins on the steps in the background.

I always bring plants to fill in the voids; the greenery on the right was a potted juniper plant that I brought with me. I believe that balancing the photo with greenery is better than having "dead space" without the plants. The plants on the left were there and I just had to fill in on the right.

Dad was sitting on one of my rocks; I used the rocks to adjust the heights of the people so everyone was not on the same plane. My posing reads as we read, from left to right. We start with the little boy and Mom's leg and move up to Mom, to the baby, up to Dad, and end with the little girl on the right.

TECH SPECS > This was photographed with Kodak Vericolor II film using a Mamiya RZ67 with an 80mm lens. My exposure was f/8 at 1/125 second, and ISO 400.

My posing reads as we read, from left to right.

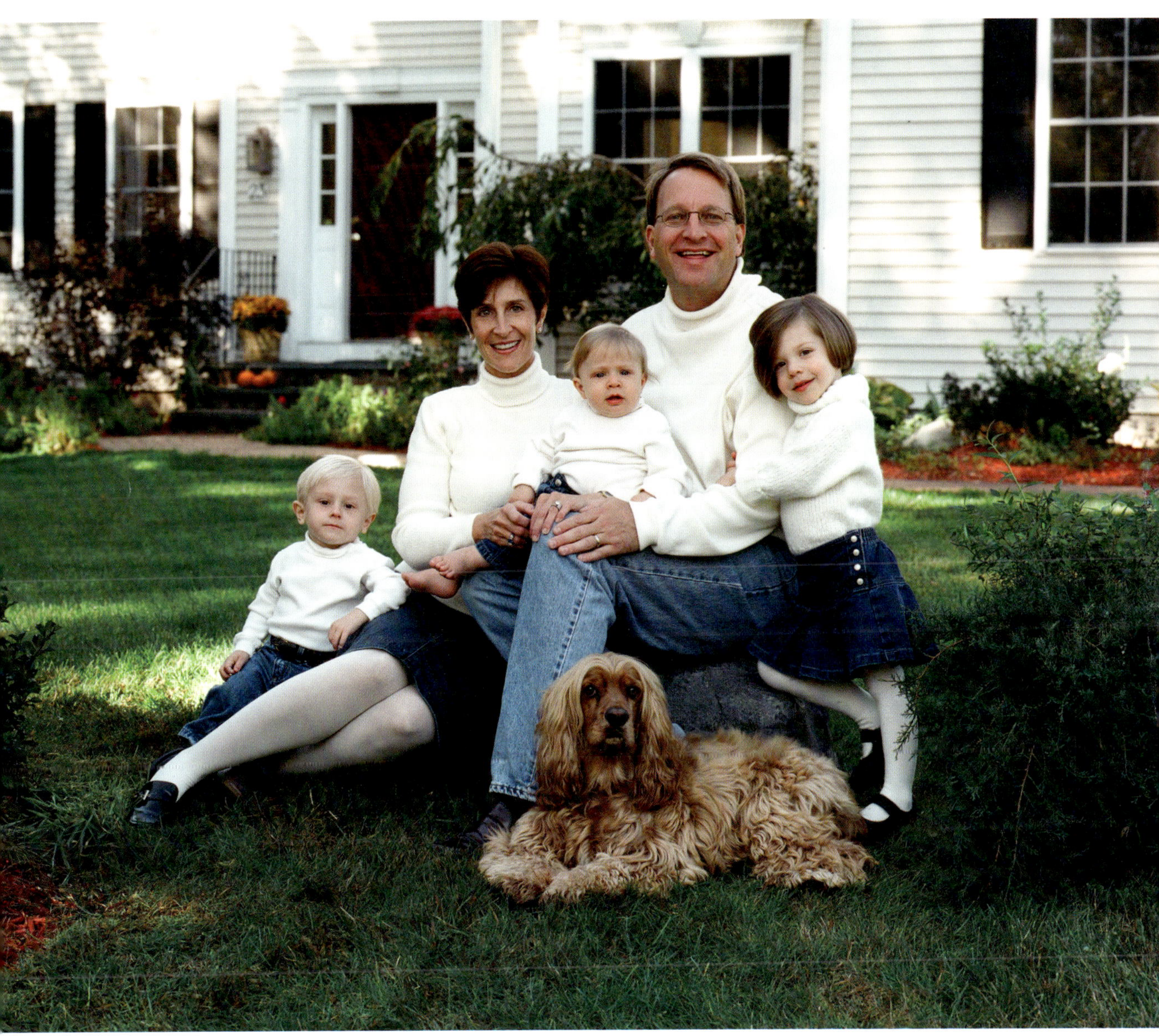

Dirt Bikes

Just for Fun

We had already finished the family portrait in their home with Mom, Dad, and two sons. We did a variety of poses, including the boys individually and together and Mom and Dad together. When we were finished with the session, Dad said that he and the boys loved riding dirt bikes. I suggested doing something a little more interesting, and since Mom does not ride—it's the guys' thing—the four of us went to a state forest nearby with the three of them dressed in complete riding regalia. This is something Dad and his two sons like to do together, and this portrait helps to capture this special time in their lives.

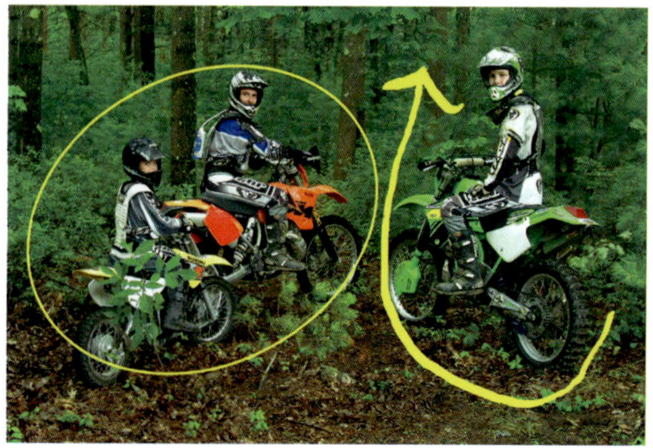

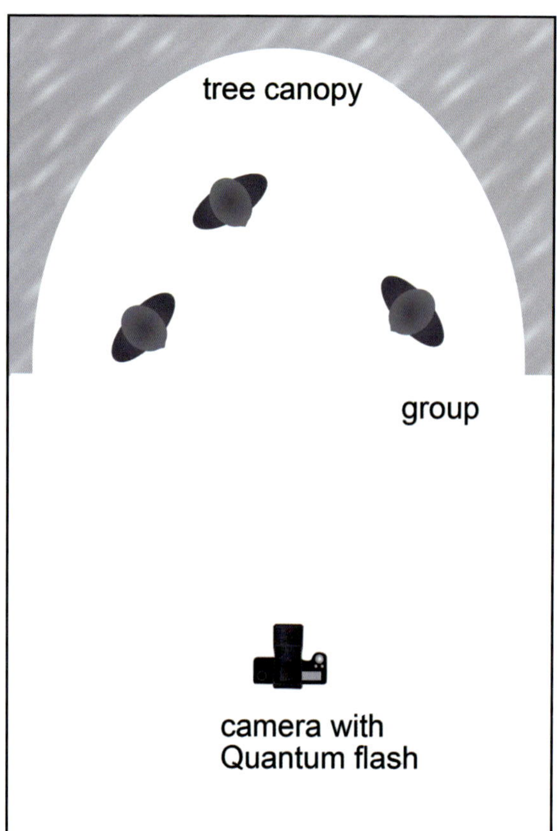

Lighting

This portrait was lit with a Quantum flash set at f/5.6 to give them a hint of light under the canopy of the trees. It was a very humid day and I had to keep drying off my lens to keep the images sharp.

Posing

I had Dad and his sons move into position so that the trees were not sticking out of their heads and had them angle themselves so that everything leads towards the center of the photograph. The portrait even tells a little story with the younger son sticking close to Dad, while the older son created some distance as if to say that he is ready to head out on his own.

When I first switched from film to digital, I used Fuji cameras. I photographed this with my camera on a tripod and used a little bit of flash. This was photographed with an ISO of 400, at f/8 and 1/30 second.

TECH SPECS > This was photographed with a Fujifilm FinePixS2Pro on a tripod using an 80mm lens. My exposure was at f/8, 1/30 second, and ISO 400.

It was a very humid day and I had to keep drying off my lens to keep it sharp.

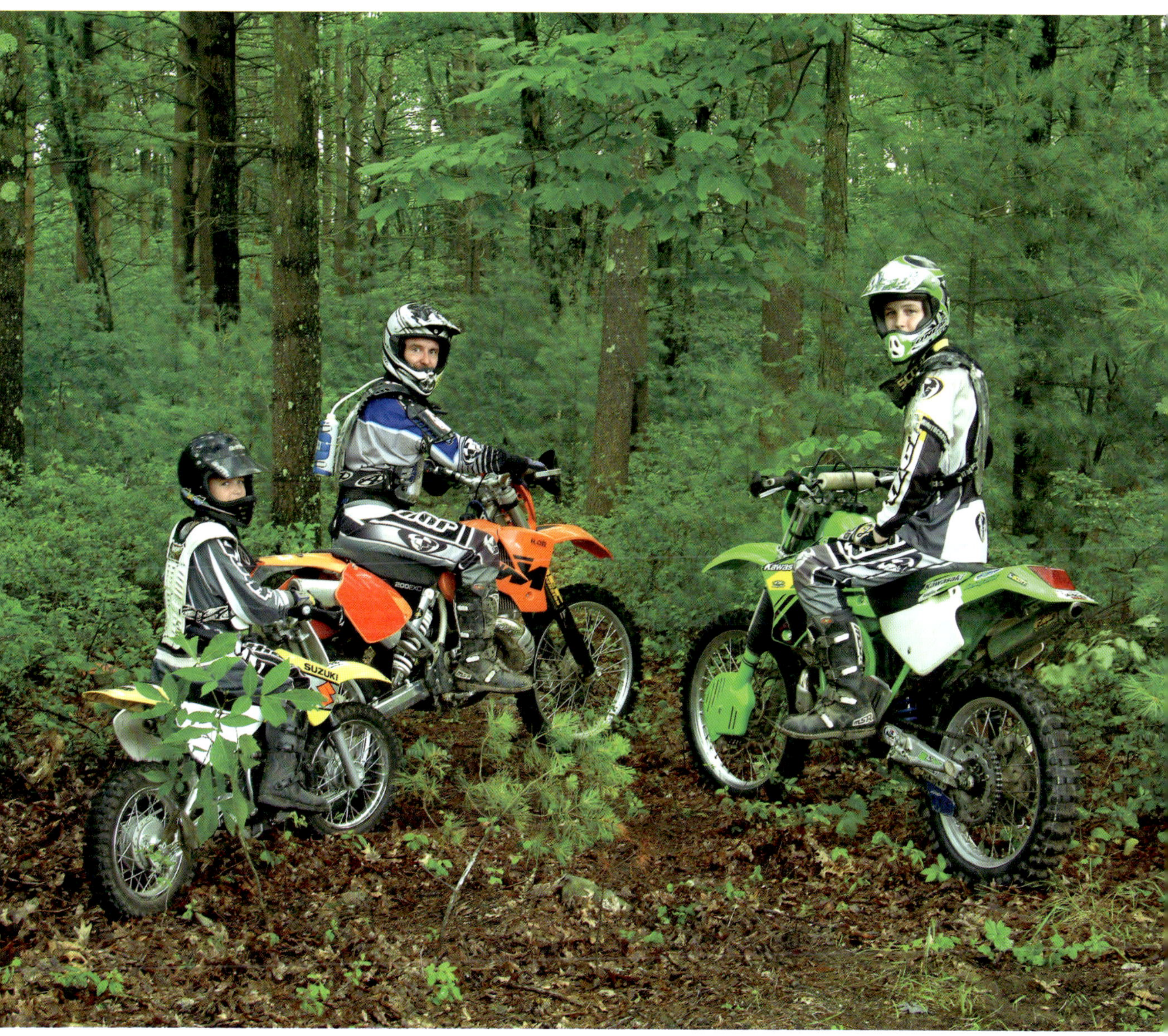

15 Ireland Meets the Fourth of July

Purpose

The parents requested this portrait be made in front of their home because their children all grew up in this house and now live out of state. Everyone came home for Dad, who was about to receive a special award. The title comes from the American flag on display in front of their home, their street address (#4), and the Independence Day holiday season. The color of Ireland can be noted in the men's green striped ties and Grandmother's green dress.

Posing

I used folding chairs for the two moms and had everyone else stand, except for the youngest child, who is sat on his mom's lap on the right. I posed the women with their knees facing in toward the center of the group, and I have the baby sit across Mom's knees, ensuring that all faces were clearly visible.

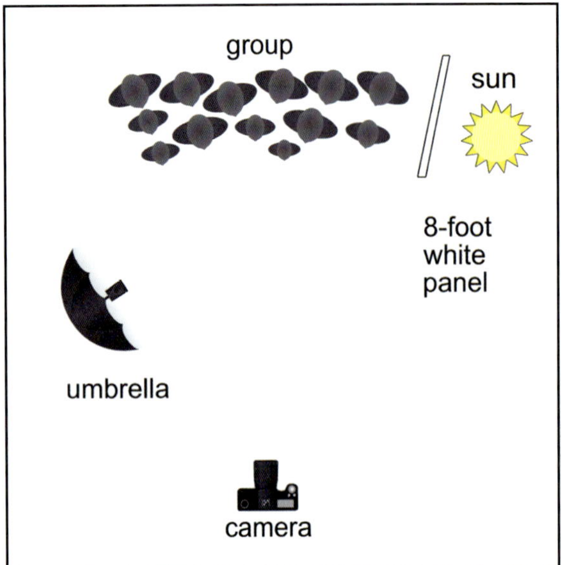

I always focus approximately a third of the way into the group; therefore, my focus was on the little boy in the middle in front of his grandmother. By photographing at this angle, I was able to avoid the flash reflecting in their front door and the flag sticking out of Dad's head.

Potted Plants. The potted junipers were placed in the front and the taller plants with a little color directly in back of the junipers to avoid dead space. This nicely framed the family. I selected plants with some red shades to complement the pink dresses.

Lighting

There was approximately 200 feet of extension cord coming from the house to my lights. I prefer a flash that is plugged in so there is little to no recycle time. I used a Photogenic umbrella to light the family. My umbrella was on the left, skimming across the faces to give me an even light across all of the subjects. An assistant held an 8-foot panel on the right side to block the sun.

TECH SPECS > This was photographed with a Canon 5D Mark II and a 24–105mm lens set at 80mm. My exposure was f/8, 1/125 second, and ISO 200.

I always focus approximately a third of the way into the group.

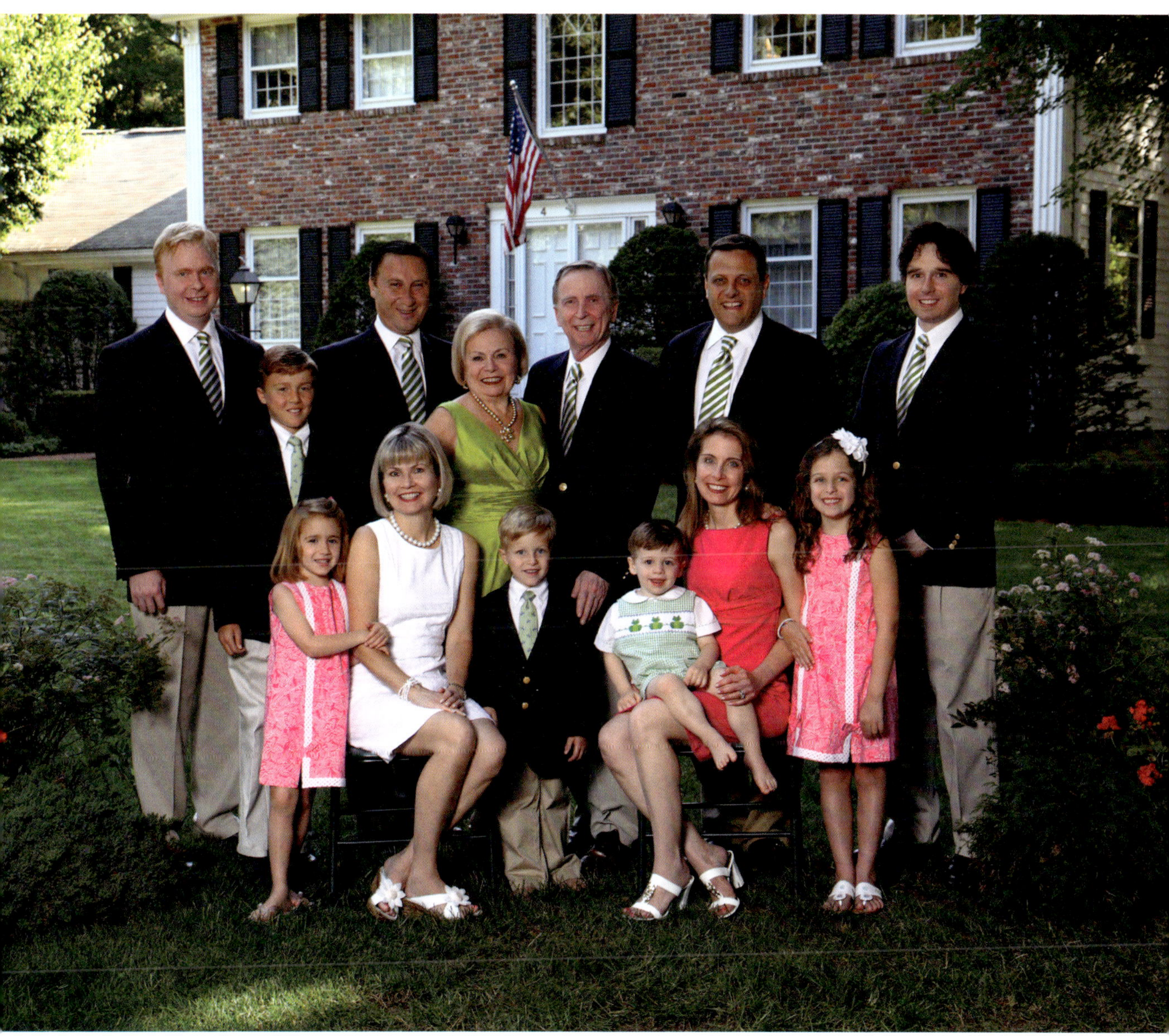

16 Follow the Diagonal Line

Purpose

Some family portraits have a lengthy story behind them; others, like this one, are very simple. Mom wanted a nice family portrait, including their cocker spaniel, in front of their house.

Clothing

While I usually prefer darker tones in clothing to bring out the faces, this portrait works with the light tones. I used the white front door as a background, and with Mom in a white dress, Dad and their son wearing white shirts and khaki slacks, and the white bib of the dog's chest, you are still drawn to their faces. The red brick walkway leads you right to the subjects.

Setup

This portrait was created on an overcast day. My fill flash to the left of the camera was a Photogenic in an umbrella, plugged into an electrical outlet.

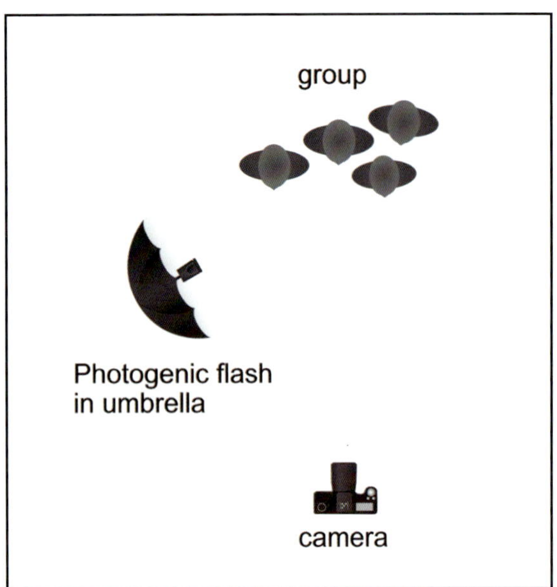

I always use a flash and do not rely just on available light for two reasons: I get extra sharpness with a flash, and the flash prevents the green cast on the faces and puts a nice catchlight in their eyes.

The flash prevents the green cast on the faces.

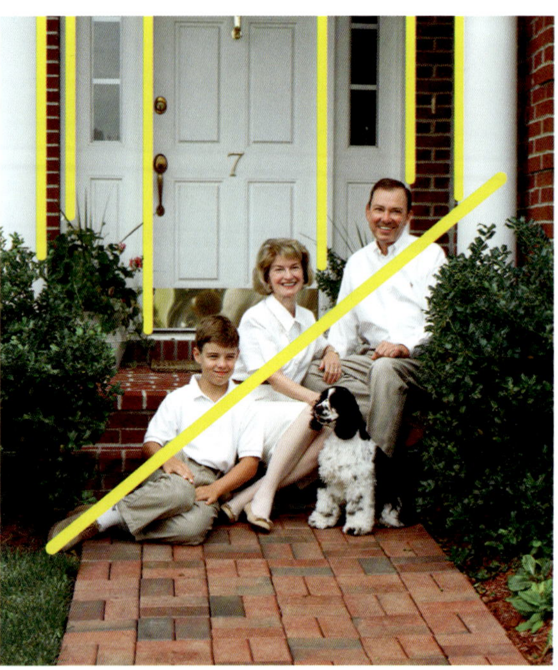

Composition. I have a nice diagonal with the boy on the ground, Mom on the first stair, and Dad on the top stair. It was important to keep the lines in background straight so they do not appear to bend left or right.

TECH SPECS > This as photographed with a Mamiya RZ67 and 80mm lens. The exposure was f/8, 1/125 second, and ISO 400.

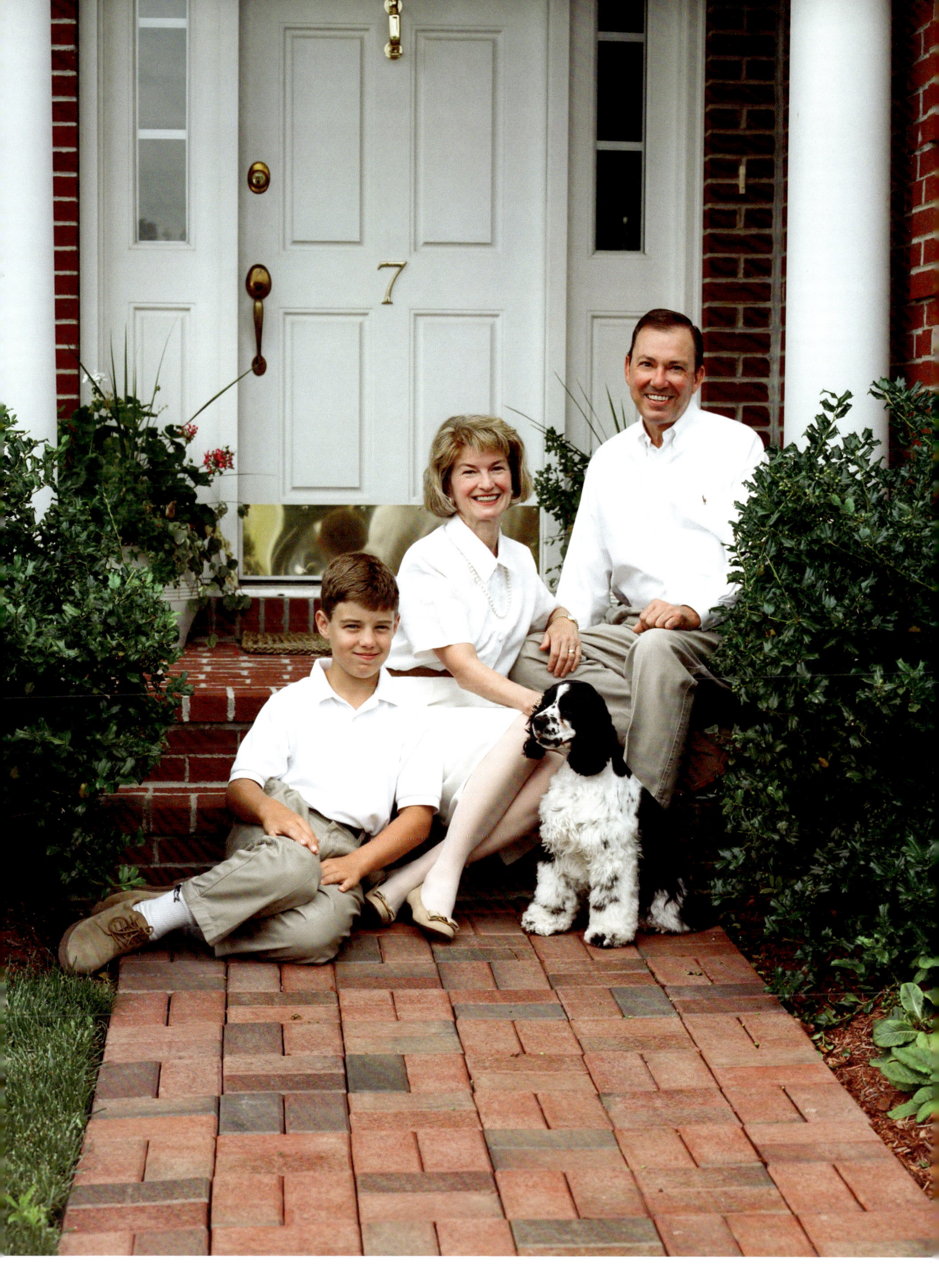
7

17 Four Generations with One Sofa

Purpose

The husband and wife on the right side of the sofa wanted a professional family portrait photographed in their home with Grandma, their children, and grandchildren.

Posing and Composing

The young man in back and the one on the left are the sons of the couple on the right. The young mom with her two daughters is the wife of the man on the left. I posed one son sitting on the back of the sofa; the other son and the dad were seated on the arms of the sofa, and the three women are sitting on the sofa. You have to use what is in the house. Sometimes you just have to improvise.

I brought the coffee table in closer to them to eliminate the dead space at the bottom of the frame. This helps to lead the eye to the subjects. This was created with film, so there was essentially one opportunity to get it right; this was photographed in the days before swapping heads was an easy task, so you wanted to make each exposure count. Their wedding photo can be seen in the background—again, another personal touch.

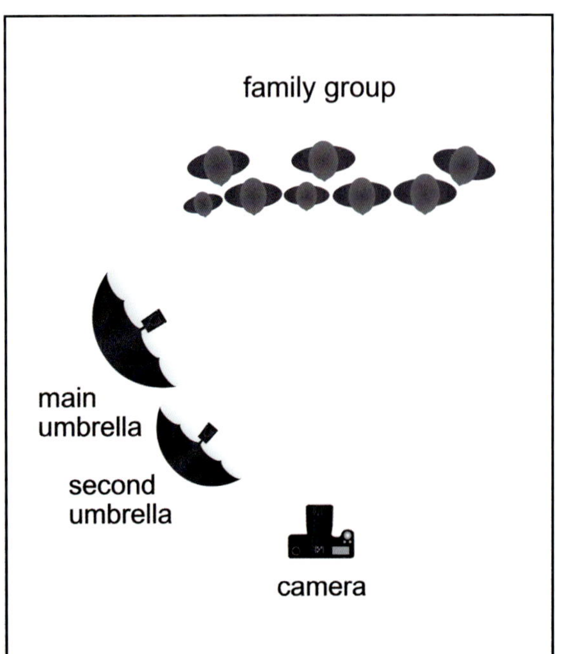

Eyeglass Glare and Tint. To avoid glass glare, be sure that the lights are at an angle to the subjects. A slight change in light angles can remedy the problem, making a postproduction fix unnecessary. Changing the angle can be as simple as moving the lights or adjusting the ear piece on the glasses.

Minor glare can be removed by retouching. However, tinted lenses cannot be lightened. Tinted and exceptionally thick lenses distort how the camera sees the eyes. One solution is to have your subjects get empty frames to wear for their portrait session.

Lighting

I used two umbrellas—a main light and a fill light—both on camera left close together. One was right next to the camera and the other was a little to the left of the first umbrella. Using the two umbrellas gave me a little more direction to the light.

TECH SPECS > This was photographed with a Mamiya RZ67 and an 80mm lens. My exposure was f/8, 1/60 second, and ISO 400.

I brought the coffee table in closer to them to eliminate the dead space. This helps to lead the eye to the subjects.

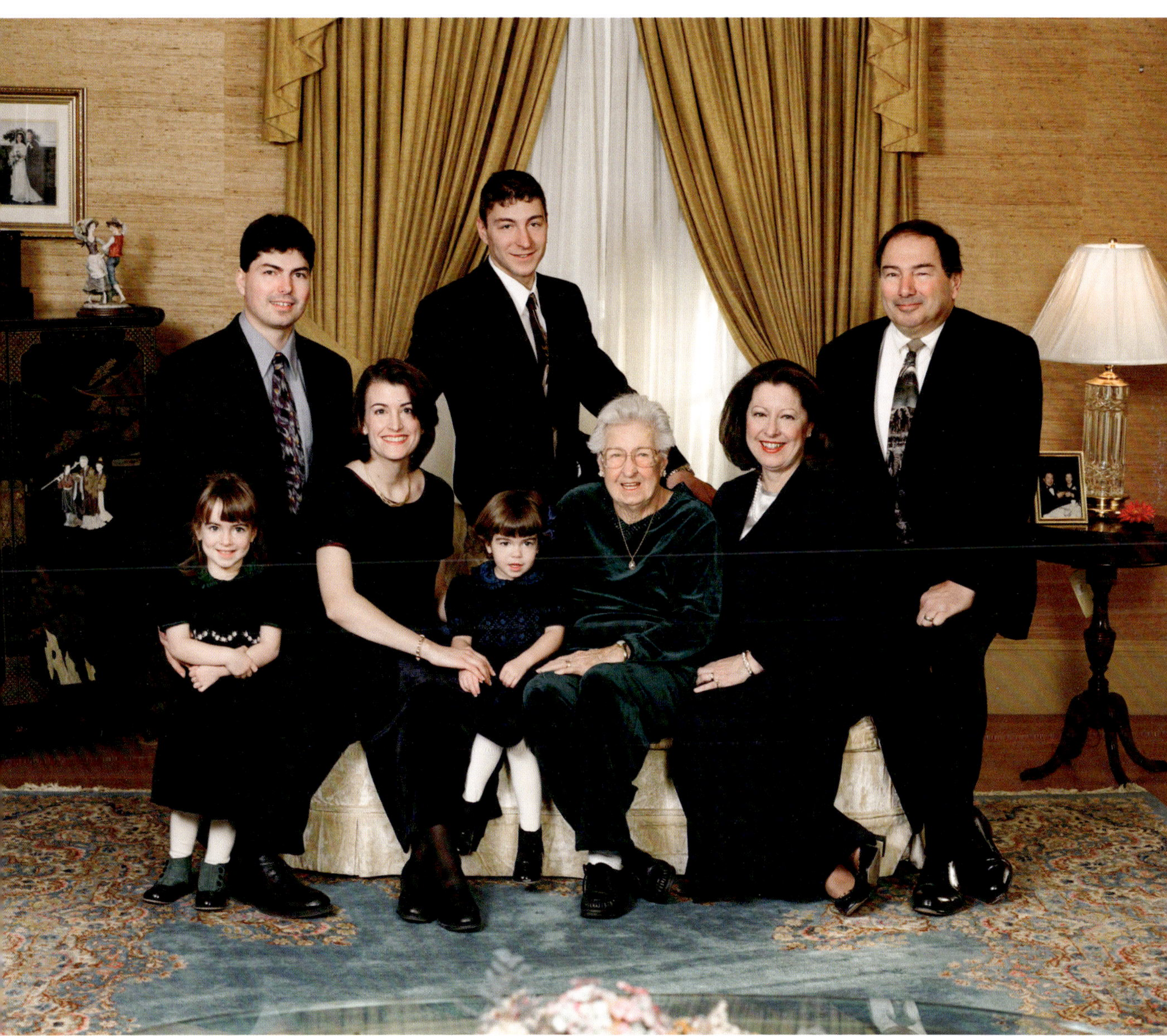

18 Outdoor Portrait with Twenty-Three People

Preparation

Approximately a week before photographing a large group, I ask for names, ages, and relationships of the family members. I prepare for the session by drawing a diagram so that I am able to place everyone quickly. Most families do not want to wait while you figure out the posing; by diagramming in advance, you cut down on the wait time. This is also beneficial because small children (and big children) get antsy if they have to wait too long.

Before making my exposures, I approach my subjects and make sure everyone's hair looks good, the jewelry is straight, and the shirt collars are neat. I go back to my camera and work to get the best expressions. I throw a stuffed toy monkey in the air, put things on my head, use squeaky toys for dogs, and just act crazy to get their attention.

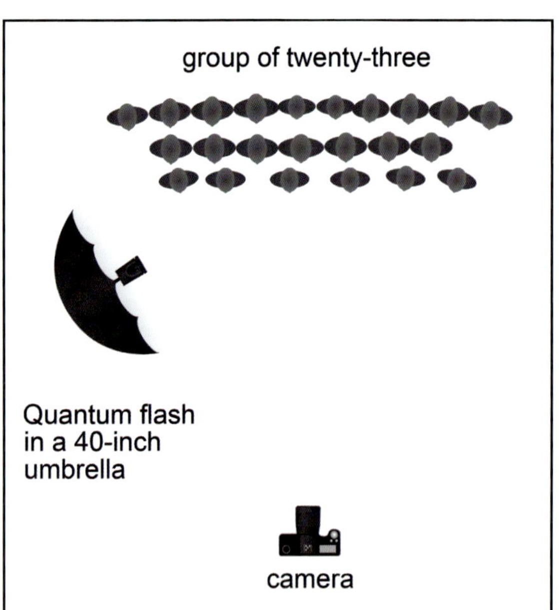

Posing and Composition

The women were seated on posing chairs; the boy in the second row on the far left and the girl on the far right were posed on my custom–made rocks. I had the row of children in front on the ground and the parents standing in the back row. I positioned the grandparents in the middle, and I tried to keep all of the families together. The potted plants on the left and right of the image are mine. I used them to create a balanced feel in the photograph.

Lighting

I used a Quantum flash with a 40-inch umbrella placed a little to the left of my camera and raised high. By placing the light a little higher, I was able to avoid glare in the glasses. I skimmed the light across the group by aiming it at the person on the far right to be sure that everyone was lit evenly. I metered for the background and filled in the faces with the light from my umbrella to give them a little sparkle in their eyes.

TECH SPECS > This was photographed with a Canon 5D Mark II and a 24–105mm lens set at 80mm. My exposure was f/11, 1/125 second, and ISO 400.

I metered for the background and filled in the faces with the light from my umbrella to give them a little sparkle in their eyes.

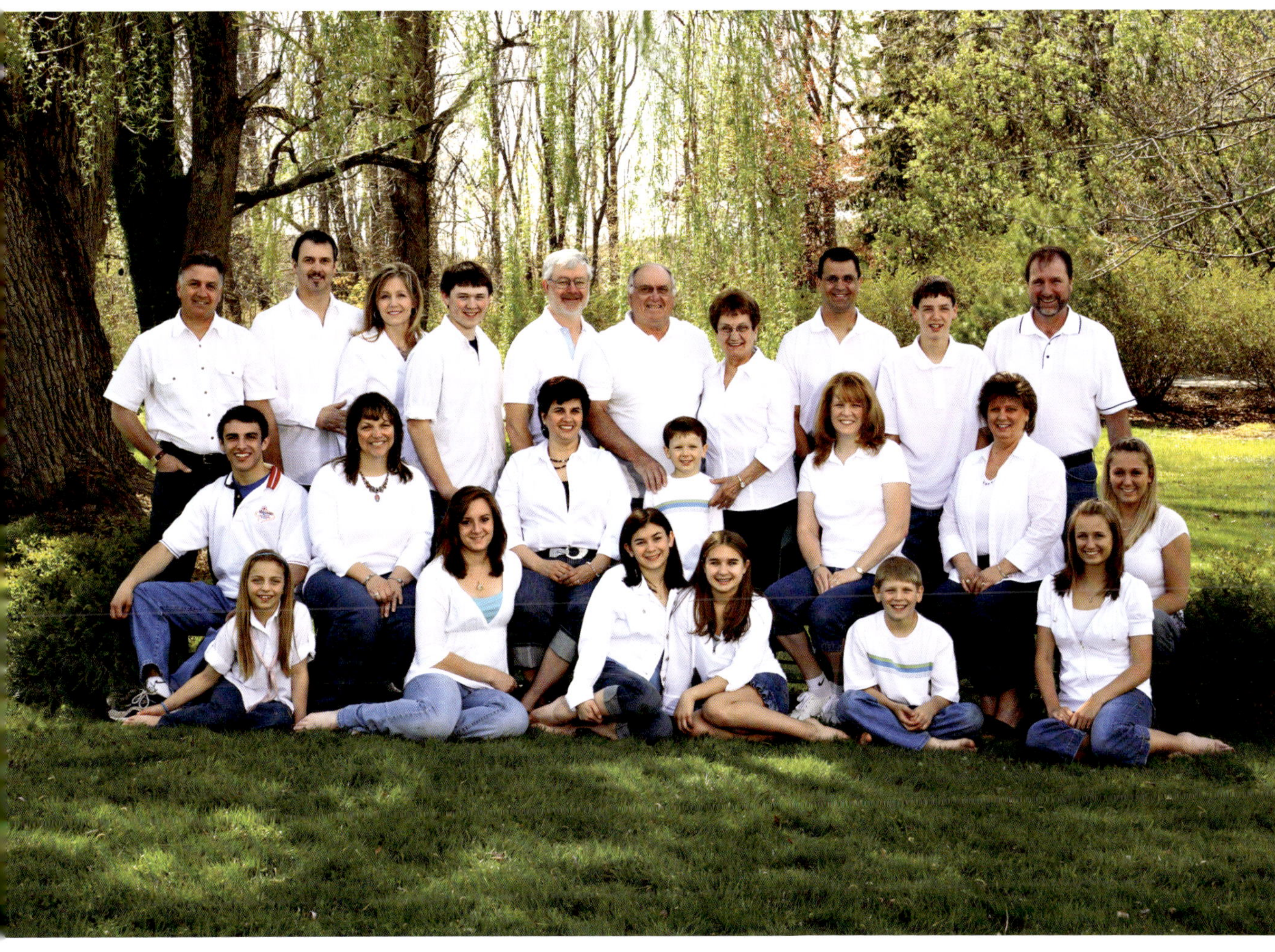

19 One Portrait Leads to Others

Posing

This is an early portrait of one of the families in the previous section. Working in their home, I found an area with a blank wall so that nothing in the background was sticking out of their heads. I kept the posing simple because of the three small children. Mom held the very active little boy, who until this point had been running all around the house; Dad held the youngest child, and the oldest daughter say on the sofa with her legs crossed at her ankles.

Exposure

My one light was an umbrella to the left of the camera, raised high to avoid glare in Dad's glasses. I made sure they were far enough away from the background so there would not be any shadows on the wall.

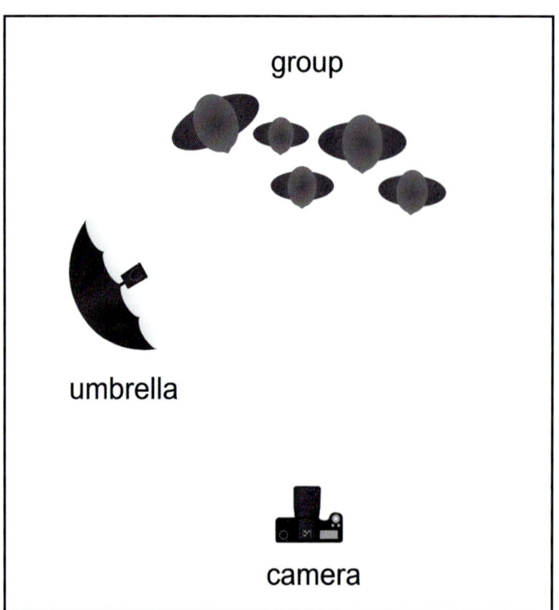

Keep Things Simple. On location in homes, it is sometimes best to keep things simple.

- Find an area with a blank wall. It will be easier to prevent lines from intersecting the heads and the background from competing for the viewers's eye when looking at the portrait.
- Keep the pose simple, especially with active children.
- Moving the furniture or a plant can make a big difference in the successful of the final portrait. It may not occur to the people who see their home every day. Just ask, "Could we move this end table to the left?"

Customers for Life

I have photographed this family group for many years, from early childhood through the kid's teen years and into adulthood. The girl sitting on the sofa is the same young woman in "Outdoor Portrait with Twenty-Three People" (see page 40), second from the left sitting in the grass with the blue top. She has served with the military in Afghanistan. My point is, if you do a good job the first time, you will be their family photographer for life.

TECH SPECS > This was photographed with a Mamiya RZ67 with an 80mm lens. The exposure was f/8, 1/60 second with Kodak Portra 400 film.

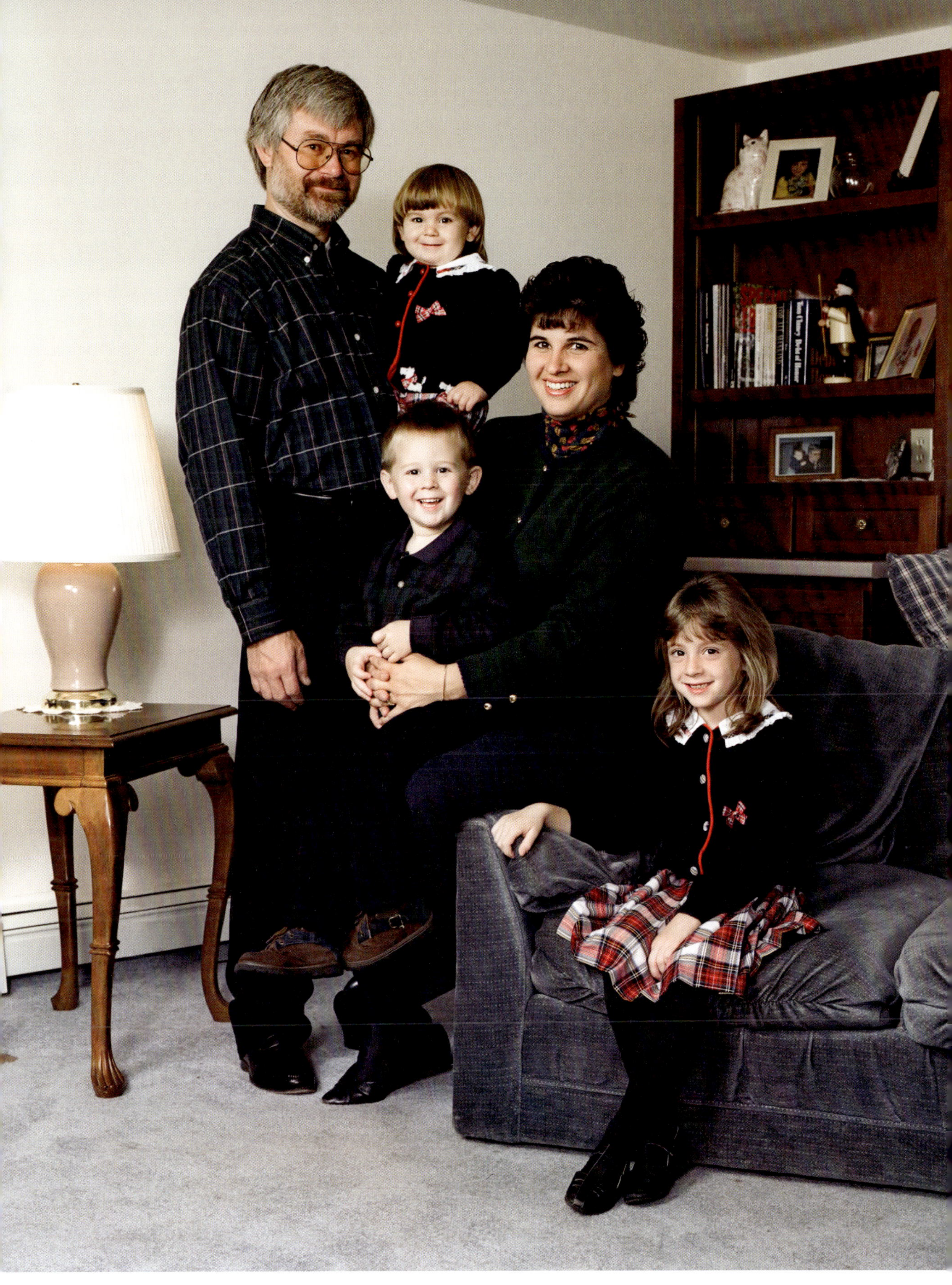

20 End-of-the-Day Portrait

Purpose

This three generation portrait was photographed in the parents' home because their older son, daughter-in-law, and two grandchildren were visiting from out of state.

Composition

In my advance visit to their house a week before the session, I noticed that when you opened the front door, you could see right through the house, through the back door, to the back yard. They said that one of the reasons they bought the house was for its openness.

The open house in the background gives this image depth. The depth was achieved without diagonal lines. It was important to keep all of the lines straight; I did not want the lines converging on the subjects.

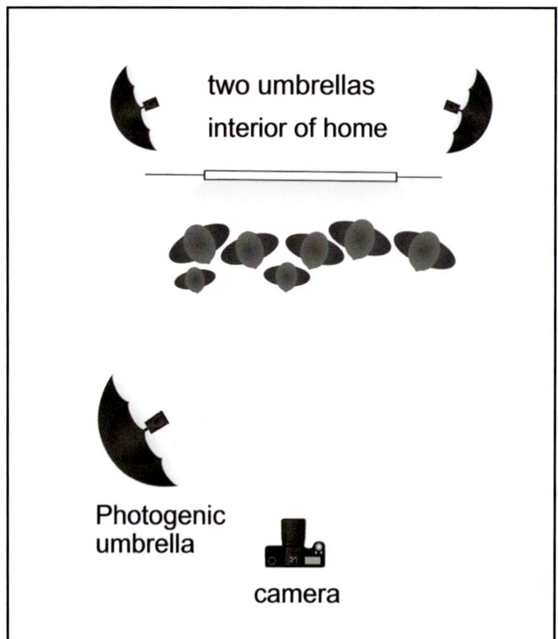

My black-eyed Susans gave the portrait foreground that added to the sense of depth. These flowers added a little color as well. This was photographed in early spring when flowers and greenery are minimal, but I always travel with my portable (real) plants.

Posing

I posed the family with the son on the left sitting on the second step holding his older son, his wife sitting next to him and the grandmother and grandfather sitting on the top step with the grandmother holding the younger grandson on her lap. The grandparent's other son is sitting on the right on the second step. They were pleased that everyone looks comfortable and that all of the faces are visible.

Lighting

My Photogenic umbrella, plugged in for a quick recycle, was raised high to the left of the camera to avoid glare in Grandma's glasses. I used two umbrellas inside the house, bouncing light off the side walls and ceiling, picking up the light on the inside of the house. This was photographed near the end of the day which is evident by the lack of bright light outside the back door.

TECH SPECS > This was photographed with my Mamiya RZ67 with a 90mm lens set at f/8, 1/60 second, and ISO 400.

The open house in the background gave this image depth and my black-eyed Susans gave the portrait a little color.

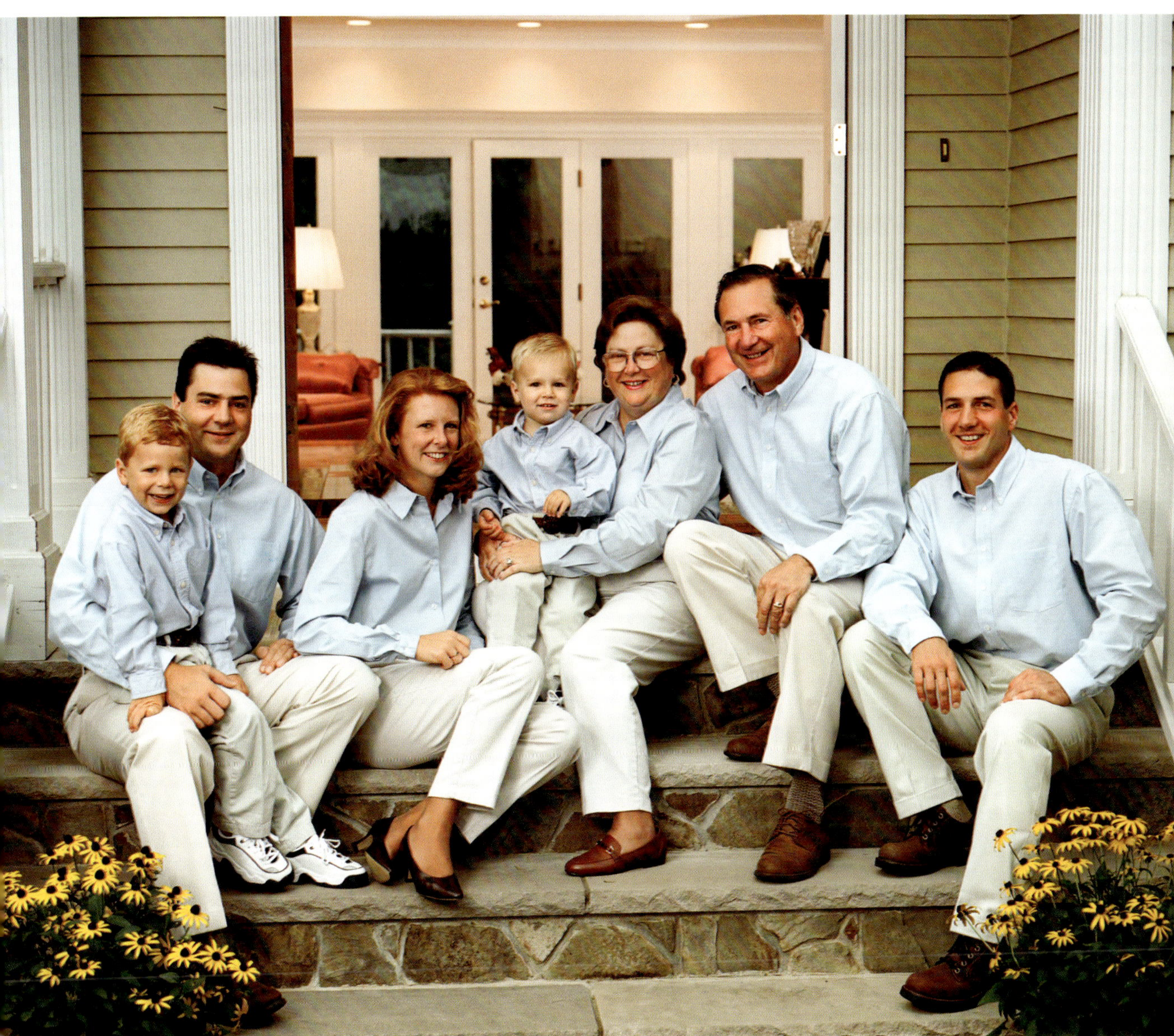

21 A Family Portrait Includes Pets

Purpose

This portrait in my outdoor garden was prompted by the daughter on the right being home from college; it was a perfect reason to gather everyone and the dog for a family portrait.

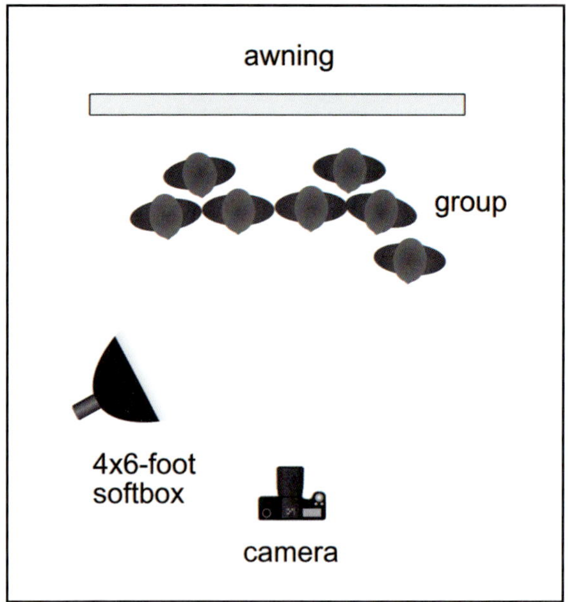

Plants Add to the Composition. I move potted plants around the family to fill in the gaps and to be sure the composition is well balanced. With potted plants, you can have a moveable garden and can change the look as needed. The grass in the foreground is artificial turf that was installed, thereby always giving the grass a nice fresh-cut look.

Posing

Photographing a family with four children can be challenging because I do not want to pose a group that is long and wide. Instead, I placed two of the children in the back creating two triangles, one with Mom and one with Dad. The four in front were seated on my custom-made rocks of different heights, and the two children in the back were kneeling on a bench.

Whenever there is a dog in the portrait, I try to work a little faster so I do not lose the dog's (or the family's) attention.

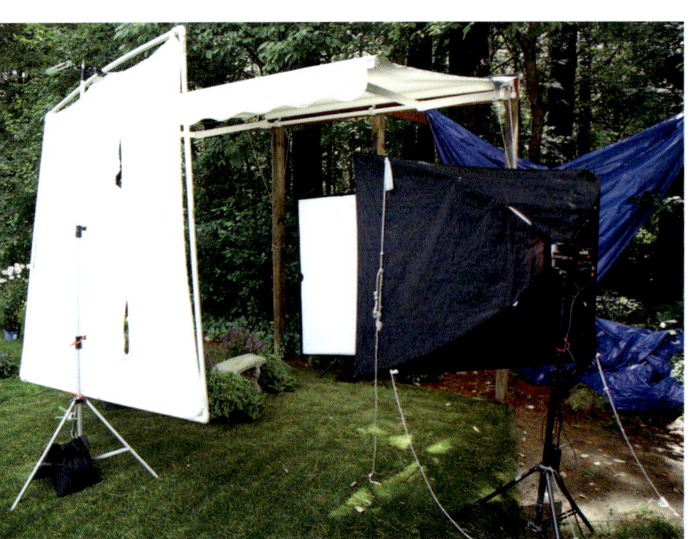

Lighting

The family was sitting under a 9x9x9-foot awning so that the overhead light was blocked. They are at the back of the awning, allowing a little bit of skylight to come through for separation for their hair. The 4x6-foot softbox on the left was aimed at the dog on the right, so that the light was feathered across the family.

TECH SPECS > This was photographed with a Canon 5D Mark II with the 70–200mm lens set at 120mm. My exposure was f/8, 1/60 second, and ISO 640.

The family was sitting under a 9x9x9-foot awning so that the down light was blocked.

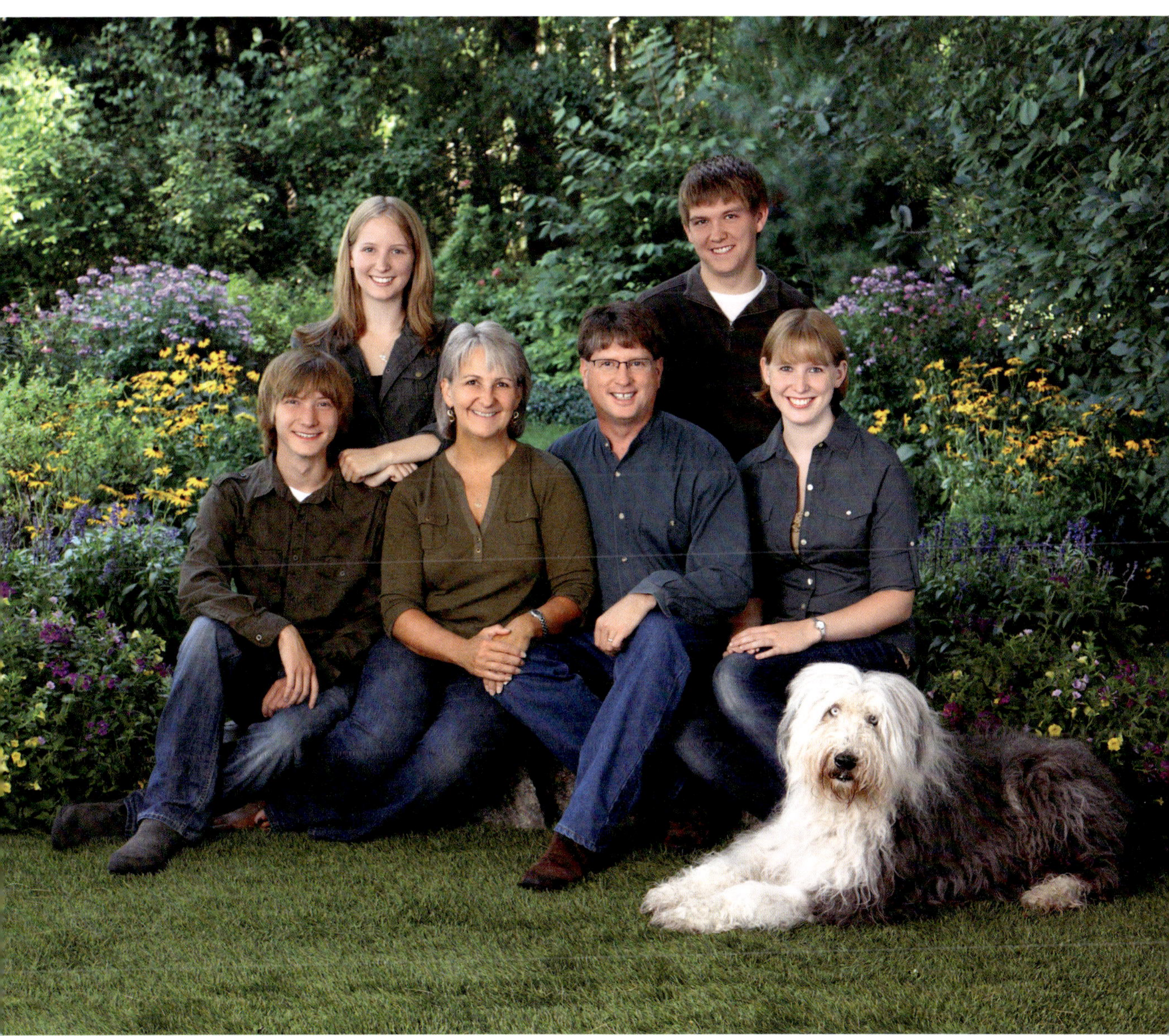

22 Relaxing in the Grass

Repeat Client

This family portrait session came about after I had photographed the son's First Communion portrait. I recently photographed the daughter's First Communion. It is a wonderful feeling to be the family photographer.

Posing and Composition

We started with the traditional sitting pose, but then switched to this fun pose. I love the little girl leaning on her dad and the little boy leaning toward his mother; this helps to make the photo. The dark clothing draws the viewer right to the faces.

This was created in my outdoor studio with an artificial field turf and a 9x9x9-foot awning over their head. I moved the potted plants on the left and right to balance the family and alleviate any dead space. The background, approximately 75 feet behind them, is landscaped and all natural.

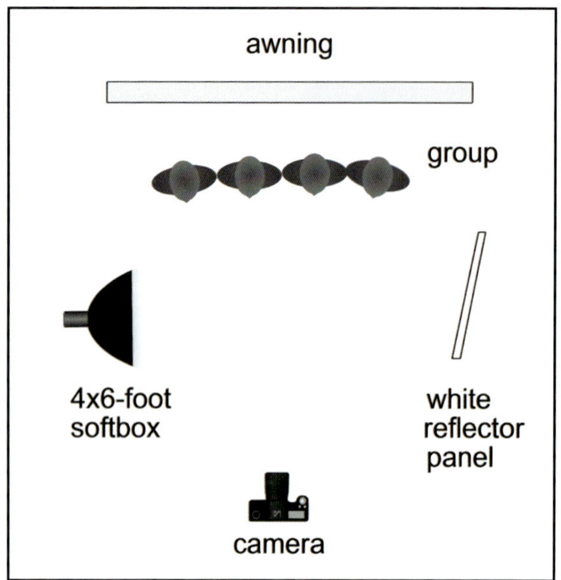

Lighting

The camera was close to the ground. I used a 4x6-foot softbox on the left, lowering it to just a little above their level, about two or three feet off the ground. Some photographers leave the softbox high, but that results in shadows under the eyes and nose. With the light at this height, you can see the catchlights in the eyes at the 10 o'clock position. The softbox was not aimed at the family, but rather at the 6-foot white reflector on the right, so the flash skimmed across the group, producing a nice, soft, even light. If I had not used the panel to reflect light back onto them, they would have a green cast from the grass and green plants.

Exposure

I based my exposure on a background reading. The subjects were at the back of the awning, allowing the light from the sky to light their hair. I set my flash to f/6.3 to balance the light on the subjects with the background.

Before I sent this image to the lab, I used the Nik Software filter called "Foliage," which just affected just the green in the photograph, making it a little bit brighter. I knocked the opacity down to 20 percent.

TECH SPECS > This was photographed with Canon 5D Mark II with the 70–200mm lens set at 180mm. My exposure was f/6.3, 1/60 second, and ISO 800.

Some photographers will leave the softbox high, but that would result in shadows under the eyes and nose.

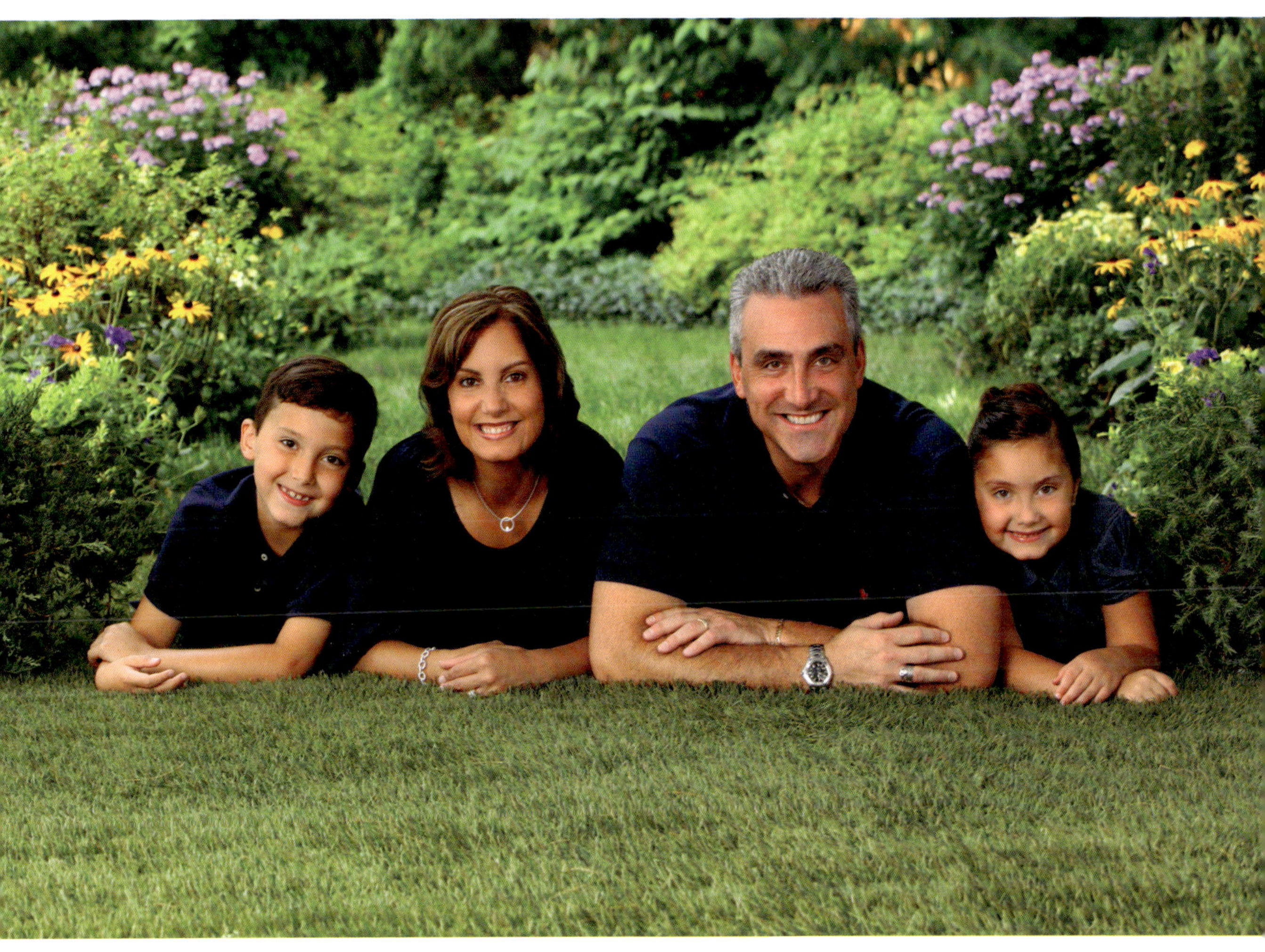

23 Plum Island Beach Portrait #1

Obstacles

Plum Island is approximately forty minutes from my home, which is one of the reasons I prefer not to photograph at the beach; it takes too much out of my day. However, since we were there, I also did some breakaways: the girls together, Mom and Dad together, and silhouettes of them pointing out to the water. We made the most of the session.

Another reason I do not photograph at the beach too often is because I find that it is a difficult place to work with the wind whipping around, blowing hair in faces and just blowing the hair in general. However, when I do photograph at the beach, it is always at the end of the day, as shown in this portrait made in late-day sun. The family loved this portrait and purchased a 24x30-inch canvas for above their fireplace.

Posing

I posed this family to follow the lines of the beach. The hill behind them went up to the right, so I posed them so that they went up to the right. The love of the family is evident with everyone touching. Their white shirts with blue jeans look great at the beach and their clothes complement the background with a combination of beach sand, sea grass, and ocean. I kept the family in the sand so you do not see the greenery coming out of their heads. This gave me a nice transition from sand to grass to water in the background. I had to make sure that the horizon line on the water remained straight.

Lighting

This portrait was made with natural light by the sun at the end of the day. The sun was directly behind me so I had flat, warm lighting.

TECH SPECS > This was photographed with a Canon 5D Mark II with the 70–200mm lens set at 150mm. My exposure was f/6.3, 1/60 second, and ISO 800.

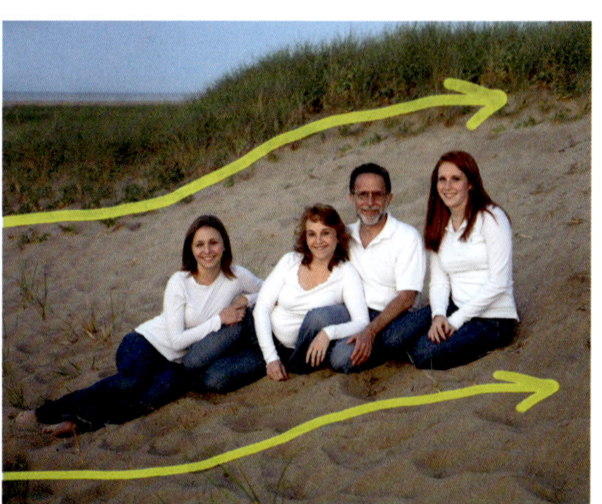

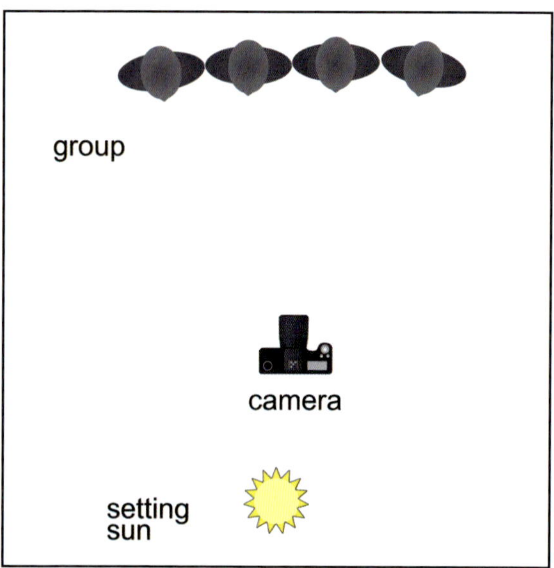

When I do photograph at the beach, it is always at the end of the day.

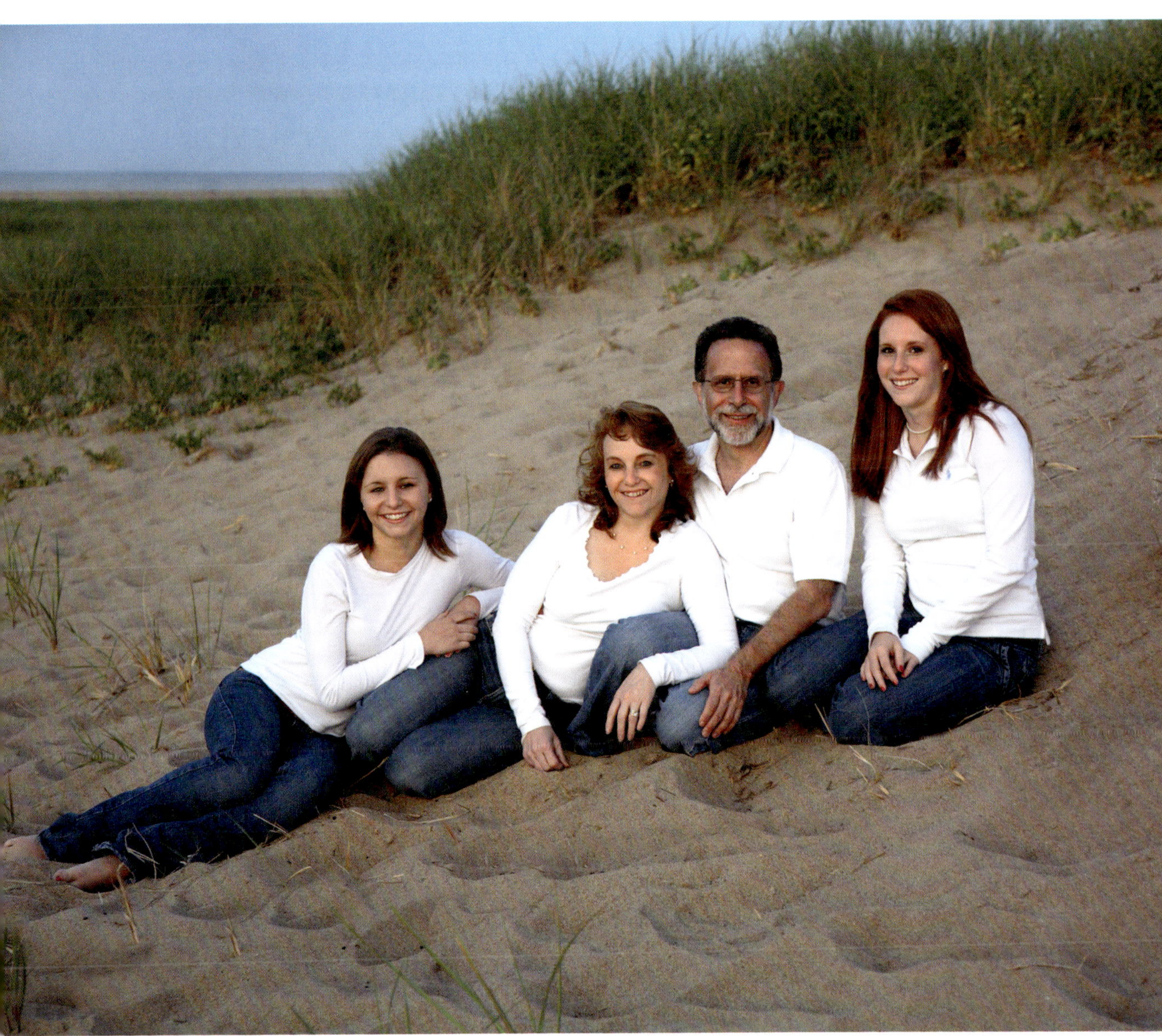

24 Studio Portrait #2

Background

This portrait session was the result of working with the family for many years. It all began with Dad's publicity photo many years ago, then Mom's publicity photo, followed by all of the kids' high-school senior portraits.

While I value my time off with my wife, I also value and respect the wishes of my clients, and this family with a dying dog could not be denied.

Purpose

I usually close the week before Christmas, but their children were going to be home from college. Also, the dog, which was probably older than all of their children, was not doing well and they wanted a current family portrait including the dog. I don't usually allow animals in my studio, but I made an exception in this case. Mom and Dad carried the dog into the studio and placed him on their laps.

They did a good job listening to the clothing suggestions; all were nicely attired in blue and black tops, drawing the attention right to the faces. The new David Maheu background complements the clothing with its dark-blue hue, again bringing the focus to the faces.

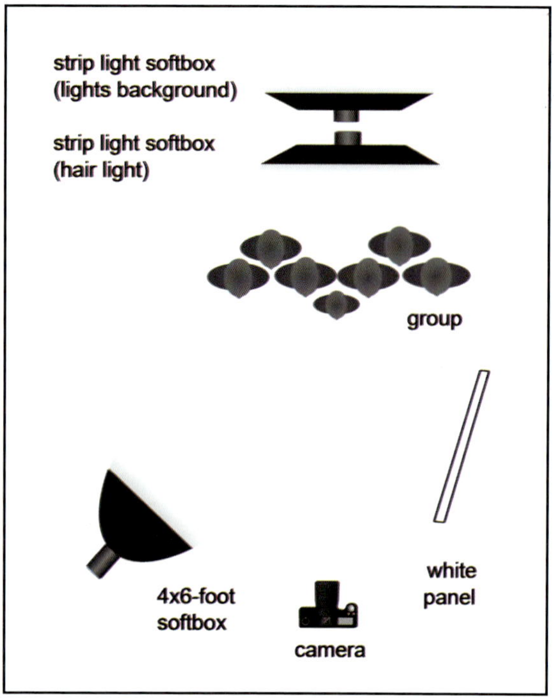

Lighting

My main light was a 4x6-foot softbox set at f/8 on my left, skimming across the group to the right. I had a Photogenic flash in a 12x36-inch strip softbox on a rail system lighting the background at f/5.6 and a Photogenic flash in a 10x36-inch Larson strip softbox as my hair light, also at f/5.6 and attached to the ceiling. I had a 6x3-foot white panel on the right side as a reflector to soften the shadows.

Posing

Mom, Dad, and the two younger children were sitting on posing stools, and you can see that I staggered the heights to avoid a static pose. The two daughters were standing in the back, positioned between two people so that everyone's face was prominent. I also created two very pleasing triangles.

TECH SPECS > This was photographed with a Canon 5D Mark II with the 70–200mm lens set at 70mm. My exposure was f/8 at 1/100 second, and ISO 100.

I staggered the heights to avoid a static pose.

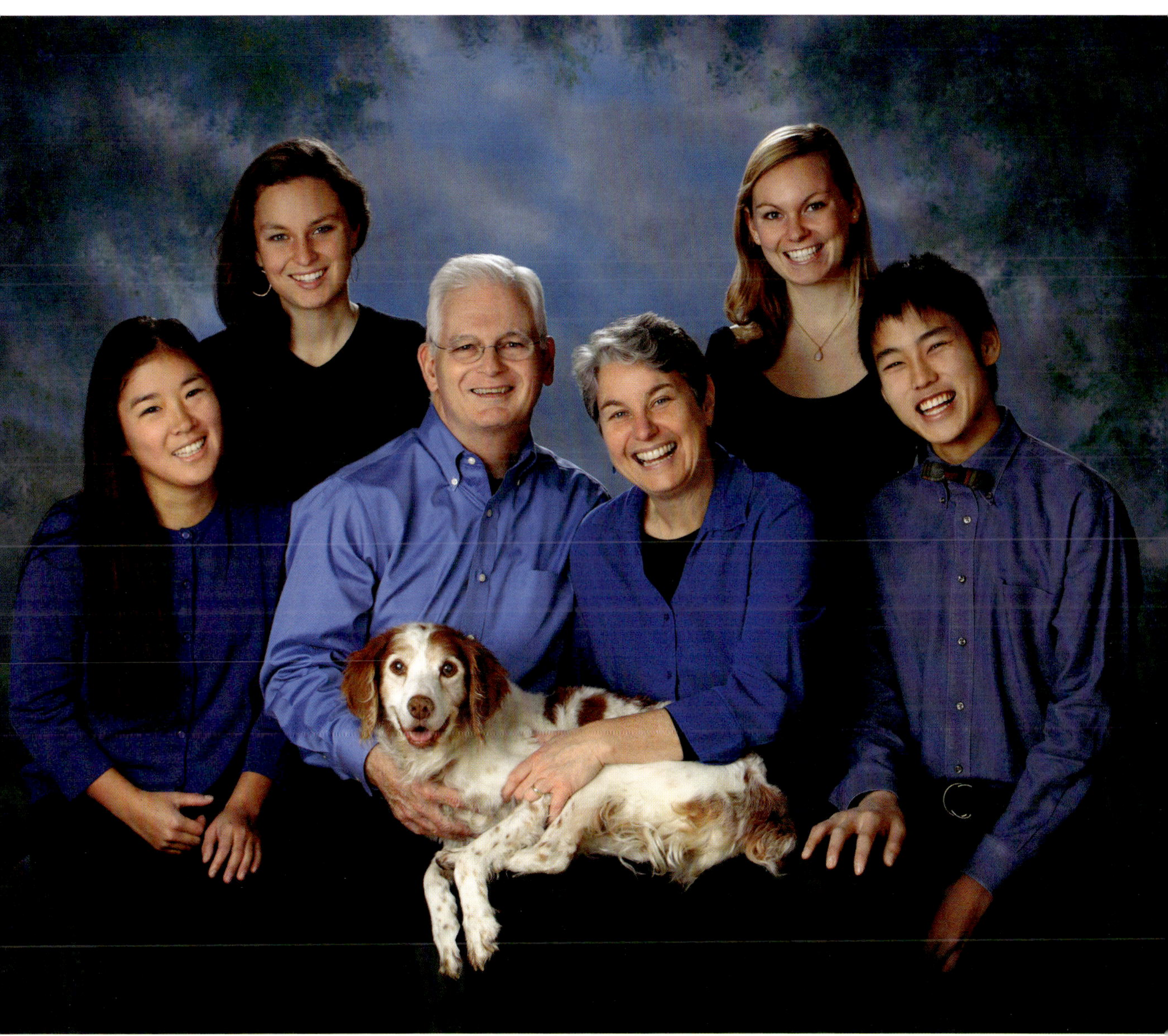

25 Eighty-Fifth Birthday Party

Purpose

This portrait came about because of the eighty-fifth birthday for the man in the suit seated in the second row, which prompted a family reunion at a family member's home. I had photographed one of the families in this portrait a year earlier and they were so pleased that they wanted me to photograph this large group. Again, one assignment leads to another.

In addition to this large group, I also did the individual families and the breakdown portraits of their children and grandchildren. There were a lot of grandparents and some great-grandparents, and I made sure to photograph all possible combinations.

Reunion Photography. Reunion photography requires a photographer to work quickly so that the crowd remains focused on your direction. Being fast and efficient is most important.

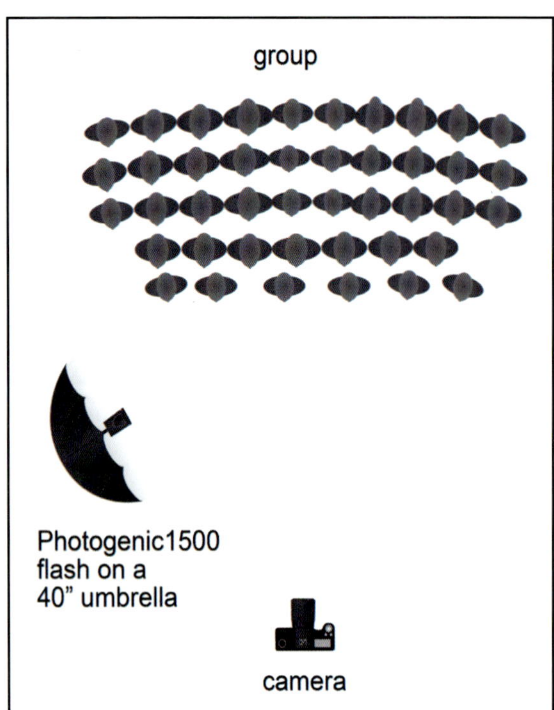

Posing

The younger set were seated on the ground in front; some of the older family members in the second row were in chairs; the girl on the far right was sitting on one of my posing rocks as were a few others for a variety of heights. The third row stood on the ground and the back row was standing on chairs or benches to elevate them a little higher. By standing on a ladder, I was able to see everyone's face in the photograph.

Lighting

My Photogenic flash was in a 40-inch umbrella,set at f/11.5, was to the left of my camera and was plugged into an electrical outlet for quicker recycling. The umbrella skimmed the light across the group from left to right. This gave me a nice even light on everyone. I exposed for the background and used the flash to light up their faces.

TECH SPECS > This was photographed with a Canon 5D Mark II with the 24–105mm lens set at 70mm. The exposure was f/11.5 and 1/60 second (to ensure everyone was in focus) at ISO 800.

To be sure everyone was in focus, my f-stop was f/11.5.

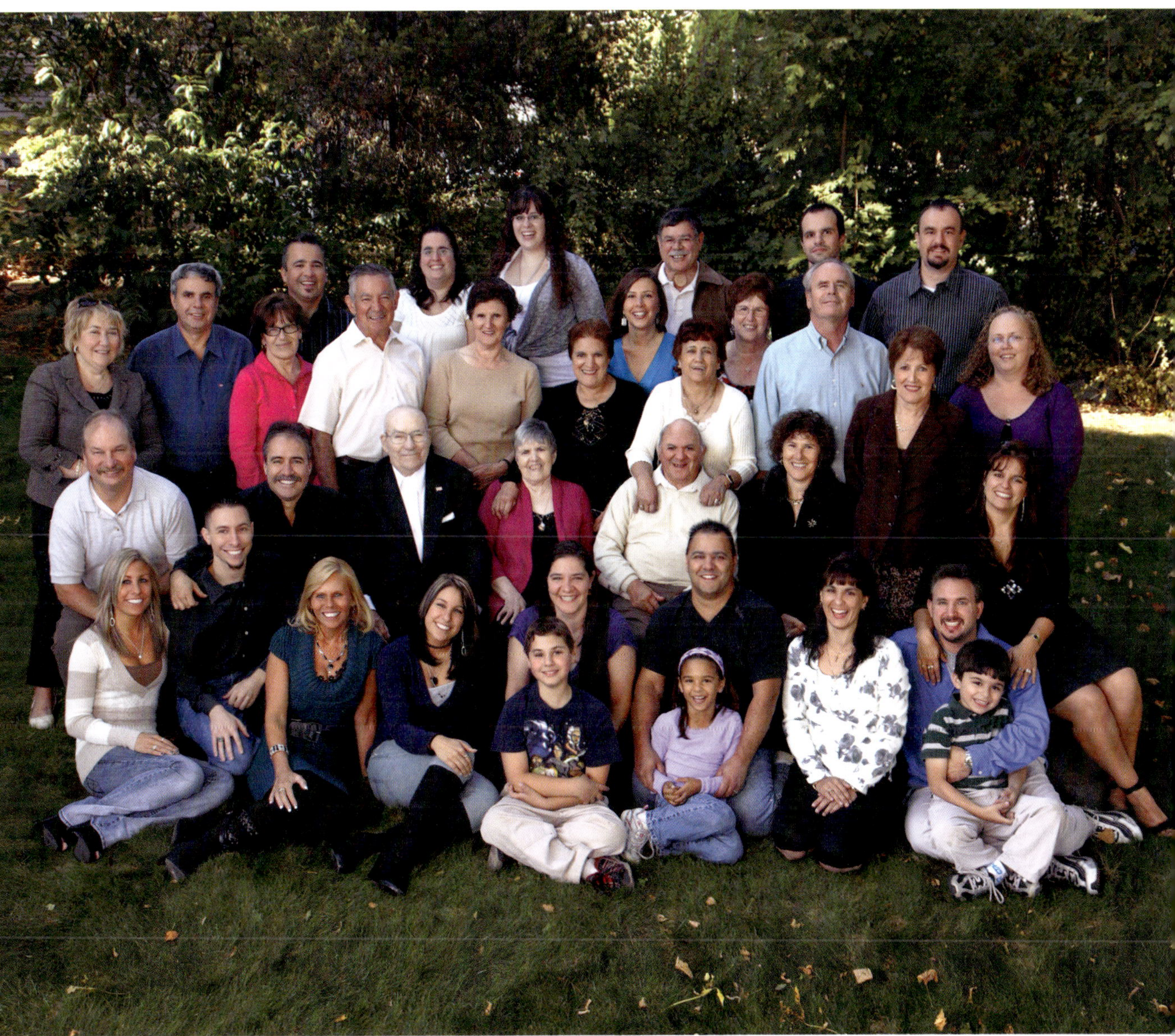

26 Three on a Sofa

Purpose

This family from New York was visiting the woman's aunt and grandmother. The aunt wanted portraits of them for the woman's mother (the grandmother) as well as for herself. We discussed clothing in my advance visit and with the light tones in the house, I thought that the tan and white clothes for the group would work well.

In addition to photographing the young family as a group, I also photographed the little boy by himself, the husband and wife, and the little boy with his great-grandmother, who was reading to him.

Setup

I liked this area between the living room and the dining room in which to photograph. With the owner's permission, I turned the leather sofa to a slight angle because of a glass case with knick-knacks behind them that I did not want coming out of anyone's head. I closed the blinds in the front so the sun did not shine through. The camera was raised on the tripod and I stood on a step stool.

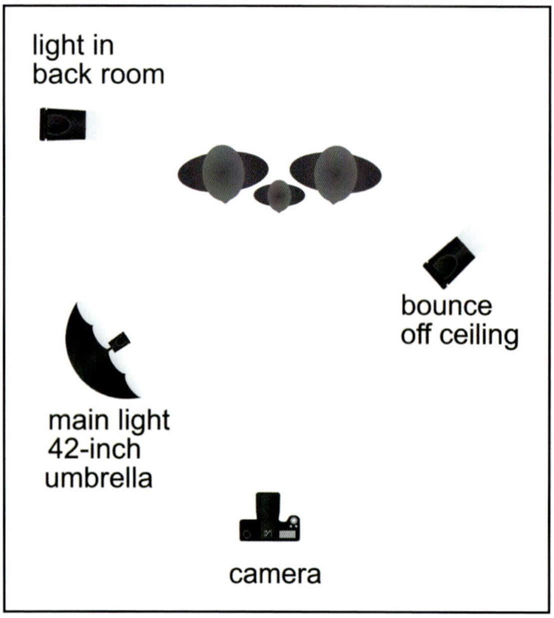

Lighting

Three lights were used in this portrait. The first, my main light, was a Photogenic flash with a 42-inch umbrella to the left of the camera. It feathered the light across the group for even lighting with a 6-foot white panel on the right to soften the shadows. My other two lights were used to illuminate the two rooms. I used a Photogenic flash on the right side of the room bouncing off the ceiling. This gave me an overall light where the family was sitting and a light in the back room bouncing off the wall. PocketWizard triggers were used to set them off.

Avoid Distracting Clothing. Stay away from bold stripes, plaids, checks, and prints because they are visually confusing and compete for the viewer's attention by drawing the eye away from the faces. Likewise, bright colors such as red and orange can detract from or overwhelm the face.

TECH SPECS > This was photographed with a Canon EOS 5D Mark II on a tripod using a 24–105mm lens set at 150mm. My exposure was f/8, 1/60 second, and ISO 400.

I used a Photogenic flash on the right side of the room bouncing off the ceiling. This gave me an overall light where the family was sitting and a light in the back room bouncing off the wall.

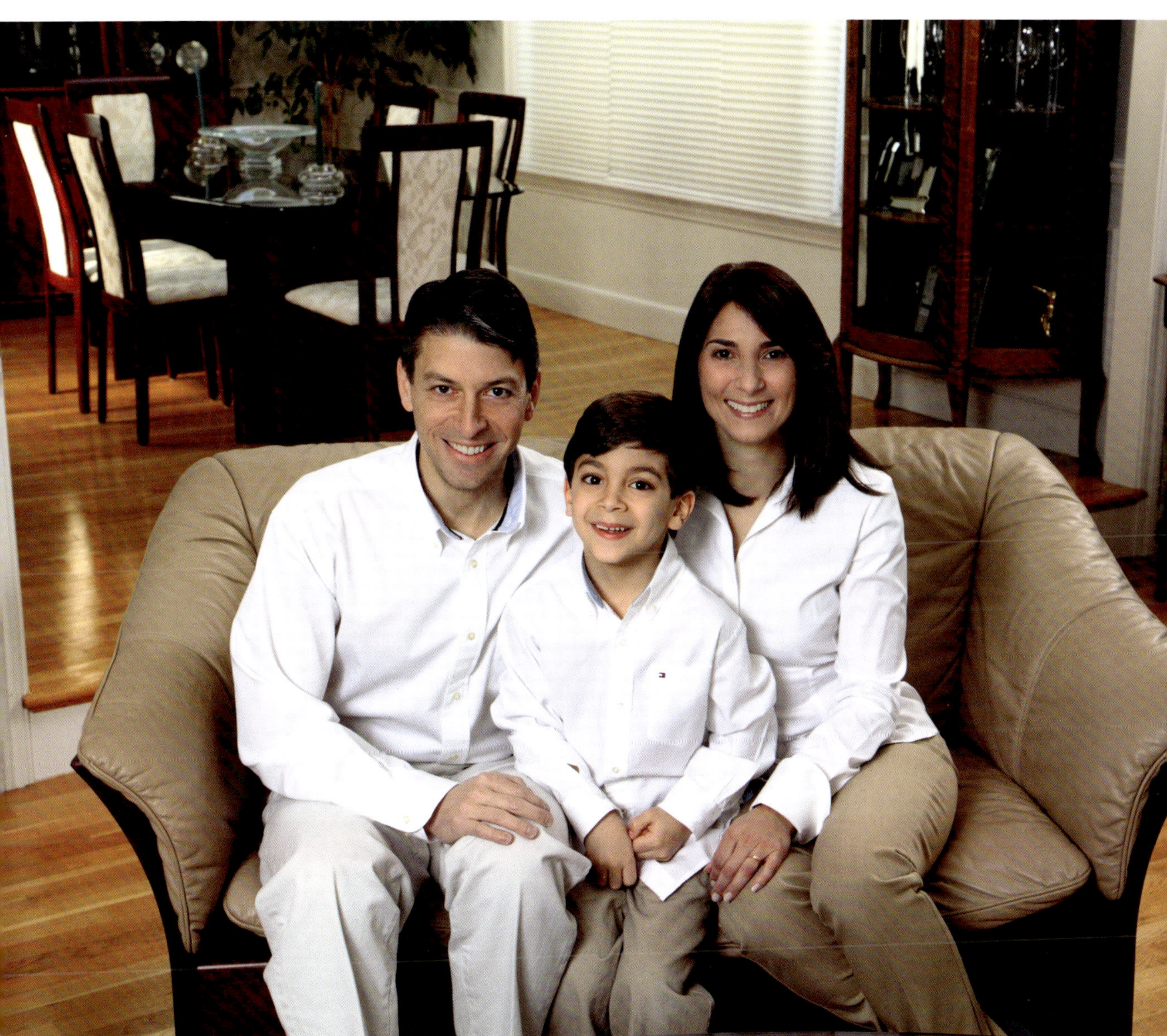

27 Breakaway: Ninety-Nine Years Young

Purpose

No, this is not a family portrait, but a portrait of a woman who is the great-grandmother of the little boy in the previous portrait, *Three on a Sofa*. It is extremely important when photographing a family portrait to also photograph any other possible combinations of groups and individuals. They may not have requested the great-grandmother to be photographed, but it is my responsibility to ensure that they have a good, current portrait of everyone in the room. A well-lit, nicely posed portrait of a 99-years-young woman is something they will cherish, and it opens the door to additional sales.

There was a Photogenic flash in a 42-inch umbrella on the left, placed high, giving me nice catchlights in Grandma's eyes.

Combinations of Groups and Individuals. When photographing a family portrait, also photograph any other possible combinations of groups and individuals. It is the photographer's responsibility to provide good, current portraits of everyone in the room.

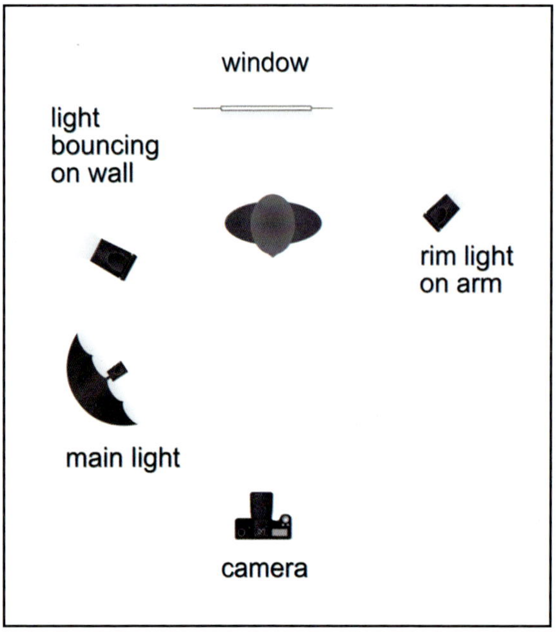

Lighting

I had a light in the corner of the room aimed at the far corner and bounced off the wall so it would come back as a big, soft light. I had a little bit of a rim of light on Grandma's arm from the one extra light. There was a Photogenic flash in a 42-inch umbrella on the left, placed high, giving me nice catchlights in Grandma's eyes. The light coming in through the blinds gave me a soft light for the back room. The owner of the house asked me not to photograph in this location because of the chipped wall paint in the back room where the painters had been working, but I fixed it in Photoshop and you would never know that the wall was chipped. I liked this angle, the open space, and the light.

TECH SPECS > This was photographed with a Canon 5D Mark II and a 24–105mm lens set at 105mm. My exposure was f/8, 1/60 second allowing for the ambient light, at f/7.1 and ISO 400.

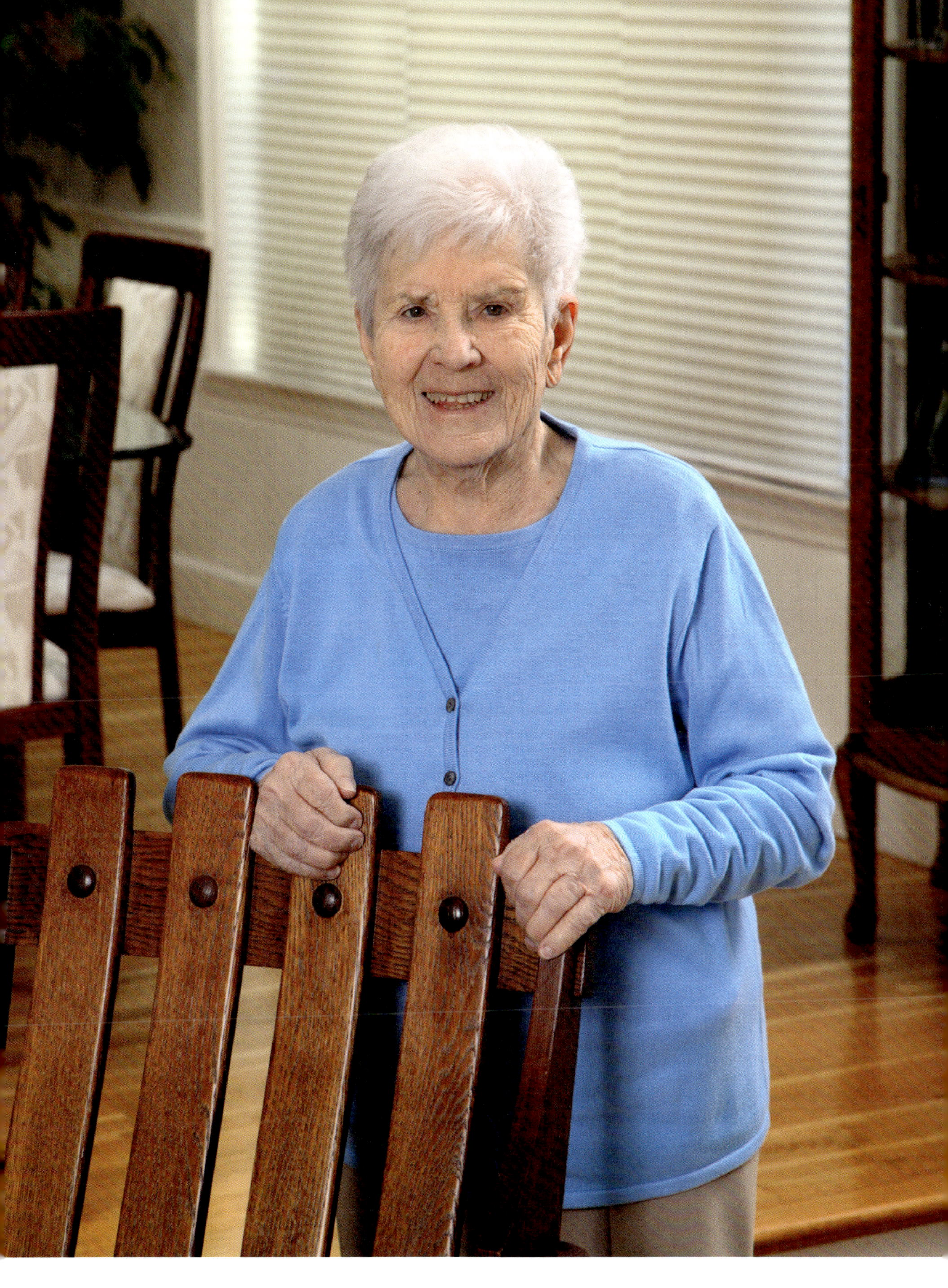

Posing

We did a variety of poses with this family, but this was their favorite. Many of my poses have the family sitting because it lends itself to a horizontal format which will fit nicely over a sofa, but I like to do at least one standing pose so the parents can look back on this time and see how small (or tall) their children were at this stage in their lives. In a year or two, they may be as tall as Mom and a few years later, as tall as Dad.

The early mornings can be dark in the tree area behind the subject; therefore, I set the ISO for 800.

I placed the son in the middle with his hands in his pockets and the girls' arms around Mom and Dad. I had each girl put a hand in their pocket and I had all of them put their weight on their back foot and point their lead foot towards the camera.

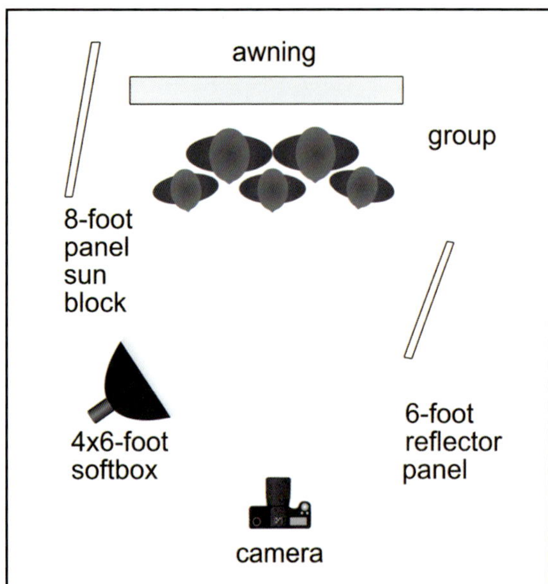

Lighting

This fall family portrait was created in my garden area with artificial turf and a 9x9x9-foot awning over their heads. A 4x6-foot softbox was on the left with a 6-foot square reflector panel on the right. My assistant held an 8-foot panel on the left to block the sunlight from shining on the family. The early mornings can be dark in the tree area behind the subjects; therefore, I set the ISO for 800 for this portrait rather than the normal 640.

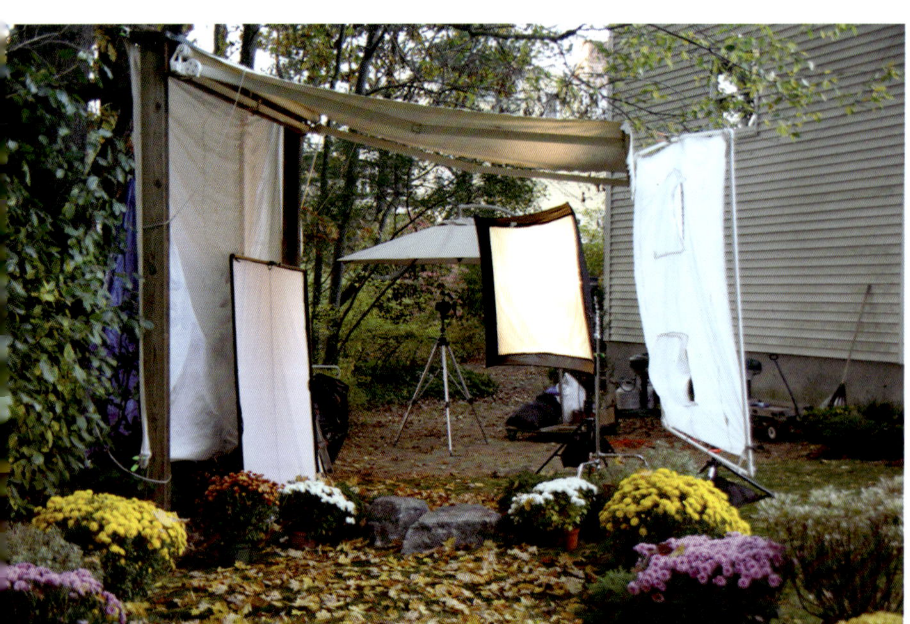

TECH SPECS > This was photographed with a Canon 5D Mark II and a 70–200mm lens set at 150mm. My exposure was f/6.3, 1/60 second, and ISO 800.

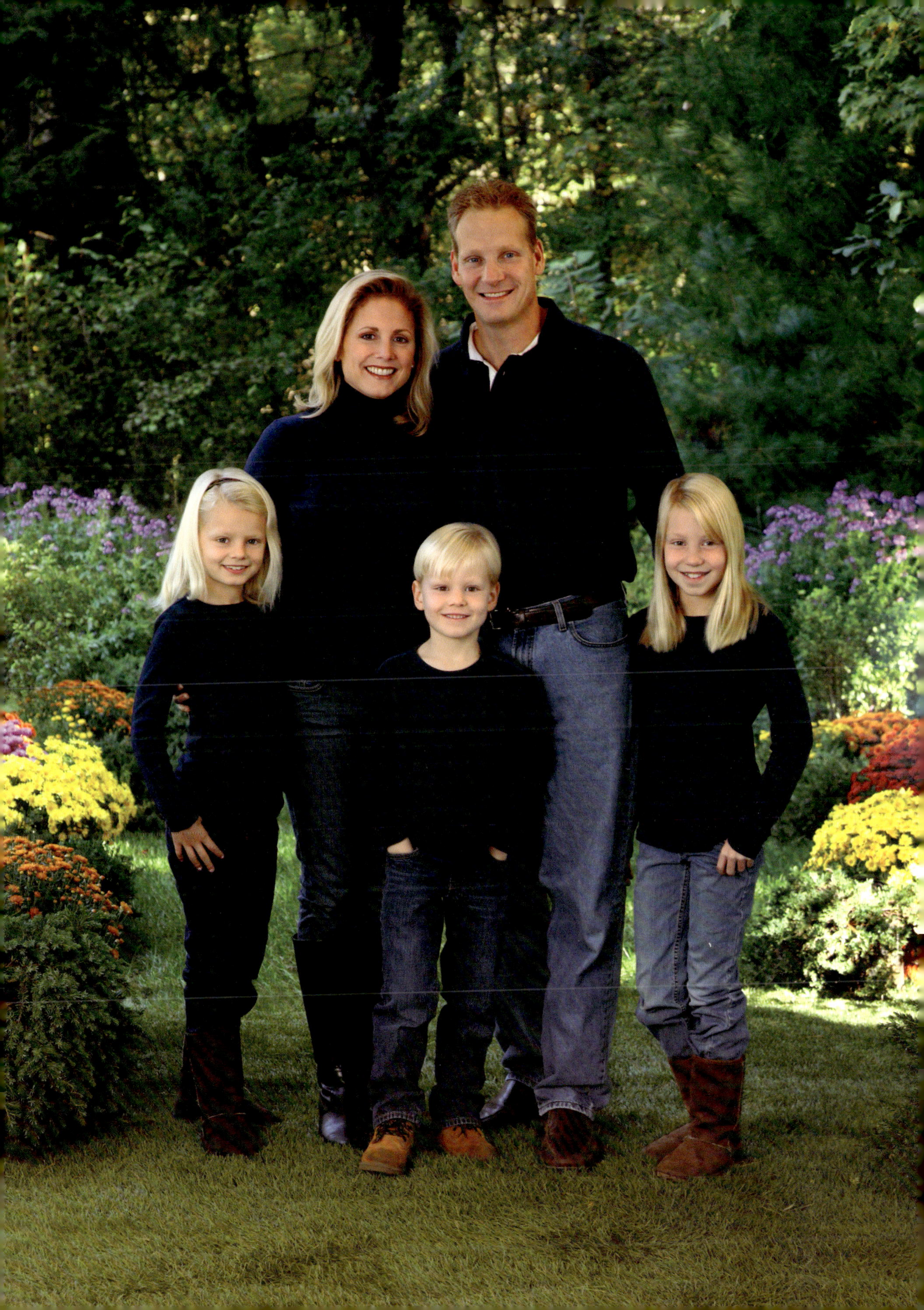

29 Three Generations, Two Steps

Getting There Is Half the Fun

This three-generation family portrait was created on the steps in front of an amazing house near the ocean. I had to drive past a gate and down a half-mile long driveway, and when I thought I reached my destination, it was only a guest house. When I finally arrived at the house, I was still confused because there were three front doors.

Obstacles

The family wanted to be photographed in the back of the house, which sat on the edge of a cliff with the ocean in the background, but the light was not good and the wind was gusting up to 50 mph. I suggested "plan B," the front of the house, and they loved this portrait. I posed them on the front steps of their home with one of their very heavy doors in the background. You always have to think about alternate scenarios and make the best of any given situation.

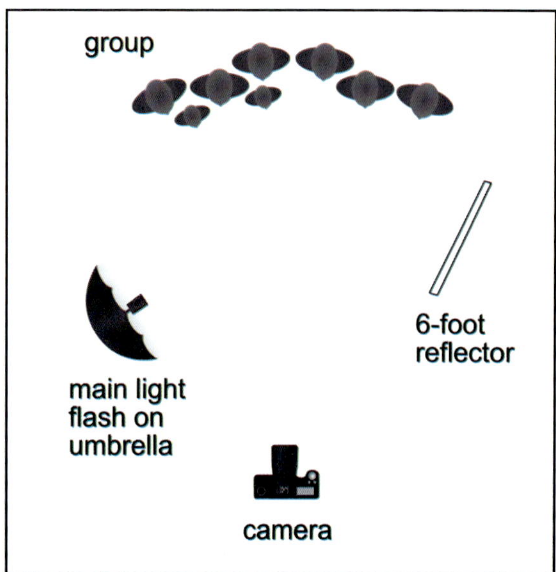

Lighting

I used an Mamiya RZ67 with a 90mm lens. A flash on an umbrella on the left skimmed across to the right with a 6-foot reflector bouncing the light back into their faces.

Alternate Scenarios. When photographing a family portrait on location, it is important to think about alternate scenarios for the portrait. The photographer needs to anticipate changes in weather or lighting and have a quick eye to observe available options for seating and lighting as well as for interesting lines, color, and other useful environmental features.

Working the Crowd

I started the session by photographing the entire group before moving to another location where I photographed the individual families, the children together and separately, as well as the grandparents and the grandparents with the grandkids. The grandparents were very reserved, and it was difficult to get them to loosen up. I was trying to evoke a smile from the grandparents when finally, I picked up the little boy and said, "Look at Michael, isn't he the cutest little boy you've ever seen?" And I got the most amazing smiles from both of them.

TECH SPECS > This was photographed with a Mamiya RZ67 and a 90mm lens. My exposure was f/8, 1/60 second, and ISO 400.

I suggested "plan B," the front of the house, and they loved this portrait.

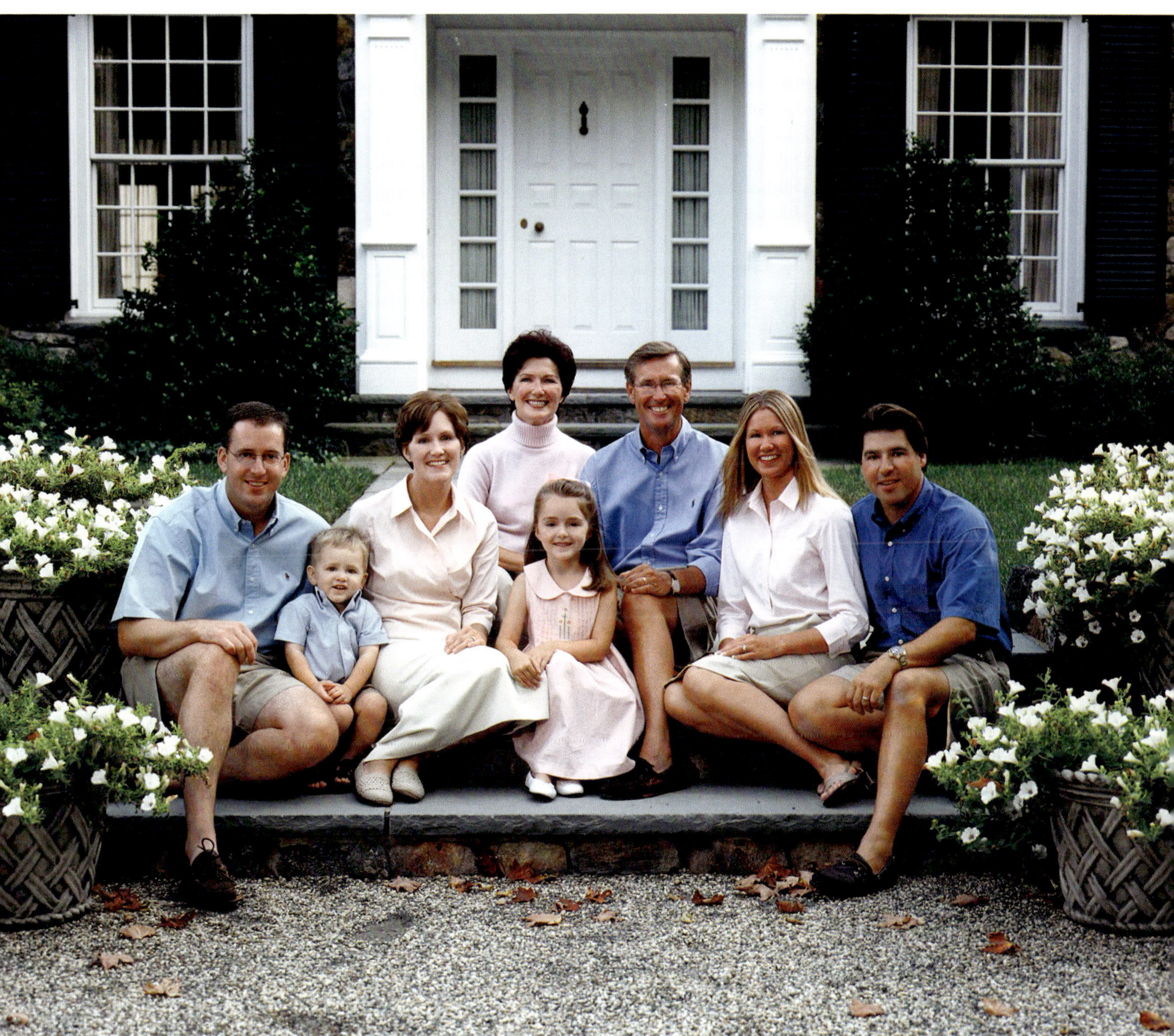

30 Fiftieth Anniversary

Purpose

The stars of this portrait are the couple standing in the middle of the group, who were celebrating their fiftieth wedding anniversary. This photograph commemorates the couple's special day and their family's celebration.

Posing

My one major concern was that I did not want the tree to appear to be growing out of the grandmother's head, so I had to be sure to position her just right. I used four chairs, angled toward the center of the group. I instructed the women to cross their legs at their ankles with the foot farthest from the camera behind the lead foot. The women on the left did this well; the woman on the right reversed what I would normally prefer, but it wasn't too objectionable in this portrait. The two youngest grandchildren were positioned in front of the grandparents, partially obscuring their midsections, and even though they are not heavy people, the grandchildren's placement has a slimming effect on the grandparents.

This was a very tight area in which to work. They were in the gazebo and I was just outside the gazebo photographing into it. I brought my potted plants to balance the group and fill in the dead space. I use junipers because they grow long and hide the pot. I placed other plants behind the junipers to give the layered effect.

Everything was set up before they came out to the gazebo; I even had my assistant sit for a test exposure. I was there to create lasting memories of this day and not to keep them from their festivities. As soon as I was ready, I had everyone come to the gazebo and placed them in position and just worked for expressions.

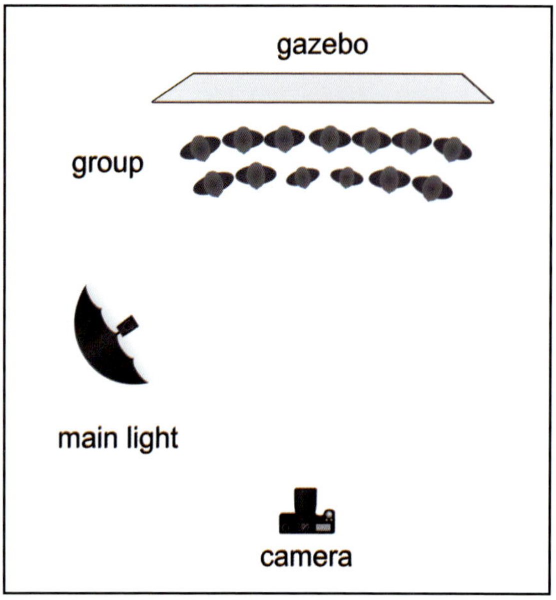

gazebo
group
main light
camera

Consistent Footwear. If the portrait is full length, ensure that stockings and footwear are consistent with the intent of the portrait.

Lighting

Because it was dark under the gazebo, I set my flash to f/8. I used a Photogenic flash with a 42-inch umbrella to the left of my camera skimming across the group. This gave me plenty of light to balance with the light in the background.

TECH SPECS > This was photographed with a Canon 5D Mark II and 50mm lens. My exposure was f/8, 1/60 second, and ISO 400.

Everything was set up before they came out to the gazebo.

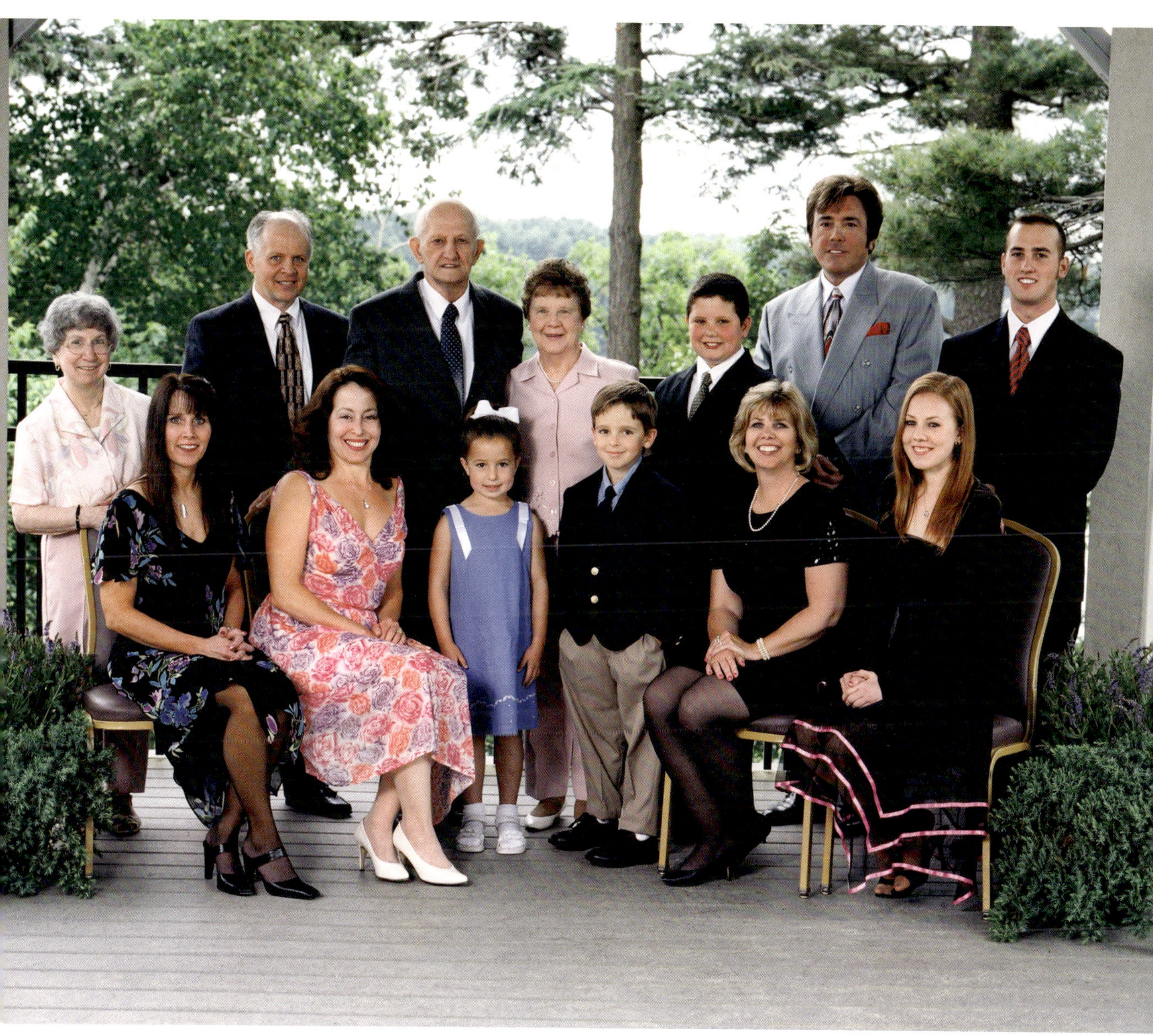

31 A New Family Portrait to Show Off Their New House

Purpose

This family found me when they were house hunting and the previous residents had their family portrait on the wall. They liked the portrait so much that they obtained my information, along with the house. I received a telephone call a year after they purchased the house to create their family portrait in front of their new home.

Lighting

I had an assistant hold an 8-foot panel on the left to block the sunlight that was coming from low in the sky so that it did not wash out my subjects. My main light was a Photogenic flash shooting into a 42-inch umbrella, placed to the left of the camera.

Posing

The women were posed so that their legs were turned in towards the center of the composition and Dad brought his left leg up and moved it slightly to his right (our left). I always have those on the outside of the group direct or lean some part of their body in toward the center; those on my left will turn slightly to my right and those on my right will turn slightly to my left. This enhanced the composition.

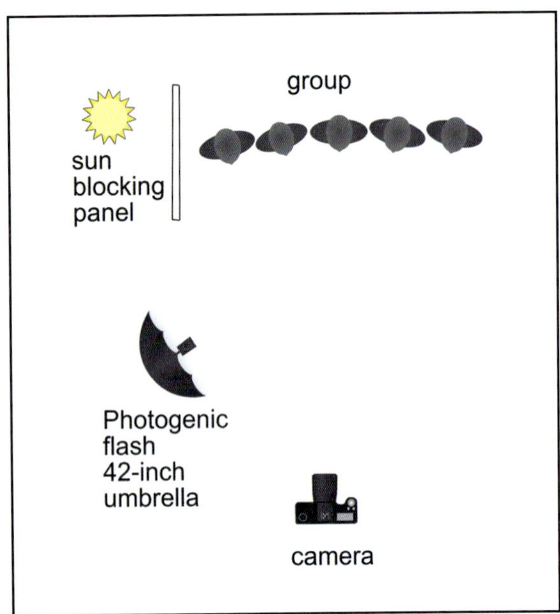

Composition and Details

I placed my plants on the left and right in front of the family for balance and positioned the camera so that the house is at an angle, making the photograph a little more interesting. The chrysanthemum in front of the house to the left of the steps had originally been on the front step. With their permission, I moved it so that it did not look like Dad was wearing the plant on his head. It is very important to pay attention to such details because the slightest error could ruin a beautiful portrait.

Mom, Dad and their daughter are sitting on my artificial rocks with the boys on the ground, building up to Dad in the middle. This created a triangle composition.

This is an example of how a refined portrait stands the test of time. Although it was taken in 2003, it could easily have been created last summer. Good photography does not go out of style. Since this family portrait was created, I have photographed the kids' high-school senior portraits.

TECH SPECS > This was photographed with a Mamiya RZ67 and 50mm lens. The exposure was set at f/8, 1/125 second, and 400 ISO.

I always have those on the outside of the group direct or lean some part of their body in toward the center.

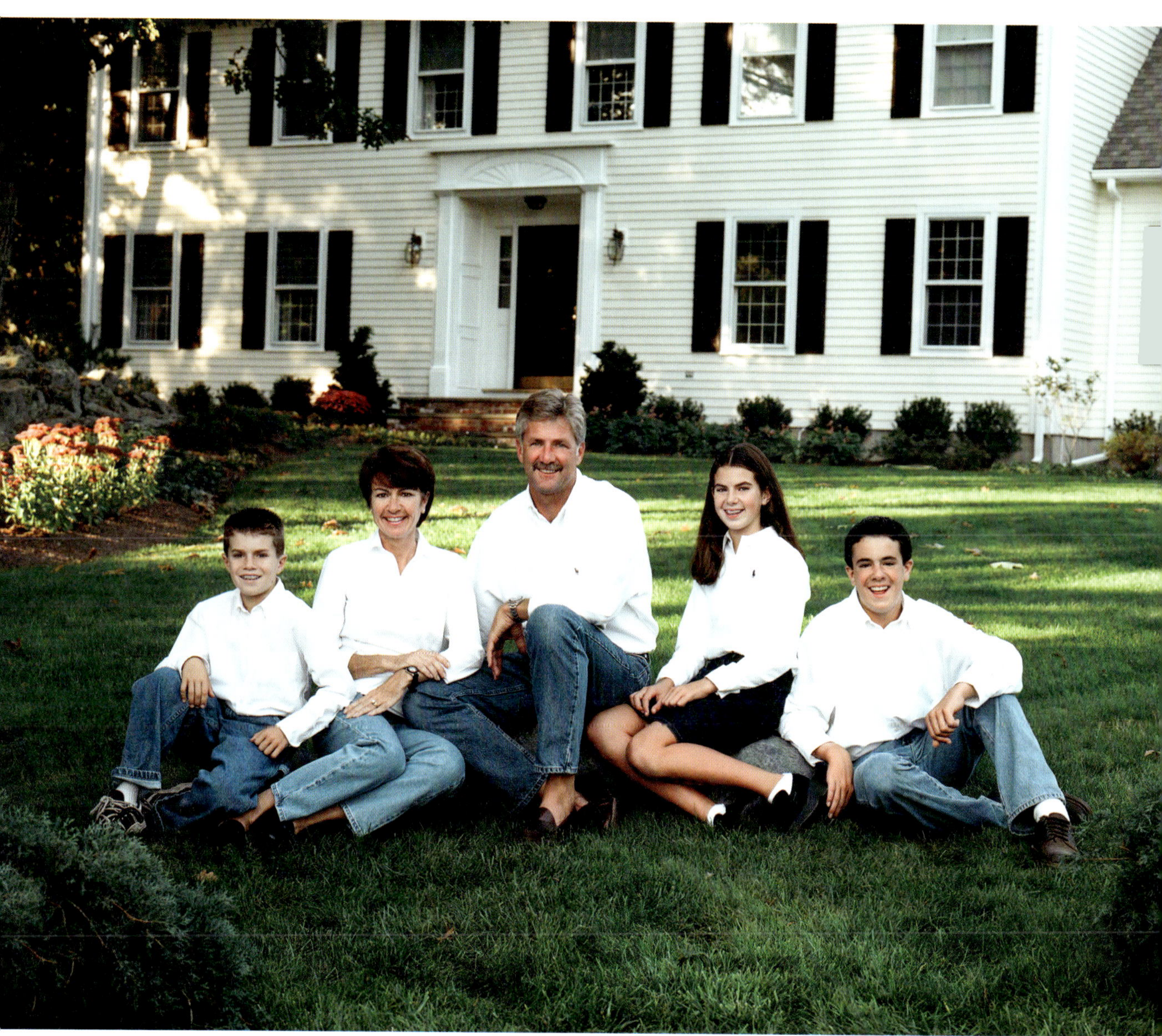

32 Relaxing in the Grass #2

How We Generate New Clients

We have portraits displayed in numerous restaurants and businesses in the North Andover area; this new client resulted from my participation in an Art-in-the-Park event. Our display always stands out because of our studio name in deep blue lettering on all four sides of the white awning. People sign up for a chance to win a $200 certificate towards a portrait, and we give out five of these at the event. By giving away a session fee or a little more than a session fee, it tends to bring the families into the studio, giving us the opportunity to sell wall and gift portraits.

Posing

This is a good pose for young people because of its relaxed nature or for heavier people (which this family was not) because it has a slimming effect. I had the little girl on the right lift her feet up and her nine-month-old brother sit up by himself between Mom and Dad. Mom liked this casual pose with Dad's arm around the little girl and everyone touching.

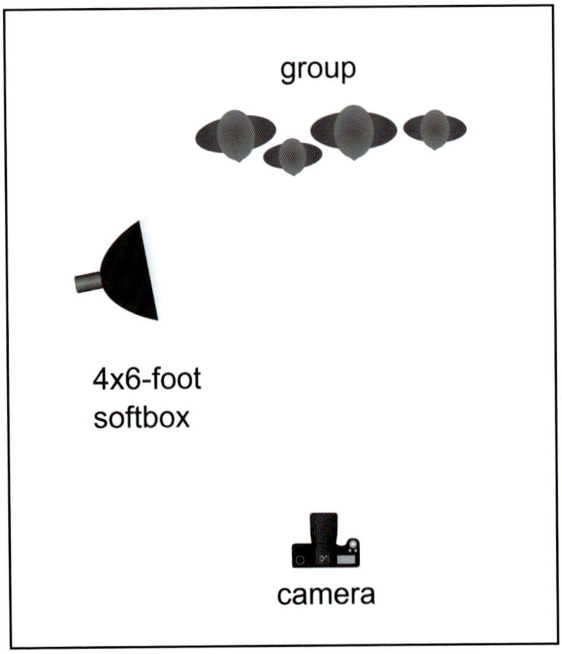

group
4x6-foot
softbox
camera

Adjust and Lower the Position of the Lights. Lower the lights to just above eye level of your subjects when the camera is lowered for a portrait that is close to the ground. Leaving a softbox high can result in shadows under the eyes and nose.

Lighting

This was created in the garden area at my studio with a Photogenic light in a 4x6-foot softbox on the left, natural light in the background, artificial field turf in the foreground, and real spring flowers. The light is came from the left, skimming across the faces to the right. I skim rather than point the light directly on them for a nice even light. Doing so allows me to avoid harsh shadows under the eyes and noses. This portrait was photographed keeping the camera and softbox close to the ground. I used a Bogen tripod, model 3051. With the push of a button, it collapses down to the ground.

TECH SPECS > This was photographed with a Canon 5D Mark II and 70–200mm lens set at 150mm. My exposure was f/7.1, 1/60 second, and ISO 800.

By skimming or feathering the light, I avoid harsh shadows under the eyes and noses.

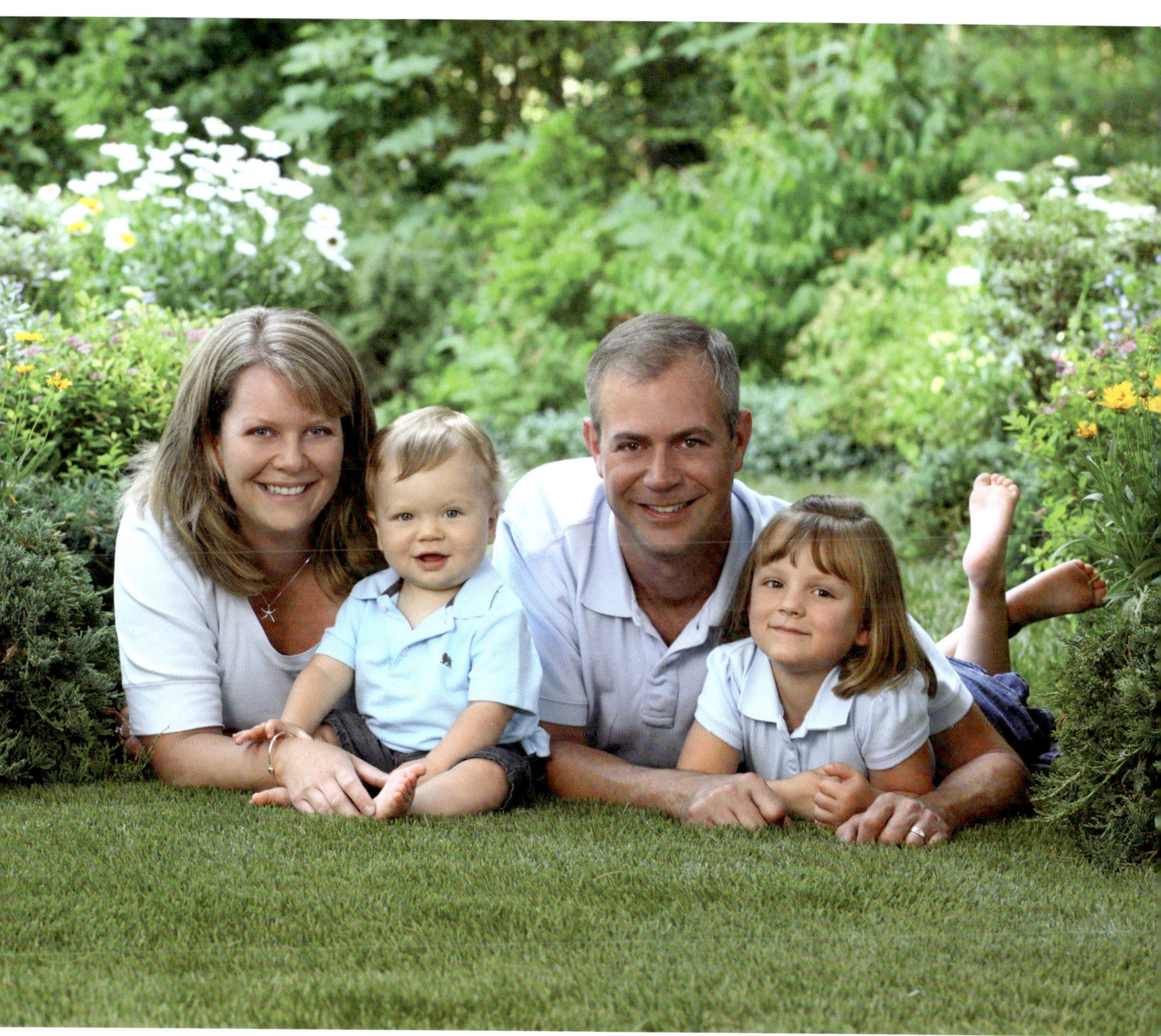

33 It's a Family Portrait with Dogs

Posing

This woman's four dogs are her kids, and she wanted a family portrait with them. I gained the dogs' attention by making high-pitched squeaky noises, which also got the woman to smile. Her husband didn't want to be in the photo but was very impressed that I was able to get such a great photo of his wife and the four dogs. Not all families have children, and many who own pets see their pets as their kids.

Potted Plants. Placing potted plants in a portrait helps to frame the subjects and create interesting textures and shapes that fills in gaps that otherwise be might be distracting.

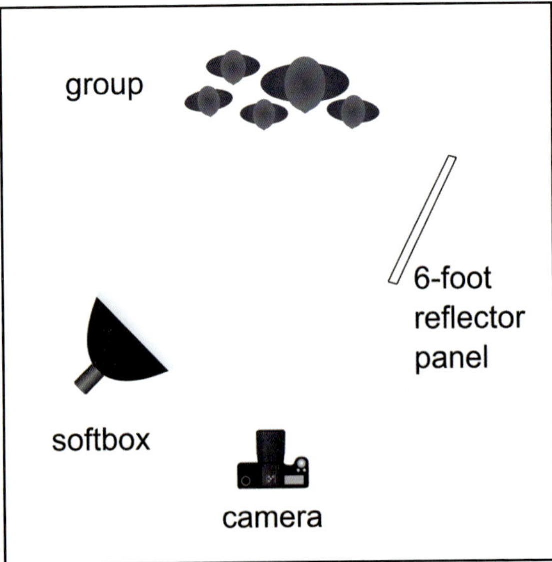

My Outdoor Studio and Its Greenery

This was photographed in my outdoor studio, which I can make look very different in each portrait because I am able to change the appearance with my portable potted plants. The background garden has many blooming plants planted in the ground, which give me a rich lush backdrop to use. Then I have a variety of plants in pots that I can select from depending on the season, the colors, and the size of plants needed. I take the area apart after each session and set it up a little differently for the next session, depending on what it calls for. I have my studio gardens blooming, but I also utilize my potted plants.

Lighting

I photographed them at f/8 so I could be sure to get all of the dogs in focus. I exposed for the background which was f/8, 1/60 second, 800 ISO. I put my softbox flash on the left set at f/8 to balance out with the background, with my 6-foot square white panel on the right to fill in the area under her eyes and nose.

TECH SPECS > This was photographed with Canon 5D Mark II with the 70–200mm lens set at 150mm. My exposure was f/8, 1/60 second, and ISO 800.

I take the area apart after each session and set it up a little differently for the next session.

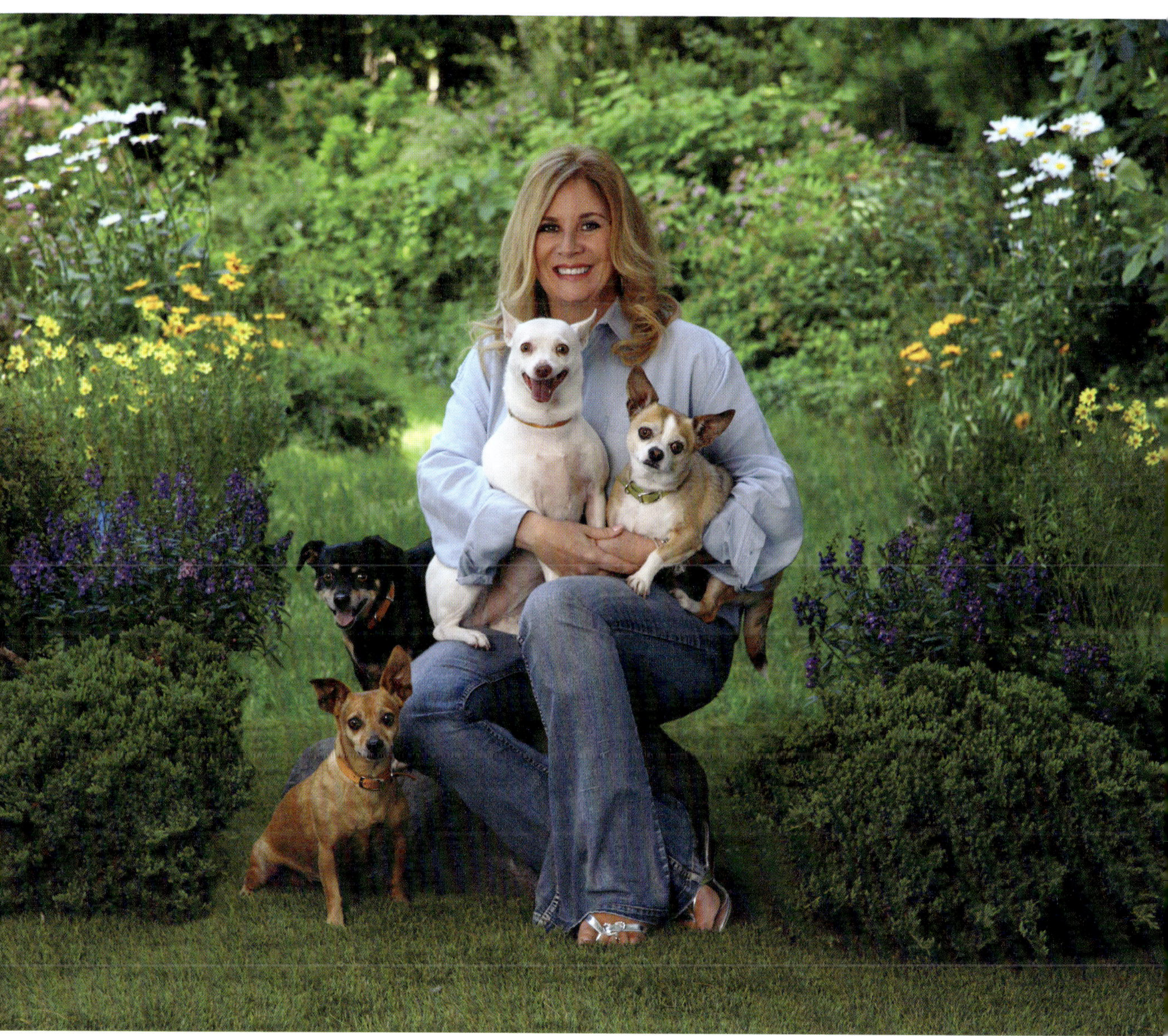

34 Three Generations in My Studio

Background

This portrait won many awards and was displayed at a national convention of the Professional Photographers of America. This is simply a nice portrait of grandparents with their married children and grandchildren. This was taken in my outdoor studio with my artificial turf; I made the area wider to accommodate thirteen people.

Posing

I placed the moms on chairs facing into the center with their ankles crossed. The little girls were seated on their moms' laps with their ankles crossed; this helped to make the moms appear slimmer. The boys on either end were seated on my custom-made rocks, and the two boys in front were on the ground. The girl in the center was also sitting on one of my rocks, partially blocking the grandparents' mid-sections. The two sons stood in the back with their hands in their pockets, adding to this casual pose. The grandfather had his right hand in his pocket and his left arm around his wife and the grandmother rested her left hand on her husband. This composition has a nice flow and all faces are clearly visible.

After photographing the large group, I photographed the grandparents alone, each of the families alone and their children separately and together. I also photographed the grandparents with the grandchildren.

Lighting

The 4x6-foot softbox was on my left, aimed at the people on the far right. My with my 6-foot-square white panel was on the right, reflecting the light back to the faces.

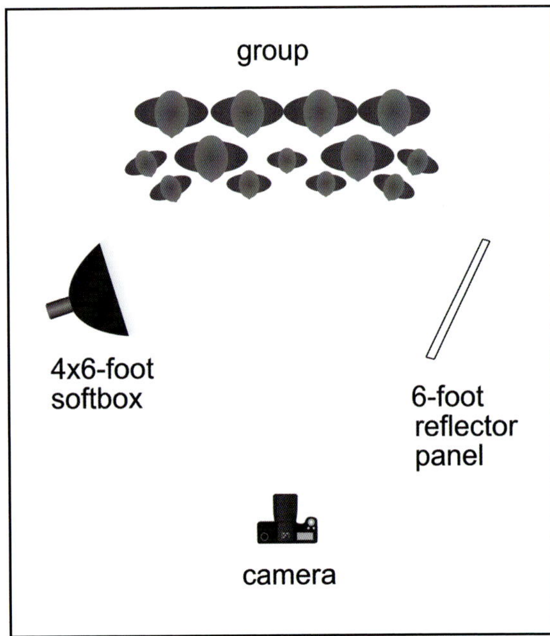

TECH SPECS > This was photographed with a Canon 5D Mark II and the 24–105mm lens set at 85mm. My exposure was f/8, 1/60 second, and ISO 640.

Skin-Tone Considerations. The main objective of a portrait is to draw the viewer's attention to the subjects' faces. Whether their complexions are light or dark, skin highlights are the lightest and brightest areas in the image. Given a medium to dark background, all subjects photograph best when wearing medium to dark tones, regardless of skin tone.

This portrait won many awards and was displayed at a national convention of the Professional Photographers of America.

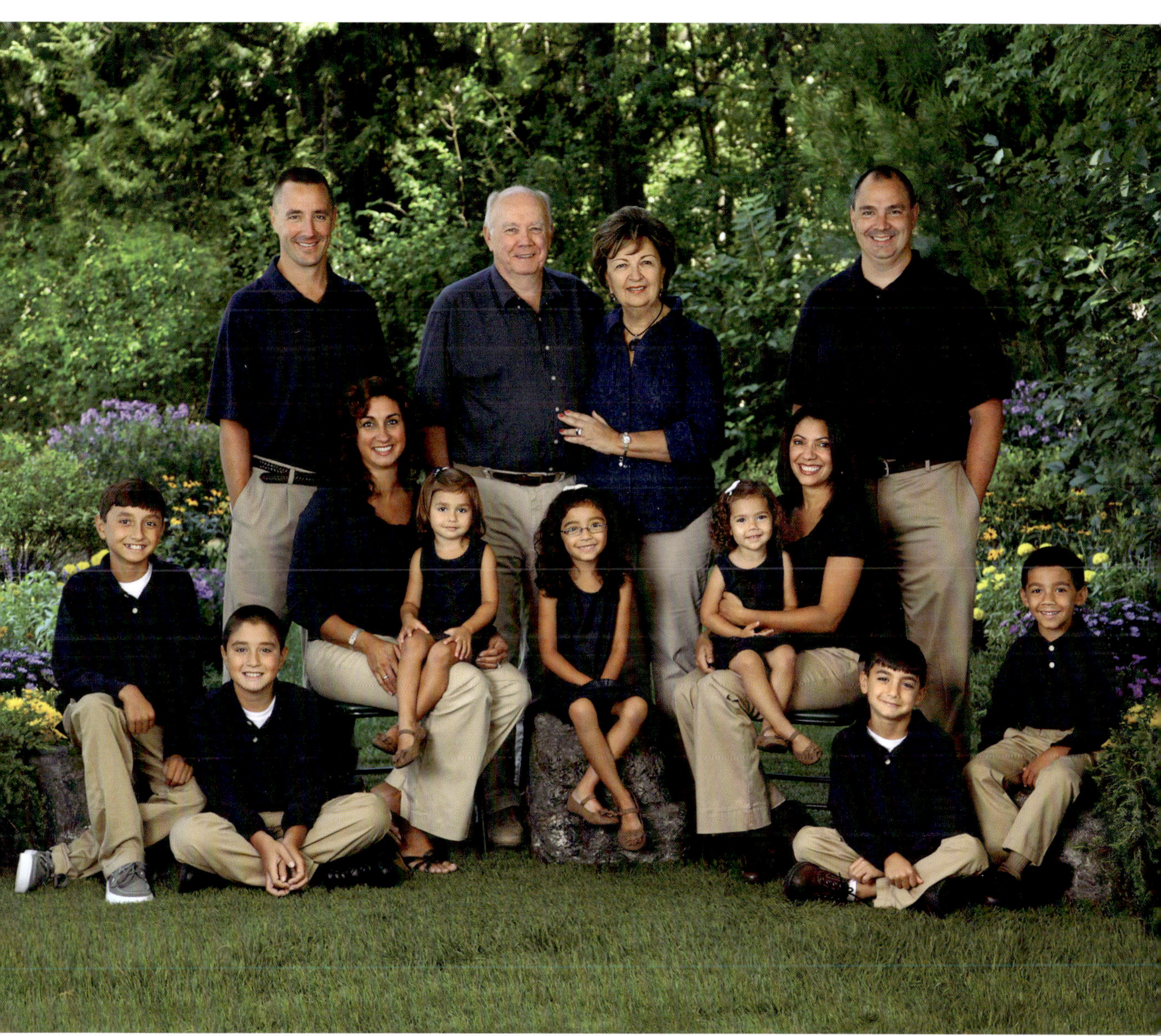

35 Studio Portrait #3

Events and Fund-Raisers

This family was photographed for a special event fund-raiser for a local Catholic school. The families paid $75, which went to the school, and they received a 5x7-inch print from the session. We photographed sixteen families in a row, one every thirty minutes. This family listened to my suggestions at the clothing consultation, and Dad was especially amazed that I got everyone looking at the camera and looking good at the same time; he didn't think I could do it with his three sons. In addition to receiving the 5x7-inch print that came with the session, this family also purchased a wall portrait of this pose, as well as other photographs for family members.

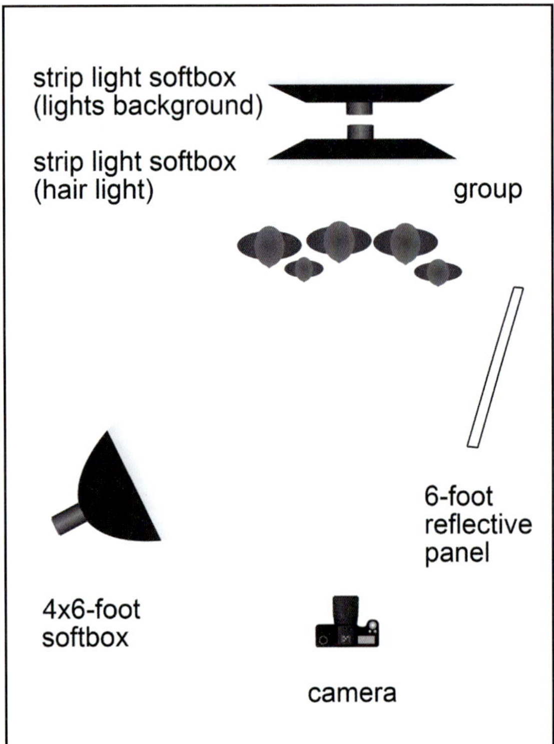

Lights

My main light was on the left and was set at f/8, with a reflective panel on the right side. I used a Photogenic flash in a Larson 10x36-inch strip softbox as a hair light, set at f/5.6. A Photogenic flash in a 12x36-inch strip softbox was set at f/5.6 to light the background. Both lights were on a rail system attached to the ceiling.

Posing

The little boy on the left stood on a box so he wouldn't have be on Dad's knees. I also put a box in the middle so Mom and Dad could lift their legs up a little bit. The box also provided a place for the littlest one to sit.

This portrait utilized two boxes—easy props for the studio. Although they can't be seen, the boxes made all the difference in Mom and Dad's comfort, pose, and the composition of the final portrait.

Time Considerations

Because of time restrictions with this project, I photographed the family and another portrait of the three kids together; I did not have time to photograph the kids individually. I did two poses of the family and the children in a half hour.

TECH SPECS > This was photographed with a Canon 5D Mark II and 70–200mm lens set at 70mm. My exposure was f/6.3, 1/100 second, and ISO 100.

My main light was on the left and was set at f/8, with a reflector panel on the right side.

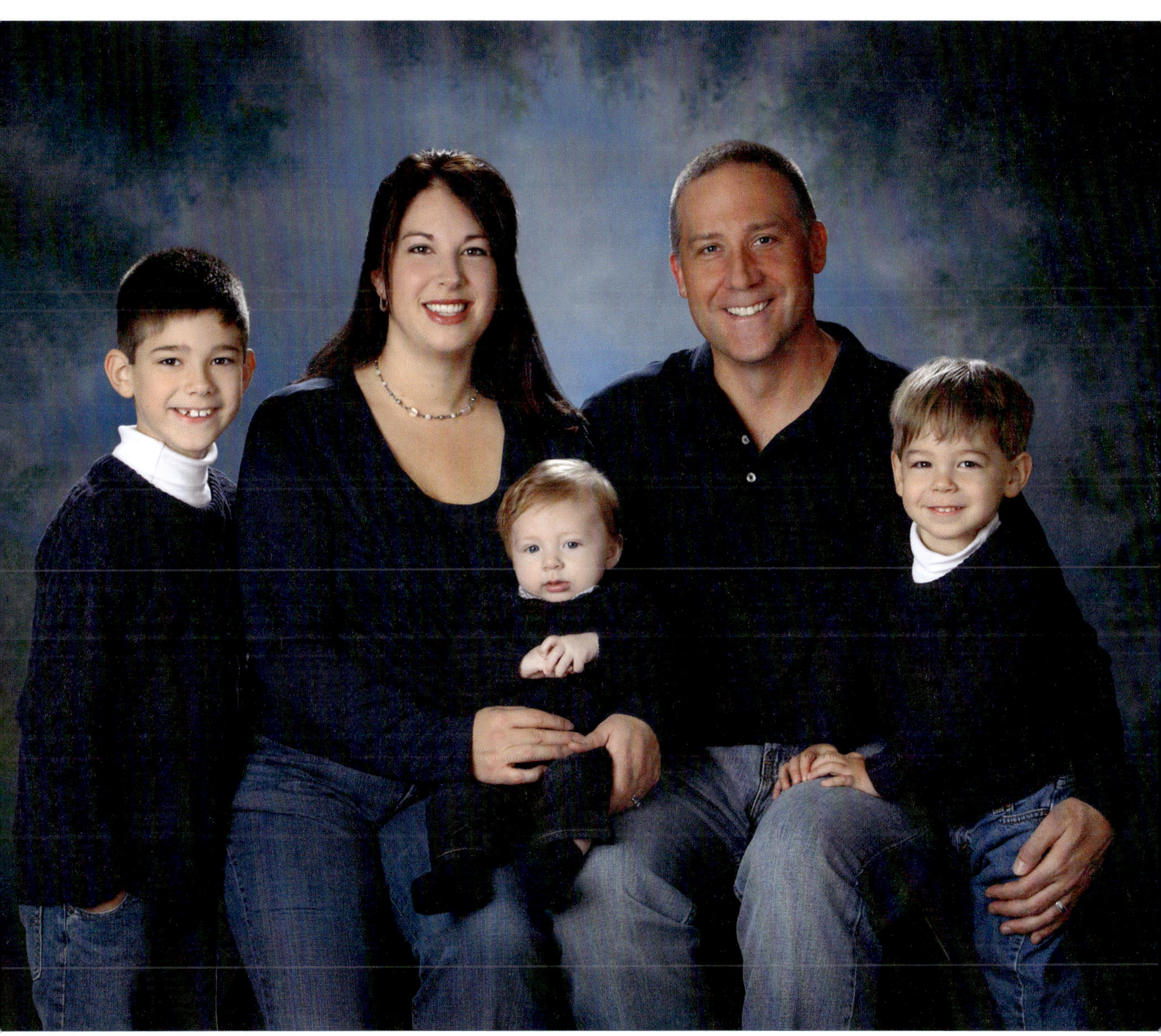

36 Fall Portrait

Leaves, Leaves, and More Leaves

The leaves are courtesy of my assistant who brings them from wherever he can find them within a five–mile radius so we can have fresh fallen leaves for our portrait sessions. We place the leaves in front and around the subjects and moved my potted plants to fill the gaps; they added some color, and balance the composition. We are able to photograph the entire month of October and guarantee beautiful leaves for every outdoor session.

Composition

The orange branch behind Dad's head was cut from another tree and placed behind him to add a little color and to fill the void; I used duct tape to attach it to a branch on the tree. I put the cut end into a water bottle and the branch lasted for a week. Not only did it add a little color, but it also picked up the colors of the chrysanthemums and formed a triangle of color, adding to the composition.

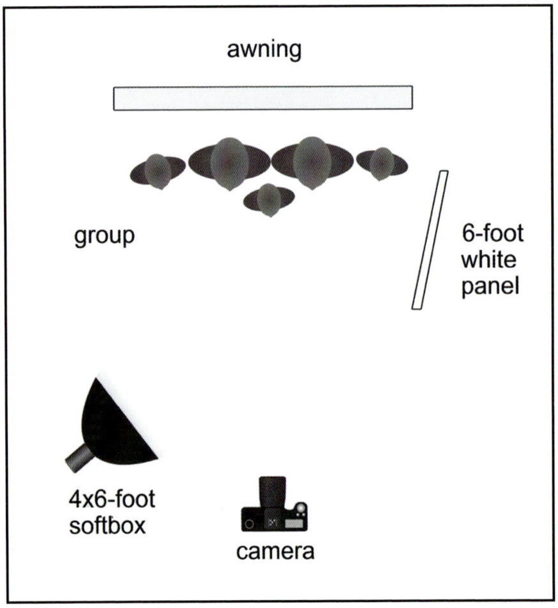

awning
group
6-foot white panel
4x6-foot softbox
camera

This family stood towards the back of my 9x9x9-foot awning with the sunlight lighting their hair.

Posing

I placed the younger daughter in the middle and gave her a leaf to hold so she had something to do with her hands. Little kids are naturally antsy, so I ran around to find the "best leaf" for her. I turned Mom a little towards Dad, with the daughter with the leaf in front hiding part of Mom. Even though Mom is slim and beautiful, she appreciated this slimming effect. The older daughter on the left held onto Mom's leg, and their son was on the right with his left hand in his pocket, looking cool.

Lighting

This family stood towards the back of my 9x9x9-foot awning with the sunlight lighting their hair. The 4x6-foot softbox was to the left of my camera, and my 6-foot-square white panel was on the right, reflecting light back to the faces.

TECH SPECS > This was photographed with a Canon 5D Mark II and 70–200mm lens set at 160mm. My exposure was f/6.3, 1/60 second, and ISO 800.

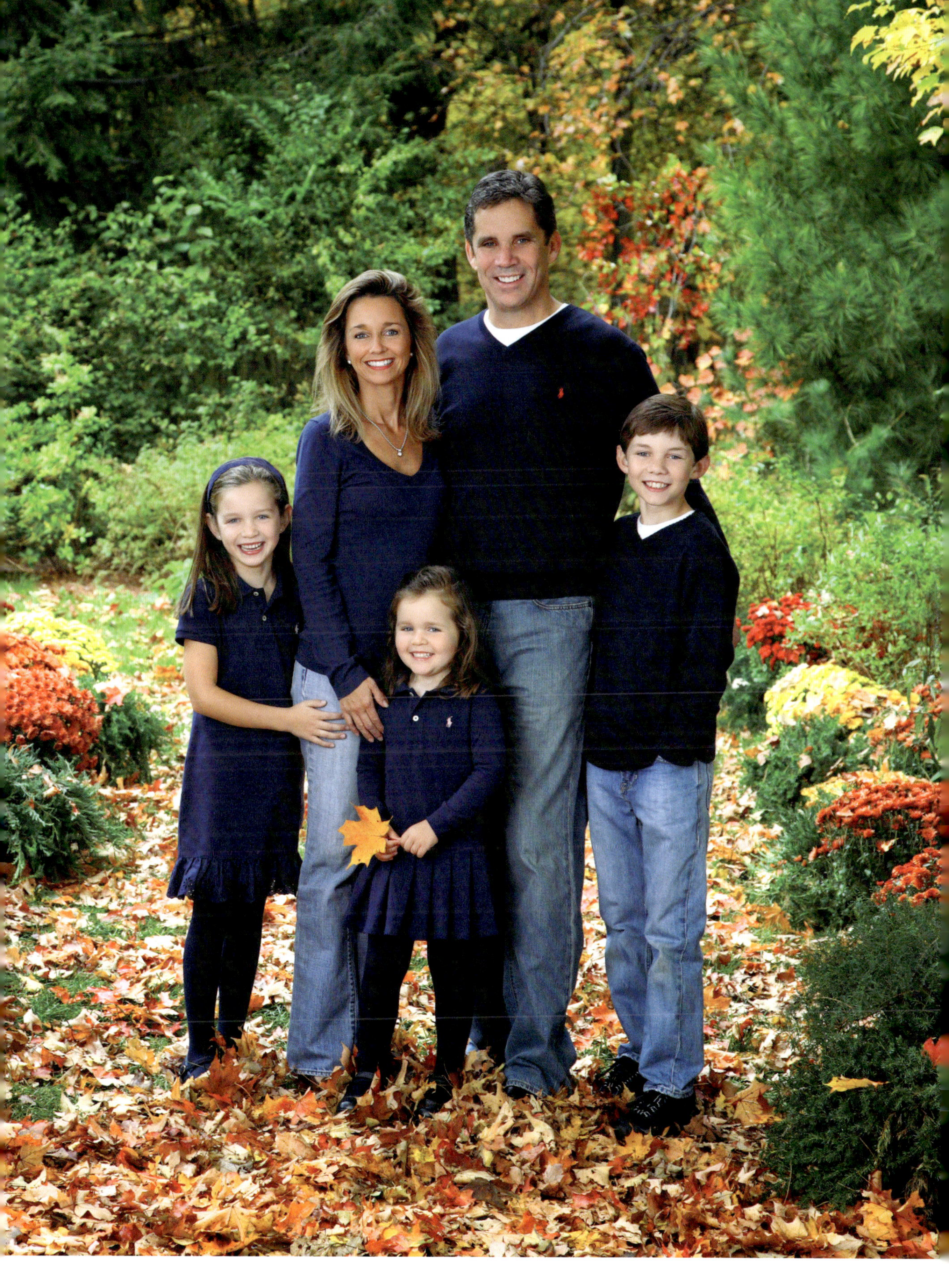

37 Portrait in My Outdoor Studio

Repeat Clients

I have been photographing this family since the oldest boy was a baby. This started as a client/ photographer relationship and has blossomed into a personal friendship.

Posing

What began as a difficult session with the youngest boy crying and the dad saying, "Good luck with this," ended with everyone being happy.

I used my three posing rocks with the oldest boy on the right, the middle child on the left, and Mom and Dad in the center with Dad holding the youngest son. I had Mom and Dad's knees turned into the center and Mom's left arm around her husband, making the faces the focal point. Again, I had everyone touching with the little boy on the left holding onto Mom and the older son held onto Dad, bringing the whole group together. I had Dad as the highest person in the group. I would have preferred everyone to be in a blue shirt like Dad, rather than a white or short-sleeve shirt because I find the white distracting. A fast look at this portrait brings you to Mom's blouse rather than their faces. White tends to add weight to people; darker tones slim them. Fortunately, they are a good looking family; she is slim and the white blouse did not adversely affect this portrait.

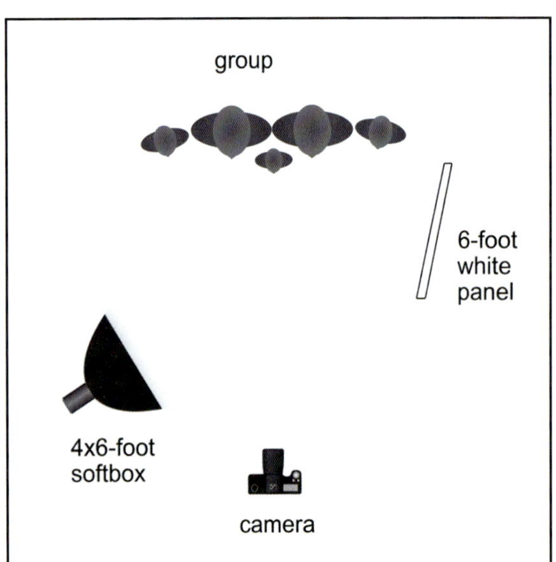

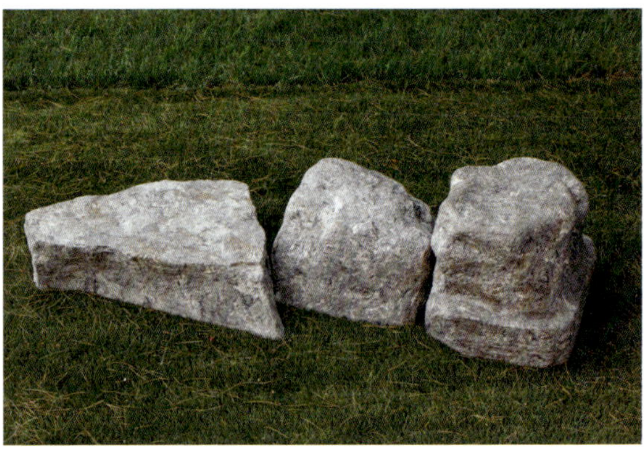

Lighting

The camera was as far from the group as possible; if it was any farther back the children would not have been able to hear me. I set my exposure to f/6.3 and 1/60 second with an 800 ISO to match the ambient light on the background. My 4x6-foot softbox was to the left of the camera. A 6-foot square white panel is to the right of the family reflecting light back into their faces.

TECH SPECS > This was photographed with a Canon 5D Mark II and 24–105mm lens set at 100mm. My exposure was f/6.3, 1/60 second, and ISO 800.

I had Mom and Dad's knees turned into the center and Mom's left arm around her husband, making the faces the focal point.

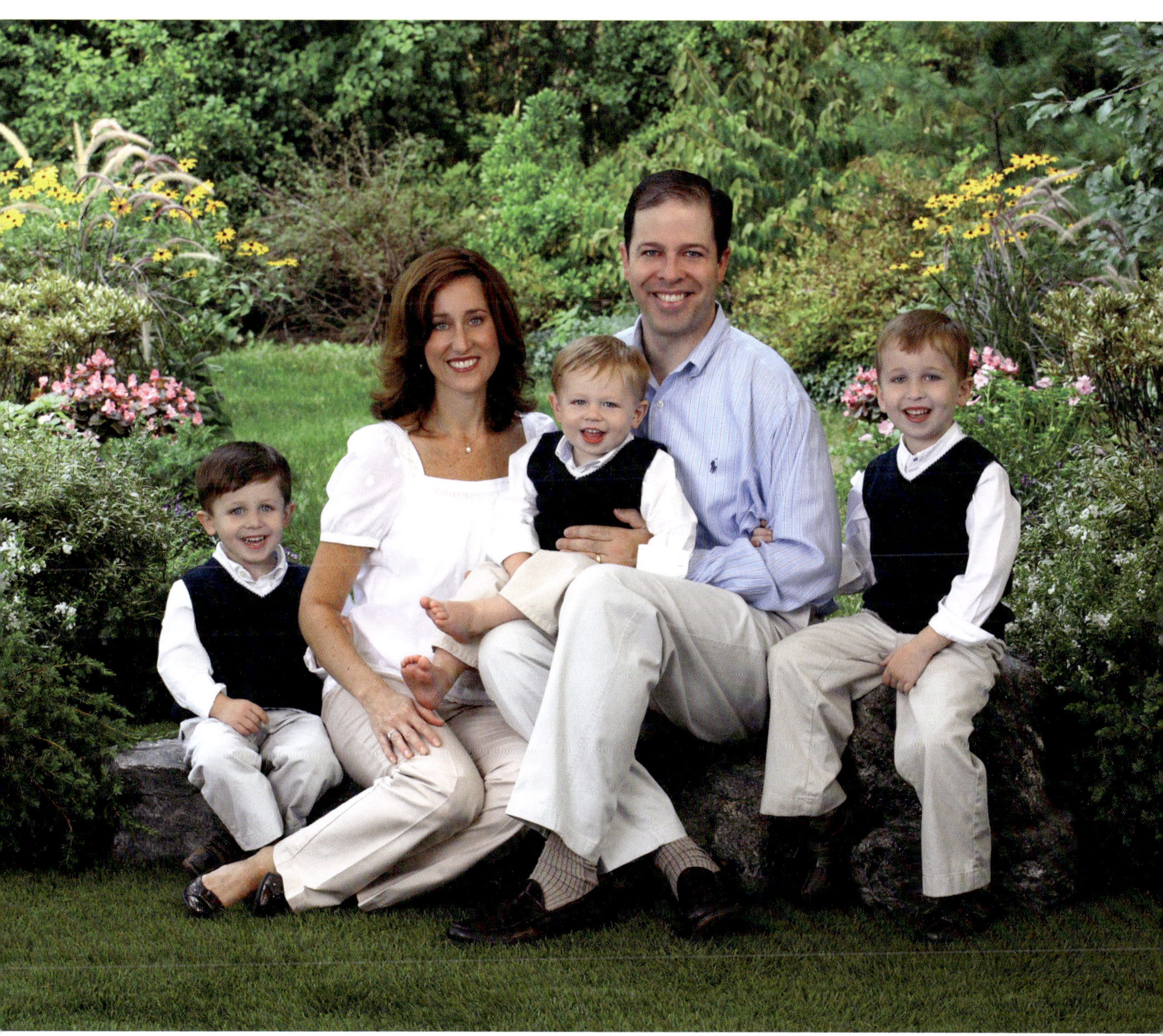

38 Plum Island Beach Portrait #2

Purpose

I had photographed this family two years earlier in my studio garden; this time Mom wanted a beach portrait. I picked Plum Island because it was not a long drive, it has a convenient parking lot, and the beach is right beyond the parking area.

They liked this spot because you can see the water in the background; it has nice sea grass and plenty of sand.

Obstacles

In spite of obstacles, I received a first place in our state competition for this portrait. This was an extremely difficult beach session. The wind was constant, whipping at 25 mph, and Mom tried to pass me a comb to fix the older girl's hair, which was not going to happen. In addition to the wind, the bugs in the sand were biting the kids' feet and they were yelping, "Ouch, ouch," which prompted Dad to ask, "Why did we come here?"

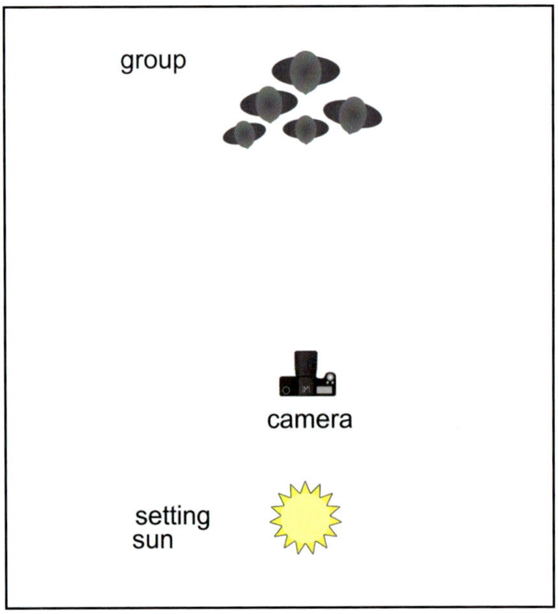

This is what being a professional photographer is all about—making good-looking images when everyone is miserable.

Posing

I liked that they were all dressed in white. I placed the son on the left, leaning into Mom blocking her sleeveless right arm. The younger daughter was in the middle partially blocking Mom's sleeveless left arm. The older daughter was on the right, with her hand gently placed on her leg. Dad was at the top of the triangle/pyramid.

Exposure

This was photographed at the end of the day with natural light. I waited until the sun dipped just below the horizon to light the family with soft, even light. You will know when it is time to photograph when the family can look at the camera and the sun behind has dropped just below the horizon and they are not blinded by the light. I had to continue to meter and change my exposure every few minutes because of the setting sun and the diminishing light. Once the sun went below the horizon, I had approximately twenty minutes to photograph the family before I lost my light completely.

TECH SPECS > This was photographed with a Canon 5D Mark II and the 70–200mm lens set at 120mm. My exposure was f/5.6, 1/60 second, and ISO 800.

I had to continue to meter and change my exposure every few minutes because of the setting sun and the diminishing light.

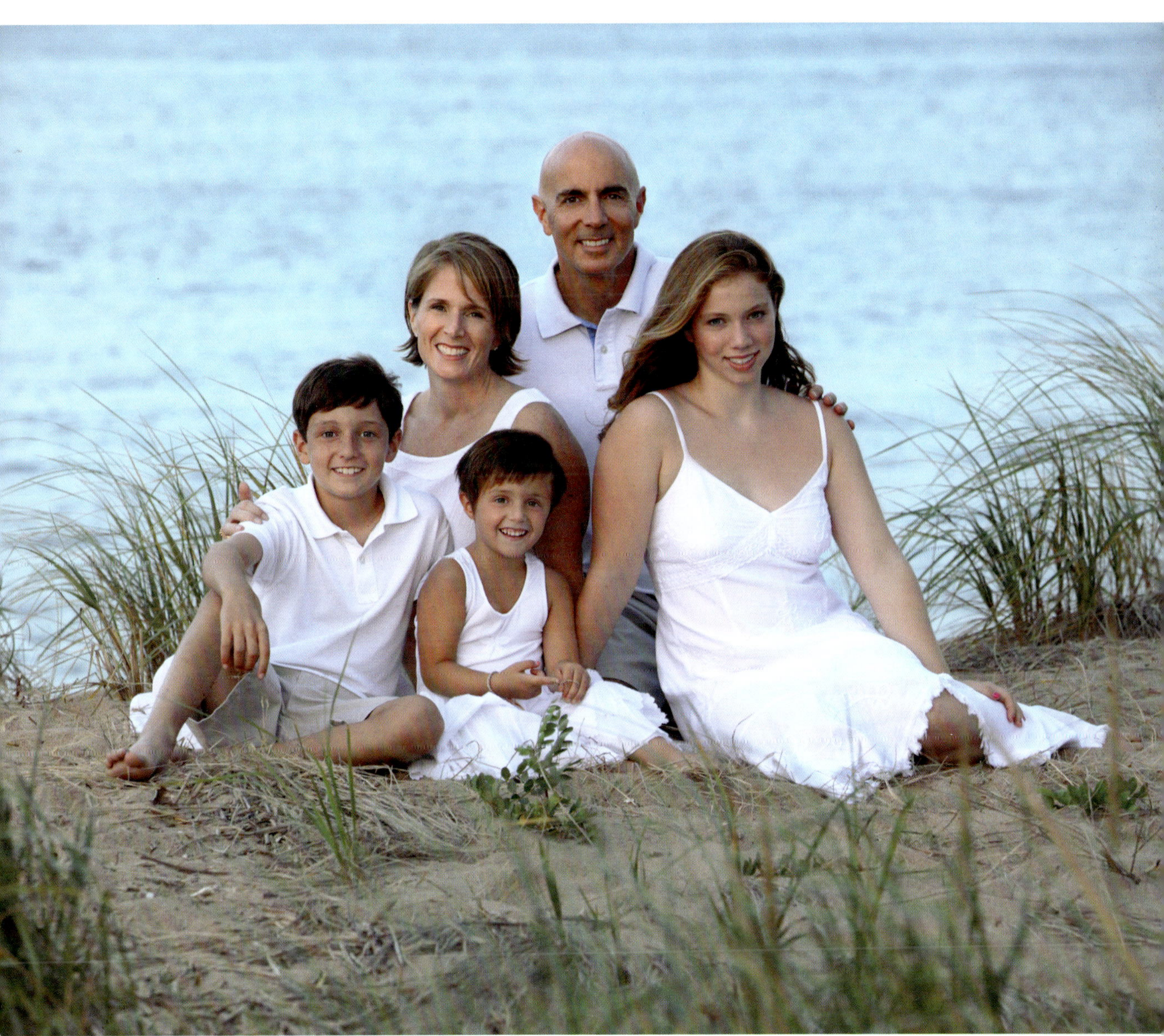

39 Photographing Photographers

Purpose

This portrait made me a photographer's photographer. This young couple owns a photography studio in a nearby town and wanted me to photograph them with their dog.

The position of the sun determines where I will photograph; this patio and steps were made for my afternoon sessions.

Deciding Where to Photograph

This was taken later in the day at my outdoor studio. Depending on the time of day, the position of the sun determines where I will photograph; this patio and steps were made for my afternoon sessions.

Lighting

My 4x6-foot softbox, placed to the left of the camera was set at f/8, and skimmed across the couple to balance the light on them to the light on the background. My house is on the right acting as a reflector; when I had my house sided, I picked a light color for this purpose. I metered the combined flash and the ambient light giving me a reading of f/8. The flash may have been set at f/5.6, but with the ambient light, the total exposure was f/8. Some meters will give you a reading of a percentage of how much flash compared to ambient light, and I feel that a 20 percent flash exposure balancing with the ambient light gives me a believable light for an image that doesn't look overly flashed.

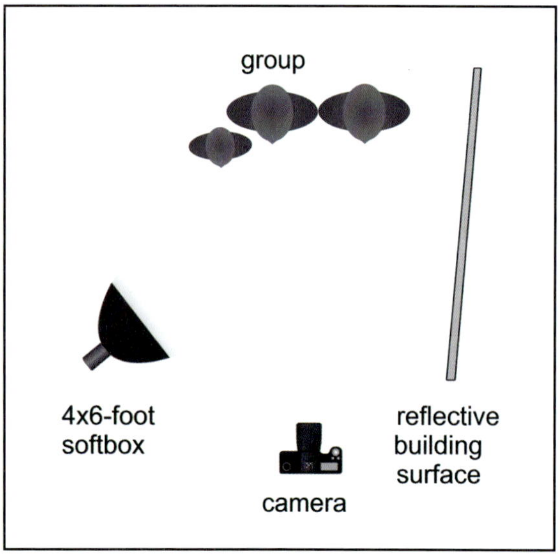

Posing

I used my portable potted plants to frame the couple. The junipers were placed in front and the chrysanthemums and other plants filled in the front and sides to balance the composition. He had one leg on the first step tucked behind the leg on the patio, and she leaned on his right leg, holding the dog. As she leaned back toward him and he leaned in toward her, their poses pulled them together. The silly noises for the dog to look at me evoked smiles from the couple.

TECH SPECS > This was photographed using a Mamiya RZ67 and Fuji NPH 400 film with a 127mm lens. The exposure was f/8 at 1/60 second.

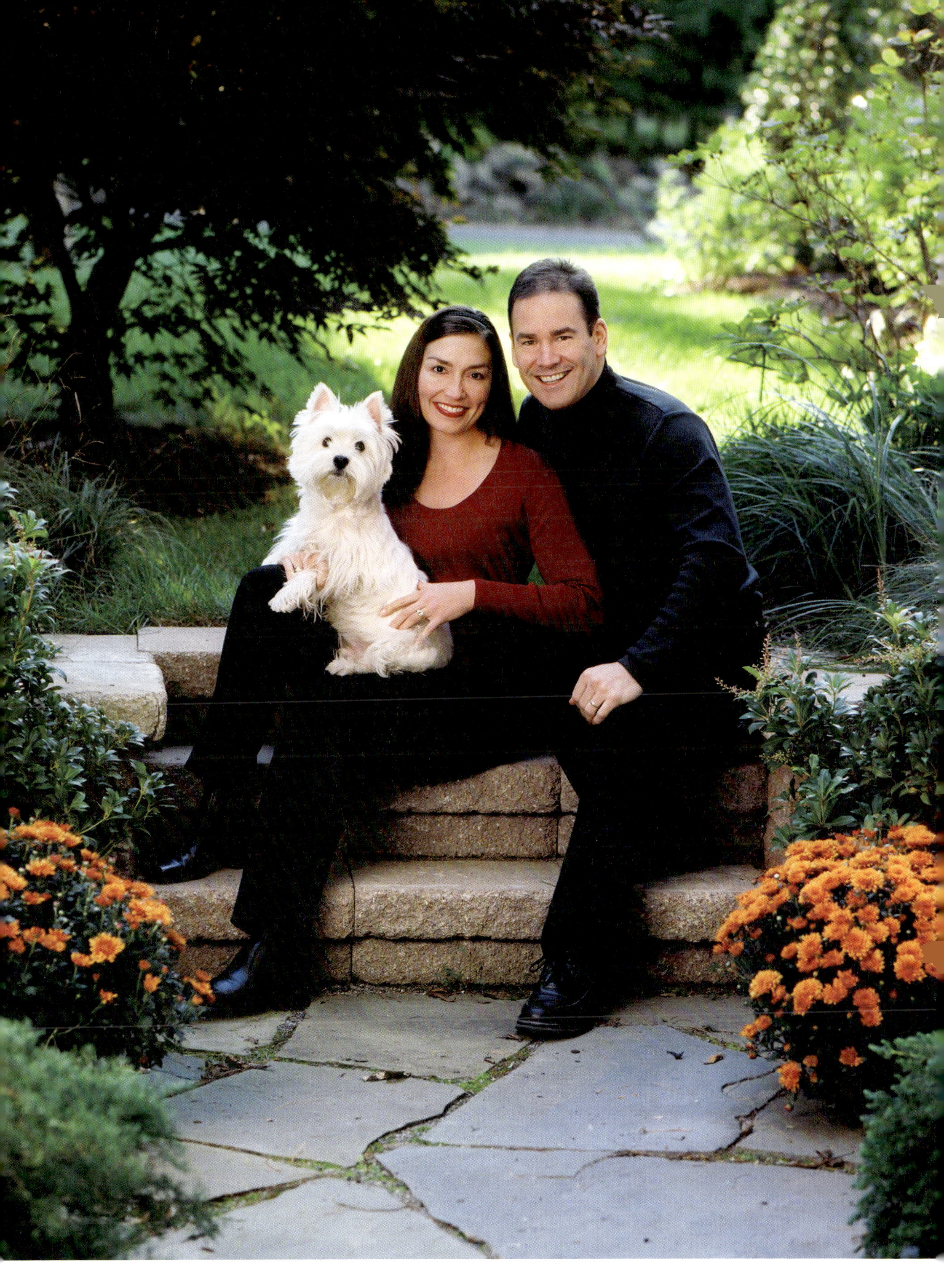

40 Overcoming a Tight Space

Purpose and Obstacles

The family was celebrating the grandfather's ninetieth birthday. He is seen in the middle, holding the baby—the oldest holding the youngest. The restaurant did not have a good area for me to photograph the family; we were in close quarters with a dark oak wall in the event room.

Posing

All of the men and two of the women were standing in back, and most of the women were seated with the grandfather. The remaining four children and one young woman were seated on the floor. I moved the dinner tables as far into the corner as possible, giving me just enough room to work. We had to work quickly because they had the restaurant for only a few hours and they did not want to take time away from the party.

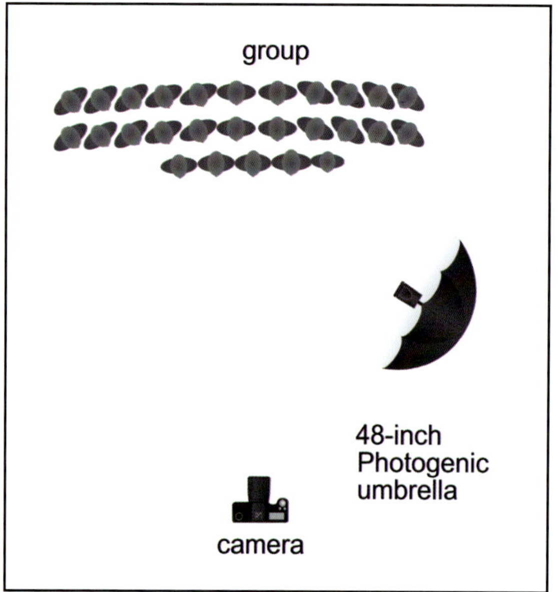

Lighting

One 48-inch Photogenic umbrella raised as high as it could extend was out of camera range on the right, skimming the light from right to left. The light was aimed at the woman on the far left holding the child on her lap. I took meter readings across the group, which if the umbrella is feathered correctly would have been an even f/16 from one side of the group to the other.

Focus

I focused on the baby in the center of the group. By focusing a third of the way into the group, I was able to keep the entire group in focus.

Breakaways

Because of time constraints, I was unable to photograph a lot of other groups, but I did photograph the grandparents and the grandparents with their four children. It is important to suggest other groups for the opportunity for additional sales, but in this case, I didn't want to take too much time away from the party.

TECH SPECS > This was photographed with a Canon 5D Mark II and 24–105mm lens set at 50mm. My exposure was f/16, 1/80, and ISO 400.

By focusing one-third into the group, I was able to keep the entire group in focus.

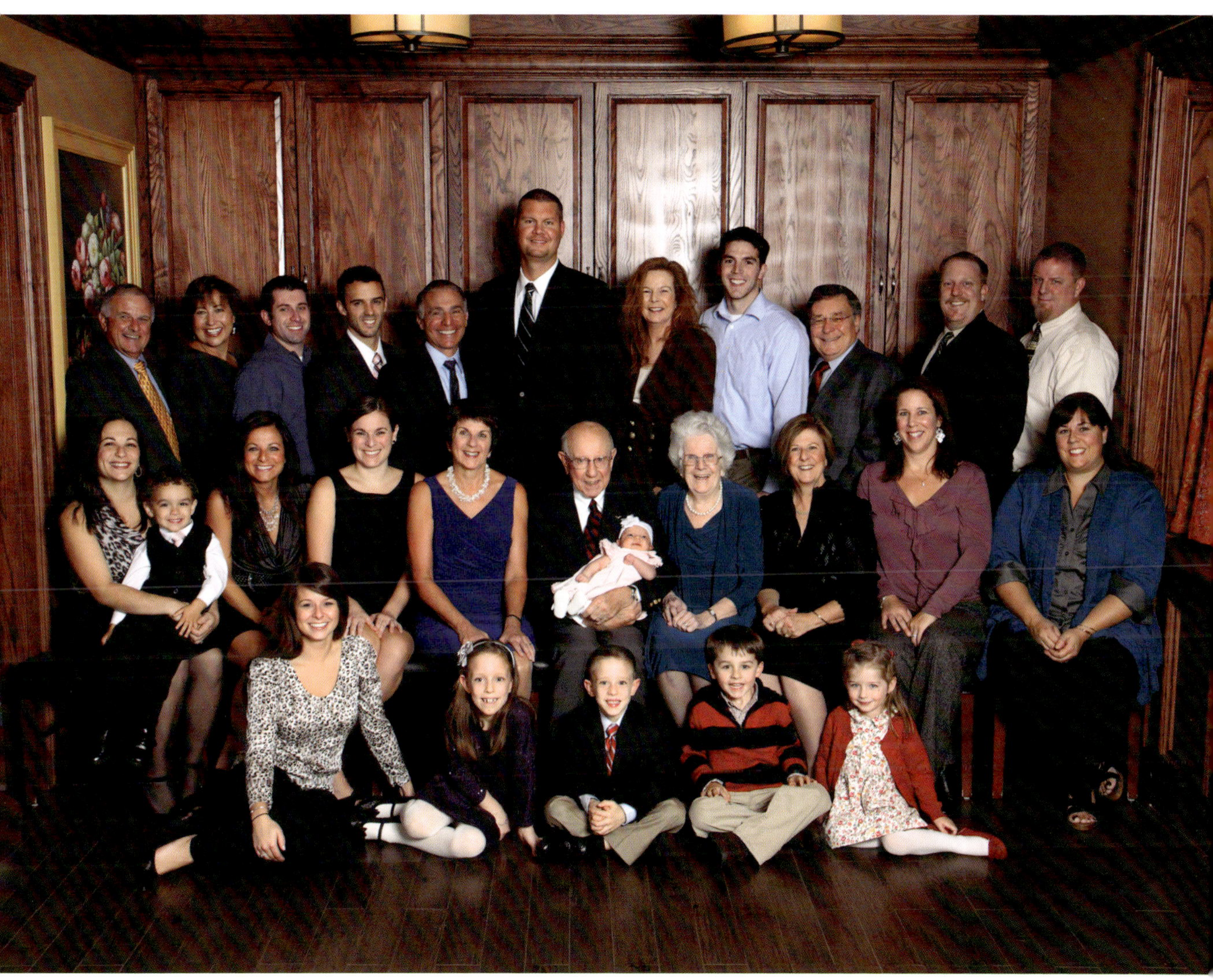

41 The "Oh!" Factor

Posing

I have the parents sitting on two of my custom-made rocks, with Dad sitting on the higher rock, making him a little taller than Mom. Mom and Dad loved their daughter nestled in between them and their son leaning on Dad. The parents were pleasantly surprised when they saw the portraits that I had captured because the little boy was very active and had been running around.

When photographing a family portrait, I try my best to show the love in the family, the "oh!" factor, and I believe this portrait has it. I had everyone touching, and I had Mom's left arm and Dad's right arm low and behind the little girl. Again, this alleviated a look of a lot of arms and helped to draw the focus to the faces. I had the little girl place her hand on Dad and the little boy lean in, holding onto his Dad. He probably would not be doing that much longer; children grow fast, so you want to capture this moment in time.

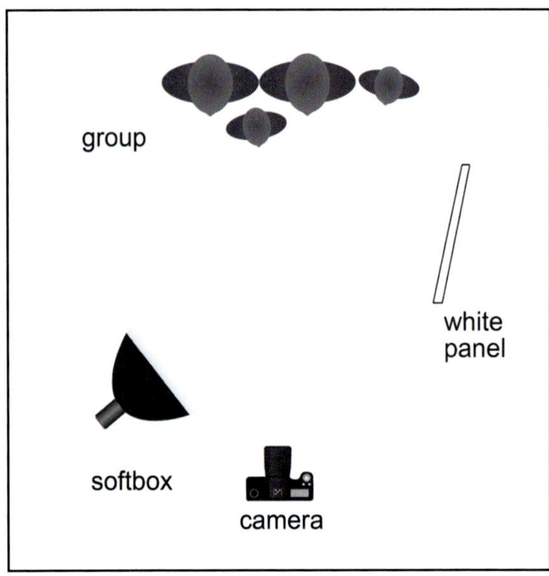

Avoid Visual Confusion. When a group of subjects wears a variety of light and dark tones, there is visual confusion. The light colors, such as yellows, come forward, and the dark colors, such as navy, recede. As a result, one person becomes more prominent than the others. Also, individuals who wear light tones can look heavier than they really are.

Clothing Choice

They wanted something "summery," which is why the kids have bare feet. Mom and Dad didn't want to take their shoes off, so I suggested that they wear something that wouldn't jump out at you when you look at the portrait. She wore sandals and he wore dark loafers without socks for the summery feeling.

Lighting

My 4x6-foot softbox was to the left of the camera with the 6-foot square white panel on the right, reflecting light back into their faces.

TECH SPECS > This was photographed with a Canon 5D Mark II and 70–200mm lens set at 100mm. My exposure was f/7.1, 1/60 second, and ISO 800.

When photographing a family portrait, I try my best to show the love in the family, the "oh!" factor.

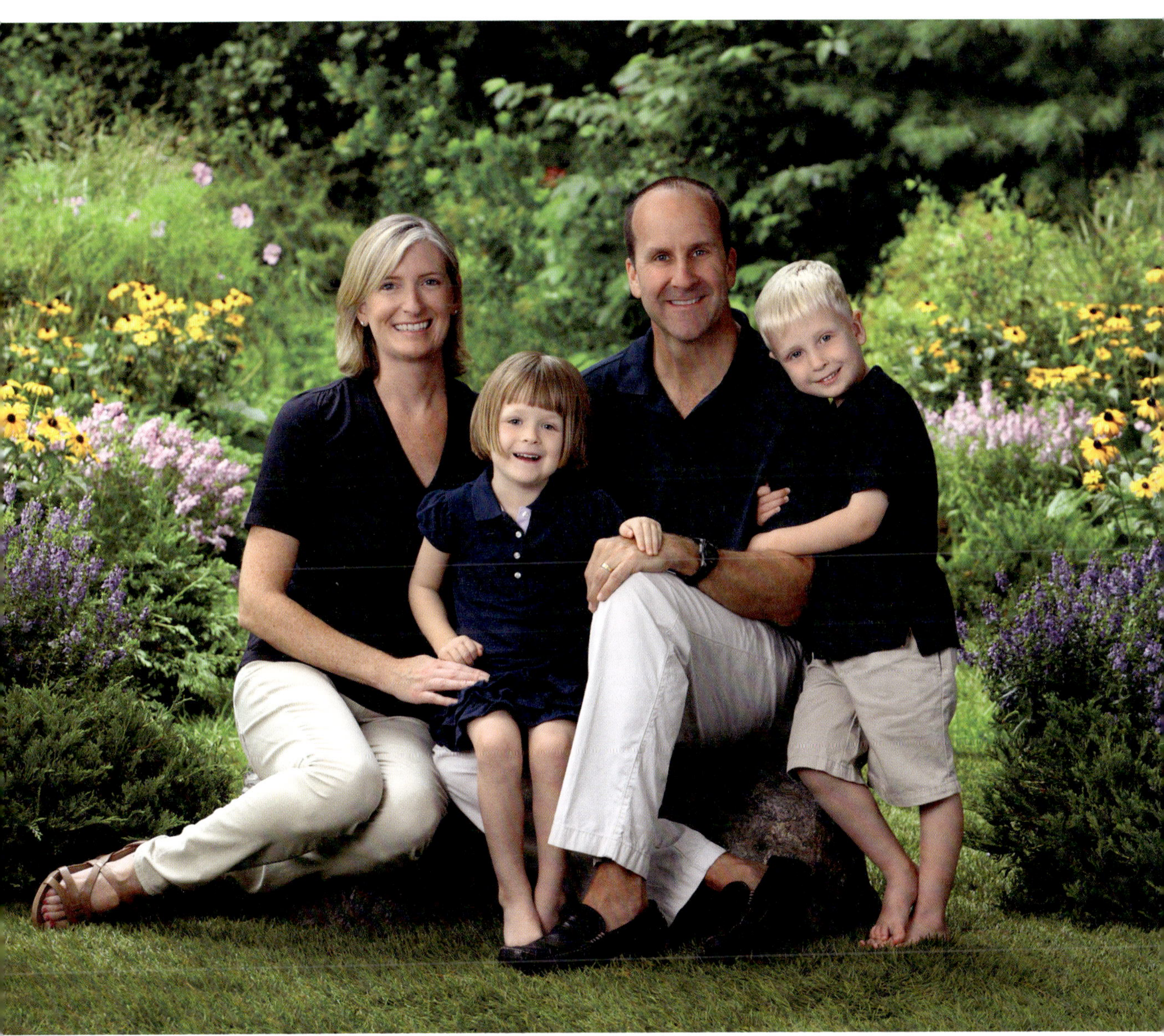

42 Life Goes On

Purpose

After raising two daughters as a single father after his first wife died, Dad remarried and had two daughters from his new marriage. He wanted a family portrait with his wife and four daughters.

The Setup

I wanted to make this portrait as autumnal as possible, and leaves do not always fall where you want them. My assistant scoured a five-mile radius looking for freshly fallen leaves the morning of this fall session; they are collected from churches, colleges, and cemeteries. The leaves were sprinkled around the area in my garden where we photographed and the chrysanthemums and other plants were placed around the family for balance and color. They snuggled together and were very cozy sitting on my 5-foot bench.

Preferred Lens for Portraiture. It is better to use a longer lens for portraiture, but you do not want to be so far away that the people cannot see or hear you. The closer you get with a shorter lens the greater the effect of distortion on the subjects, so I try to work from a distance.

Lighting

The family was at the edge of my 9x9x9-foot awning with my 4x6-foot softbox on the left skimming light across the faces. My 6-foot white panel on the right to kick light back to the subjects' faces. There was an 8-foot scrim on the same side as the softbox, placed next to the family to block out the ambient light. This scrim has wind panels in it so the wind can blow through it and not knock it over. The scrim also reduced the intensity of the light down about a half a stop (See page 60 setup).

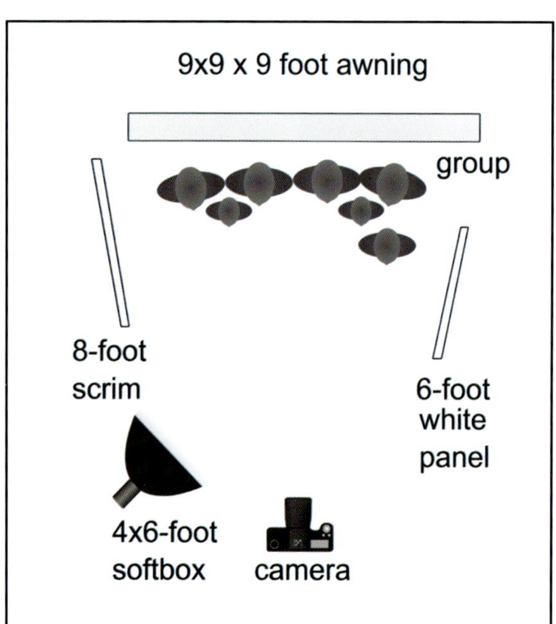

TECH SPECS > This was photographed with a Canon 5D Mark II and 70–200mm lens set at 150mm. My exposure was f/7.1, 1/60 second, and ISO 400.

This scrim has wind panels in it so the wind can blow through it and not knock it over.

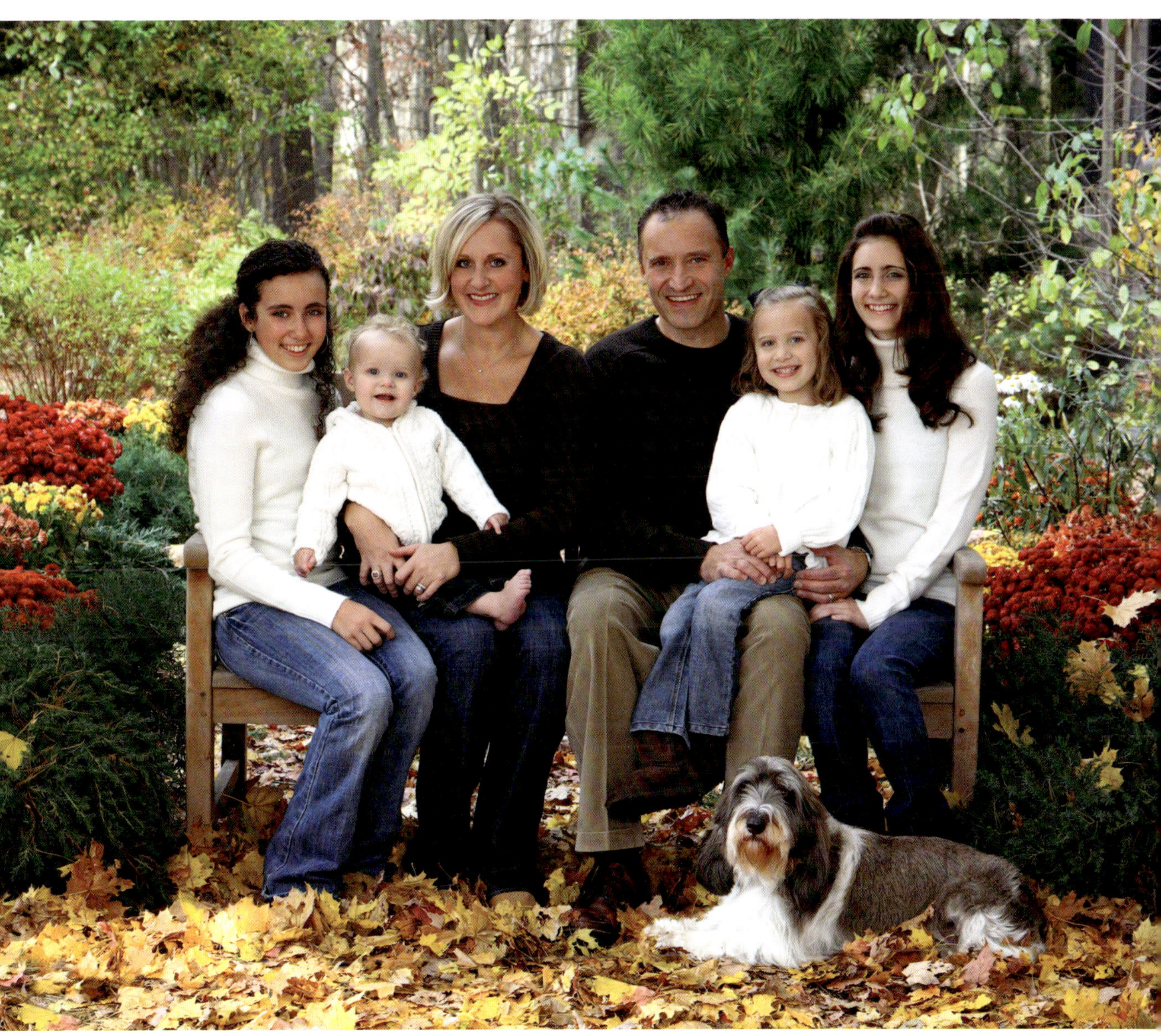

Hot Car

Repeat Clients

I had photographed this family a number of times over the years prior to this session, beginning when the girls were very little. They came back to me recently and wanted something different at their home. I am their family photographer, and that is a title I proudly display.

Lighting, Composition, and Camera

I had initially photographed them on my rocks with the walkway to the house in the background. They also wanted to do something with their new car. They brought out this beautiful, new, red Corvette, and I asked them if we could park it on the grass. I liked this angle and preferred the car in this position.

This was photographed near the end of the day. The sun was going down behind me, giving me sweet light as my primary light source. There is one Photogenic light in a 42-inch umbrella to the right of my camera to fill in the shadows on their faces and put a little sparkle in their eyes. The difficulty was keeping the family and the car in focus.

Composition

The composition intrigued me, with a line leading from the front of the car to Mom, continuing to the girls, and up to Dad. I liked Mom's position behind the steering wheel. The younger daughter leaned on the car, and both girls posed with their left hands in their pocket. Dad leaned on the seat of the car while standing in a pose of protection over his two daughters.

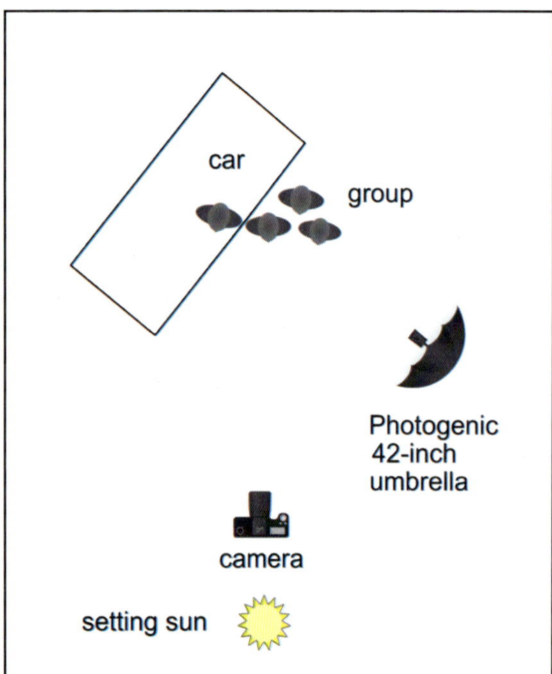

TECH SPECS > This was photographed with a Canon 5D Mark II with the 70–200mm lens set at 80mm. My exposure was f/8, 1/60 second, and ISO 400.

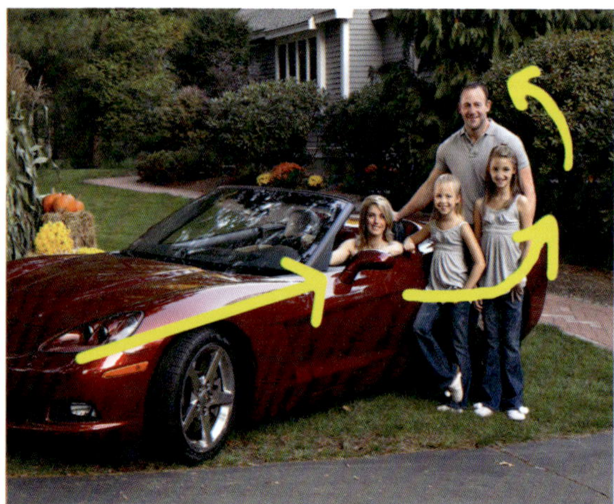

The sun was going down behind me, giving me sweet light as my primary light source.

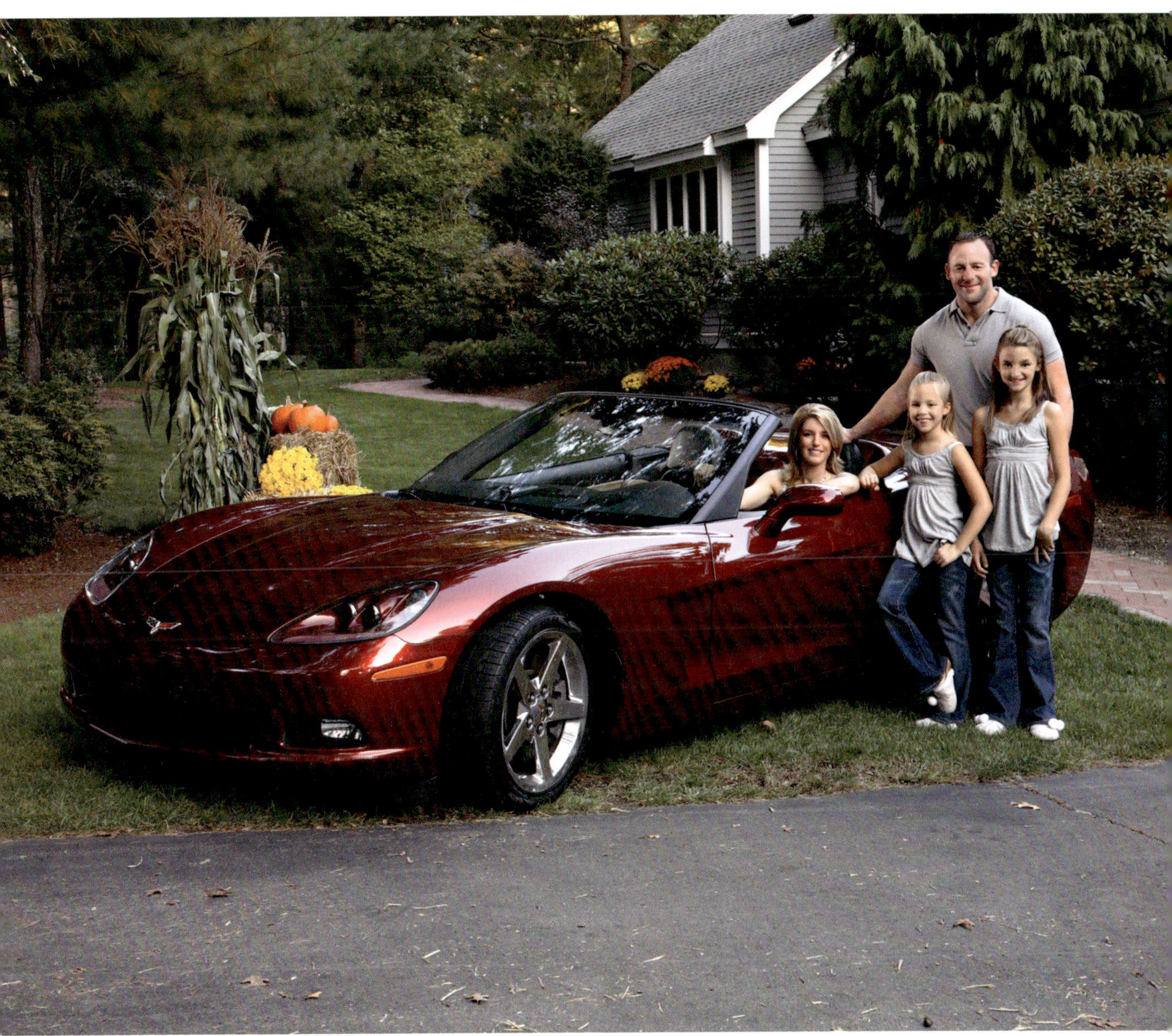

Studio Portrait #4

Repeat Client

I had previously photographed the girl on the right for her senior portrait. She is very shy and Mom said that she usually does not like her photos, but she really loved what I did for her. They called me for the family portrait session as a result of her senior portraits.

The Tallest One in the Portrait. I almost always make Dad the tallest one in the portrait, even if he isn't the tallest. Give some thought as to how to achieve the overall composition that you have envisioned in regard to apparent height and placement. Then, use chairs, rocks, stools, or whatever you have to arrange everyone's height and placement according to your plan.

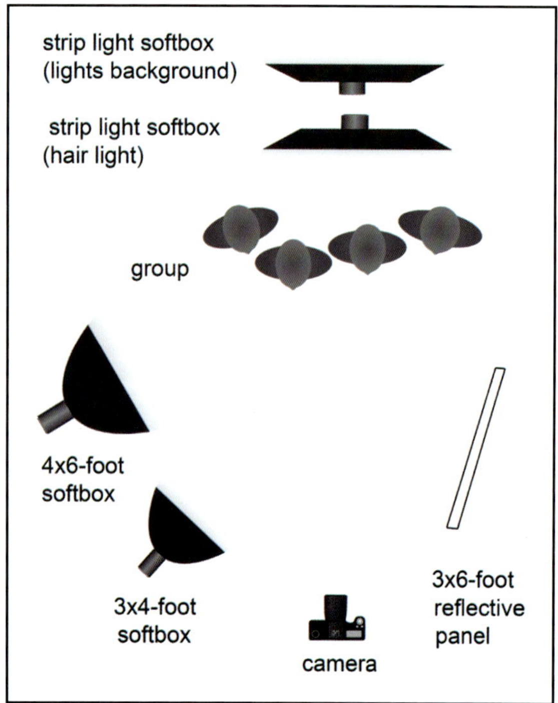

Posing

I placed the younger sister in the middle on a stool so the family hovered around her as if protecting her. The mom was a little higher on a stool, the older sister leaned on her mom, and the dad—posed as the protector of his girls—was the tallest point in the photograph.

Background

I had planned on using my blue background, but Mom thought that blue would not go with their home so I selected this David Maheu background. The tones of the background worked well with the tones in their clothing.

Lighting

I used a double main light—a 3x4-foot softbox placed horizontally and a 4x6-foot softbox set vertically between the first light and the background. My 3x6-foot studio reflective panel was on the right to soften the shadows on the faces. I had two strip lights attached to a rail system on the ceiling: a Photogenic flash in a Larson 10x36-inch strip softbox for the hair and a Photogenic flash in a 12x36-inch strip softbox for the background,. Both were set at f/5.6.

TECH SPECS > This was photographed with a Canon 5D Mark II and 70–200mm lens set at 70mm. My exposure was f/7.1, 1/80 second, and ISO 100.

The tones of the background worked well with the tones in their clothing.

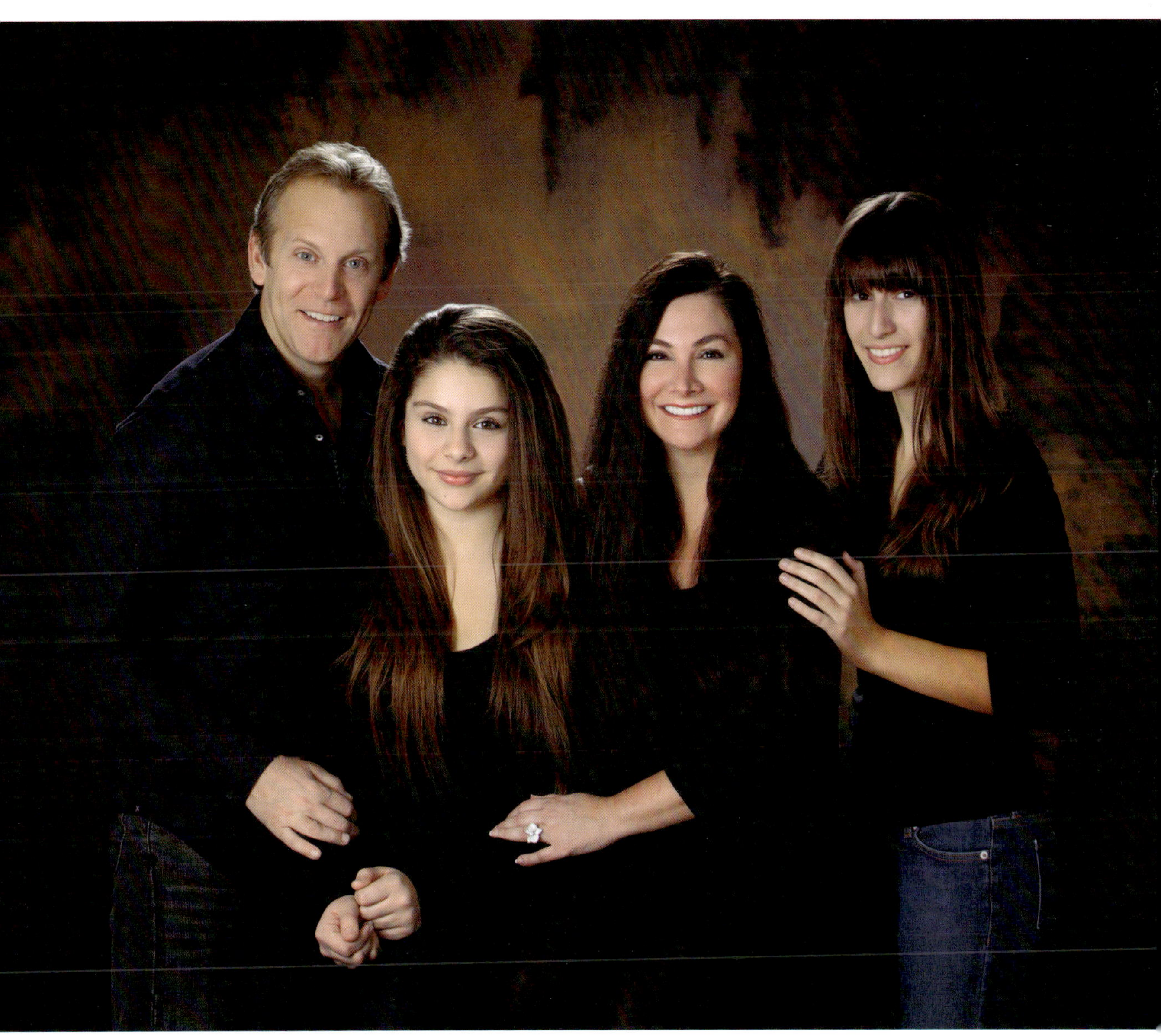

45 Family in the Woods

History

This family originally discovered me through a fund-raising auction a number of years ago. After a few years of traditional family portraits, they wanted something different. Many of our family portrait clients come back every four to seven years, and you have to be creative so you are not always doing the same pose.

Preparation

You need a plan before the family arrives because they do not want to hang around while you figure things out; Know in advance what you plan to do and the session will move quickly and efficiently.

Clothing Selection. Long sleeves are recommended for teens and adults. Bare arms compete visually with faces for attention because they have a similar color and tone.

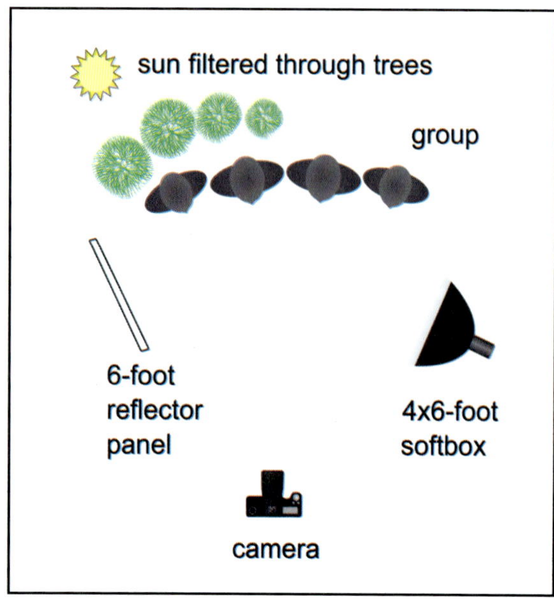

Have your assistant stand in for them before they arrive so you know that your exposure is good. This dad was very pleased that we were able to photograph the family and all of the breakdowns and we were finished in less than an hour.

Posing

The early poses in this session had them sitting on the patio steps. Later, we moved to this wooded area. There was not much sunlight there, and when the sun went behind the clouds, it became very dark. However, when the sun came out and filtered through the trees, backlighting the family, it gave a nice separation on Dad's shoulder and arm, the mom's hair and arm, the daughter's right shoulder, and the son's hair and left shoulder.

Lighting

I used the 4x6-foot softbox approximately eight feet off the ground on the right side of the camera. My 6-foot reflective panel was on a light stand just in front of them on the left. I placed all of my potted plants in front of them and to the sides to block unsightly natural growth, fill in voids, give the photograph additional color, and balance the composition.

TECH SPECS > This was photographed with a Canon 5D Mark II and 70–200mm lens set at 180mm. My exposure was f/7.1, 1/60 second, and ISO 800. The background was lit by the sun.

There was not much sunlight there, and when the sun went behind the clouds, it became very dark.

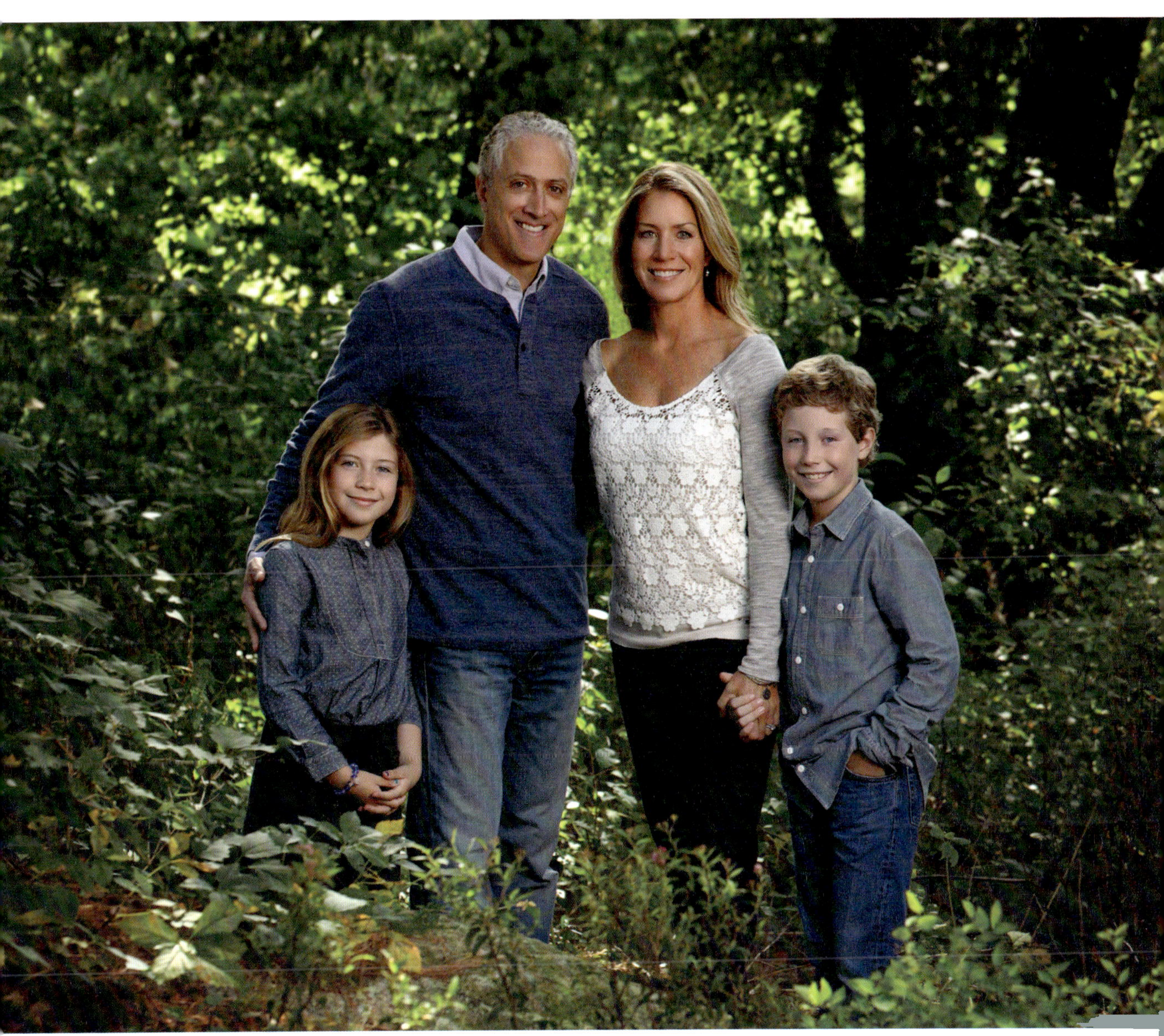

46 Breakaway: Kids, Pond, and Fish

Breakaway Photographs

With family portraits, I almost always do additional photographs of the kids separately and together and of Mom and Dad without their children. There is no extra fee to photograph them; they just pay for any portraits that they purchase.

Posing

This breakaway portrait from "Family in the Woods" was created at my pond. I posed the brother and sister close together by the edge of the pond. The key was to get them to look at the same place at the same time. I asked them to put their finger near the water but not in the water, so the fish would gather near them.

Popular Setup

The kids had a good time hanging out by the pool and feeding the fish. Many of my clients have purchased wall portraits of this popular setup.

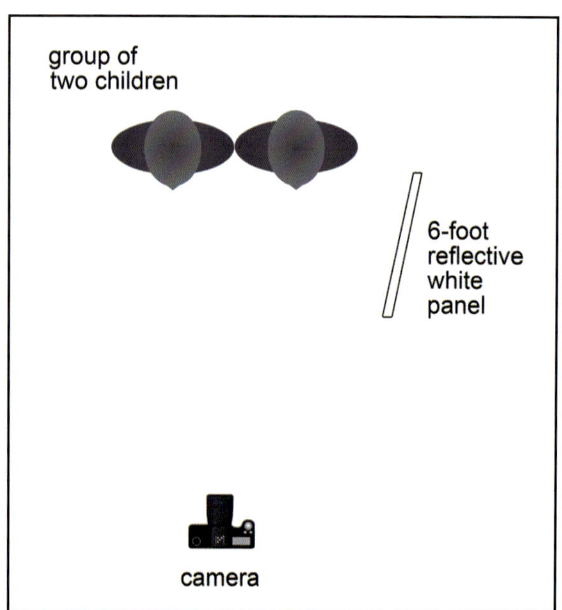

This provides a relaxed setting, a reflection of the subjects, and captivates subjects.

Lighting

My exposure settings of f/7.1, 1/40 second, and ISO 800 allowed me to ensure the scene was in focus from front to back and detail would be visible throughout the image. Photographed with natural light, I used only a 6-foot reflective white panel on the right side of the pond just outside of view of the camera, angled backwards a little bit so it picked up the sky and bounced the light back to their faces.

Shutter Speeds and Falling Water

The falling water retained some of its detail at 1/60 second. A faster shutter speed would capture more detail. A smoother waterfall texture is produced with a slower shutter speed such as 1/30 second. I used 1/60 second because I wanted to show the water movement and pick up some of its detail.

TECH SPECS > This was photographed with a Canon 5D Mark II and 24–105mm lens set at 80mm. My exposure was f/7.1, 1/60 second, and ISO 800. Photographed with natural light.

The key was to get them to look at the same place at the same time.

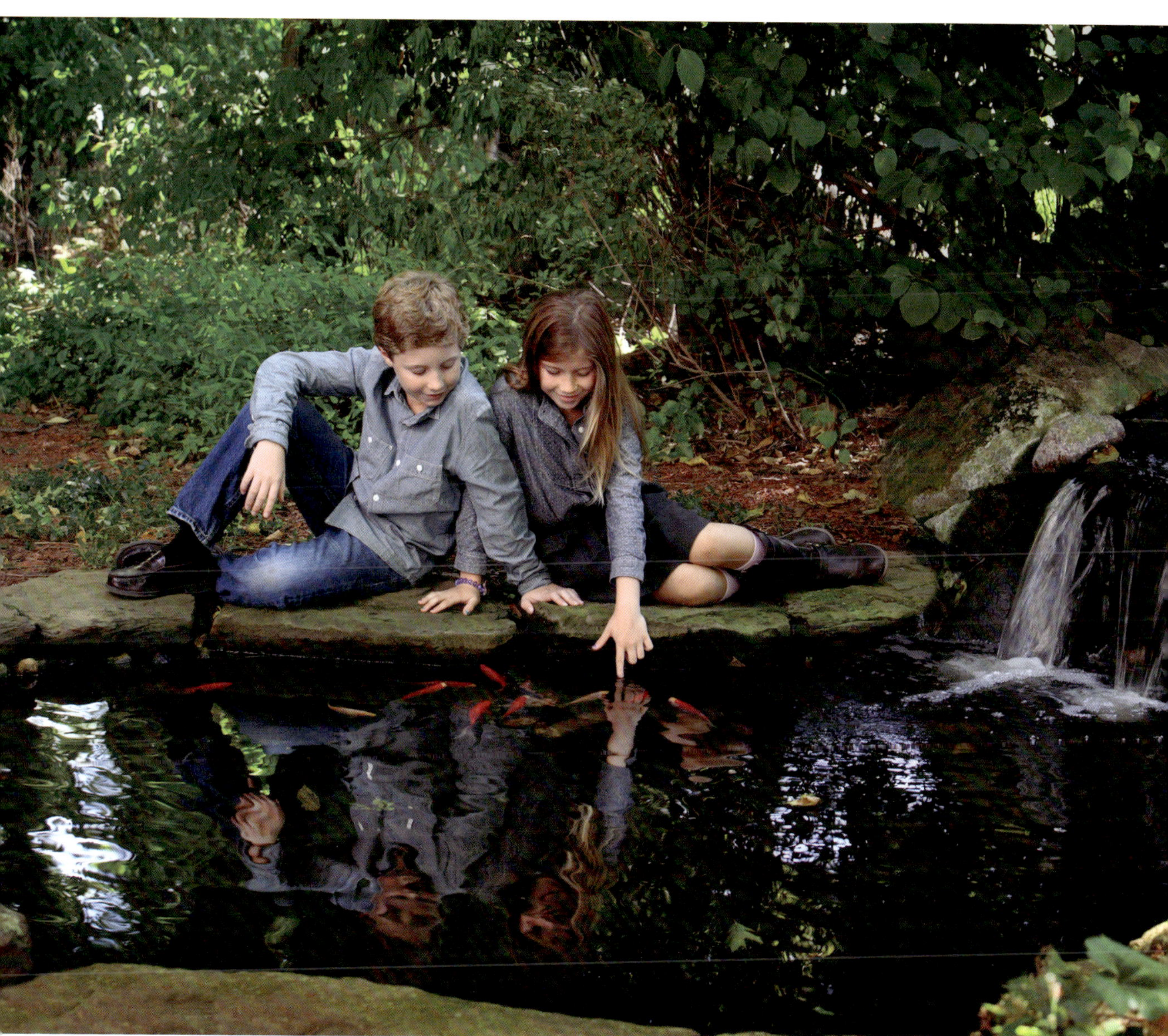

47 Family of Four with Two Dogs

Clothing

This family did a great job coordinating their clothes. They selected long-sleeve blue shirts and khaki slacks and skirt. Even the two dogs had blue kerchiefs to match their outfits.

Lighting

My 4x6-foot softbox on the left was set at f/6.3 and skimmed across the group. My 6-foot white panel on the right reflected light back to their faces. I also used my 8-foot wind panel on the left to block out extraneous sunlight. They sat at the back of my 9x9x9-foot awning, allowing the sun to act as a hair light as well as a background light.

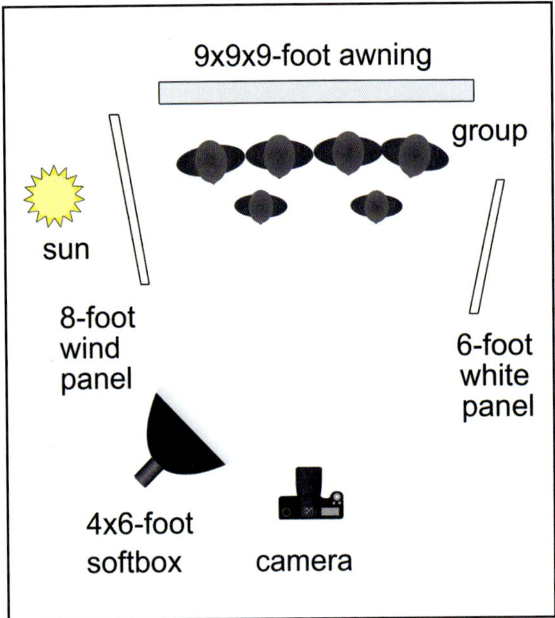

Overcoming Challenges

The primary challenge with this portrait was to get four adults and two dogs looking good and at me at the same moment. It was not an easy task. You can "swap heads" more readily now than in the days of film, but we did not do that for this portrait.

Working with the Dogs. I had them walk the dogs before we began and then lead the dogs to sit down facing the softbox. This gave a nice light in the dogs' eyes. Once I had them seated, I had the daughter hold the collar. The son held down the other dog's back while Dad held the dog's collar. I had them pet the dogs to keep them calm and stationary and then instructed the family that I was going to make a squeaky noise so the dogs would look at me. I told them that when I squeaked they should let go of the dogs, move their hands quickly, and place them on their leg and look at me.

TECH SPECS > This was photographed with a Canon 5D Mark II with the 70–200mm lens set at 150mm. My exposure was f/6.3, 1/60 second, and ISO 800.

The primary challenge with this portrait was to get four adults and two dogs looking good and at me at the same moment.

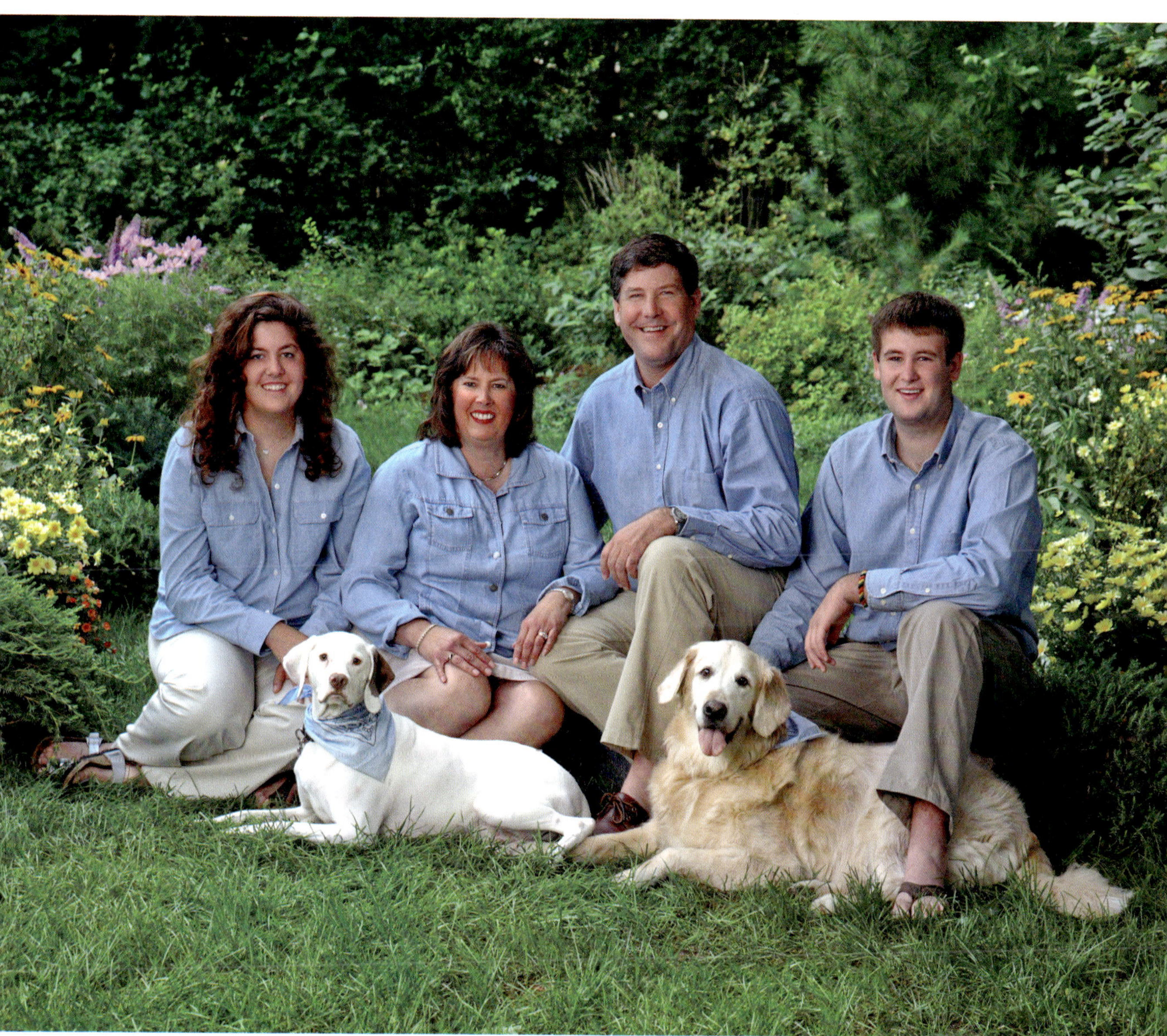

48 Mom and Her Four Children

Purpose

Mom had raised her four children alone after her husband passed away, and she wanted a family portrait now that they were almost adults and getting ready to leave home.

Outdoor Studio

Creating an outdoor studio is very important in New England because it gives you flexibility to photograph outside in three of the four seasons. However, it is important that you are able to work with your entire property and not just a slice of it. Light changes during the course of the day and with the seasons; you have to utilize different areas depending on the situation.

Posing

Mom was seated with her youngest daughter and her son on a sturdy 4-foot fiberglass bench that I purchased at Home Depot. The two older sisters stood behind them, making two triangles. Their dark-toned clothing was perfect for this portrait.

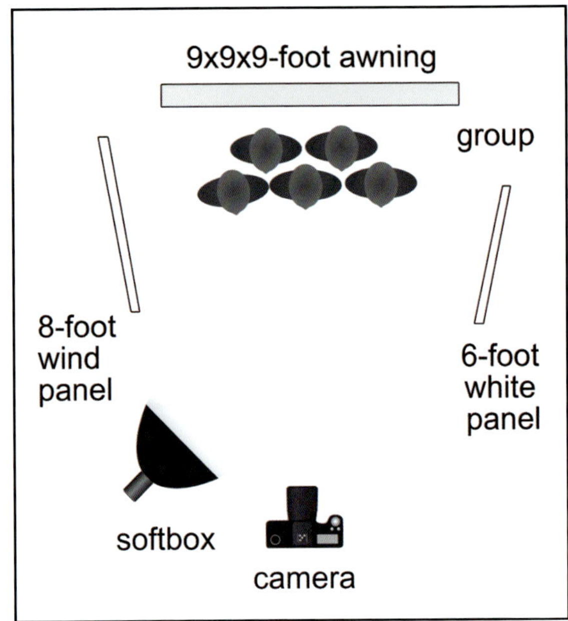

Camera and Lighting

They were at the edge of the 9x9x9-foot awning with the 4x6-foot softbox to the left of my camera and the 8-foot windowed wind panel to the left of the softbox blocking any extra light. My 6-foot-square white panel was on the right reflecting light back into the faces.

Changing the Outdoor Studio Look. When you photograph people in your studio, you change backdrops according to the clothes your clients are wearing; why not do the same with an outdoor studio? You can use fall flowers and plants from late September until late November (or until you can no longer photograph outside), spring flowers from April through June, and summer flowers and plants in July, August, and early September. You can also change the look in your outdoor area from one session to the next by moving portable plants and flowers so that no two portraits look alike.

TECH SPECS > This was photographed with a Canon 5D Mark II and 70–200mm lens set at 180mm. My exposure was f/7.1, 1/60 second, and ISO 800.

My 6-foot square white panel was on the right reflecting light back into the faces.

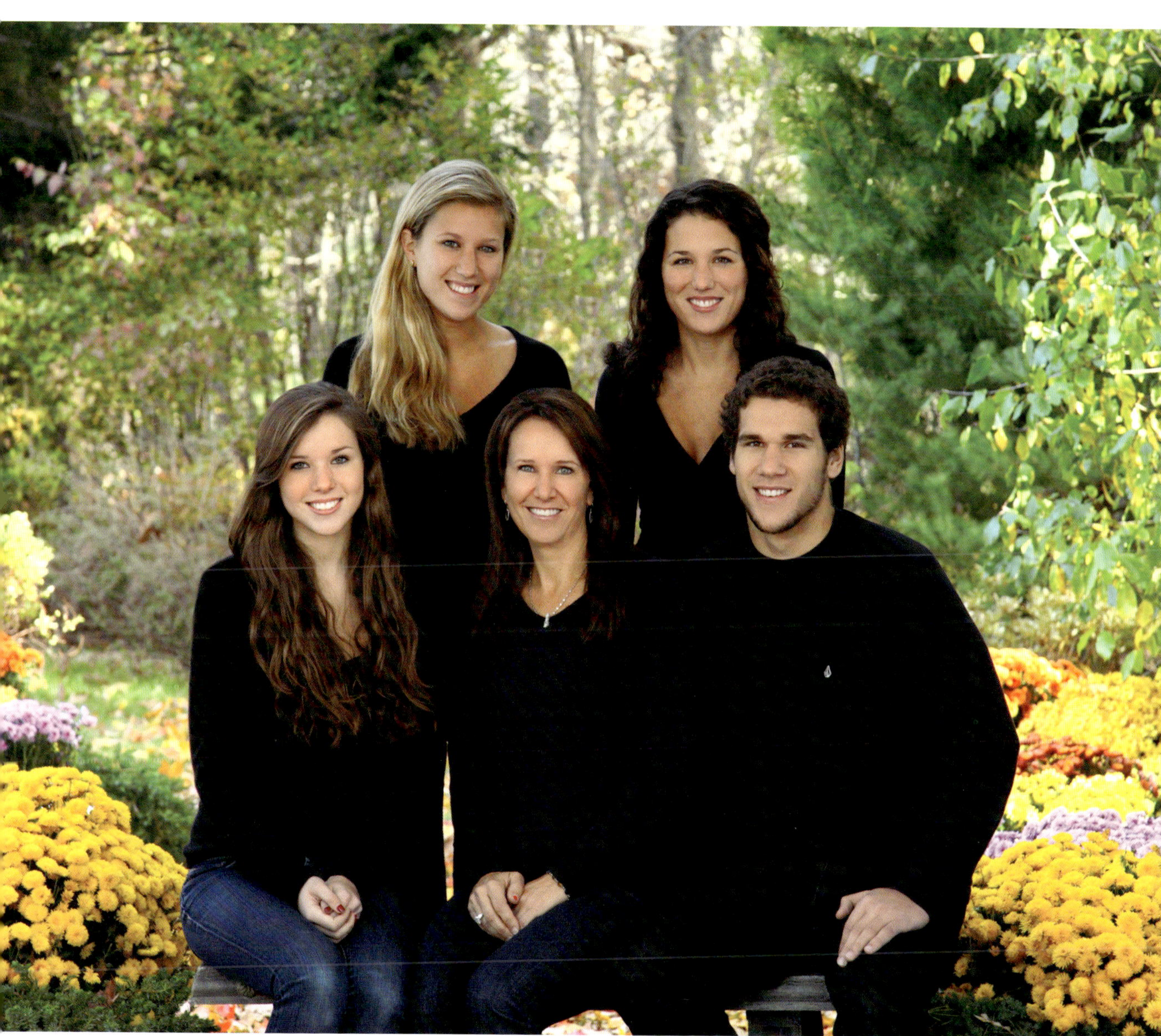

49 Celebrating a Seventieth Birthday

The Challenges of Scheduling

The patriarch of this family was celebrating his seventieth birthday and wanted a family portrait with all of his children, their spouses, and his grandchildren. He had to reschedule three or four times and was getting frustrated because family members would cancel at the last minute.

A Portrait Seating Plan. I always plan the seating in advance and even draw a diagram so that when they arrive, I can easily and quickly move people into position. Even though I was working with a group of nineteen, I was able to pose this entire group in less than three minutes. When I present programs, I use this portrait as an example, with the first slide being just the chairs and rocks in position and the next slide having everyone in place.

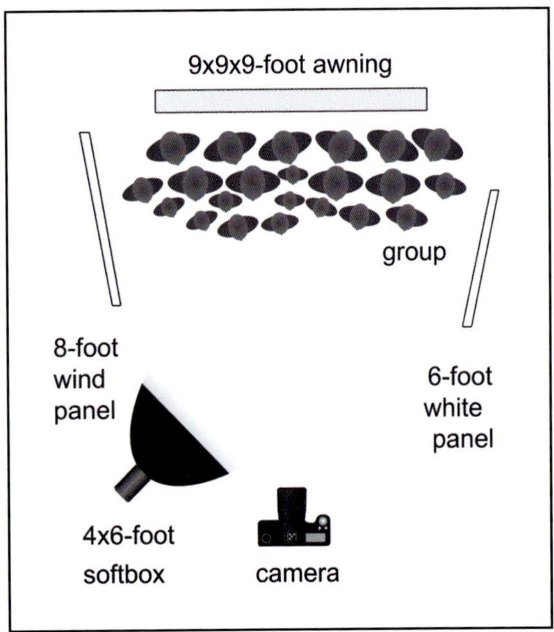

Clothing

I normally suggest darker tones but the grandfather liked the light colors. He bought the same Ralph Lauren shirt for everyone in the family for this event.

Posing

The women were seated first, then the men and the grandparents in back and finally the children in front. The children were posed last because they often did not want to sit still. After everyone was in place, I finessed the pose by having people move slightly to the left or right as needed.

Those great, natural expressions came from having everyone look at me while I worked quickly with a toy monkey on my head and a remote control in my hand.

Lighting

My 4x6-foot softbox and 8-foot wind panel were on the left and the 6-foot square reflective white panel was on the right.

TECH SPECS > This was photographed with a Canon 5D Mark II and 24–105mm lens set at 75mm. My exposure was f/11, 1/60 second, and ISO 800.

The women were seated first, then the men and the grandparents in back, and finally the children in front.

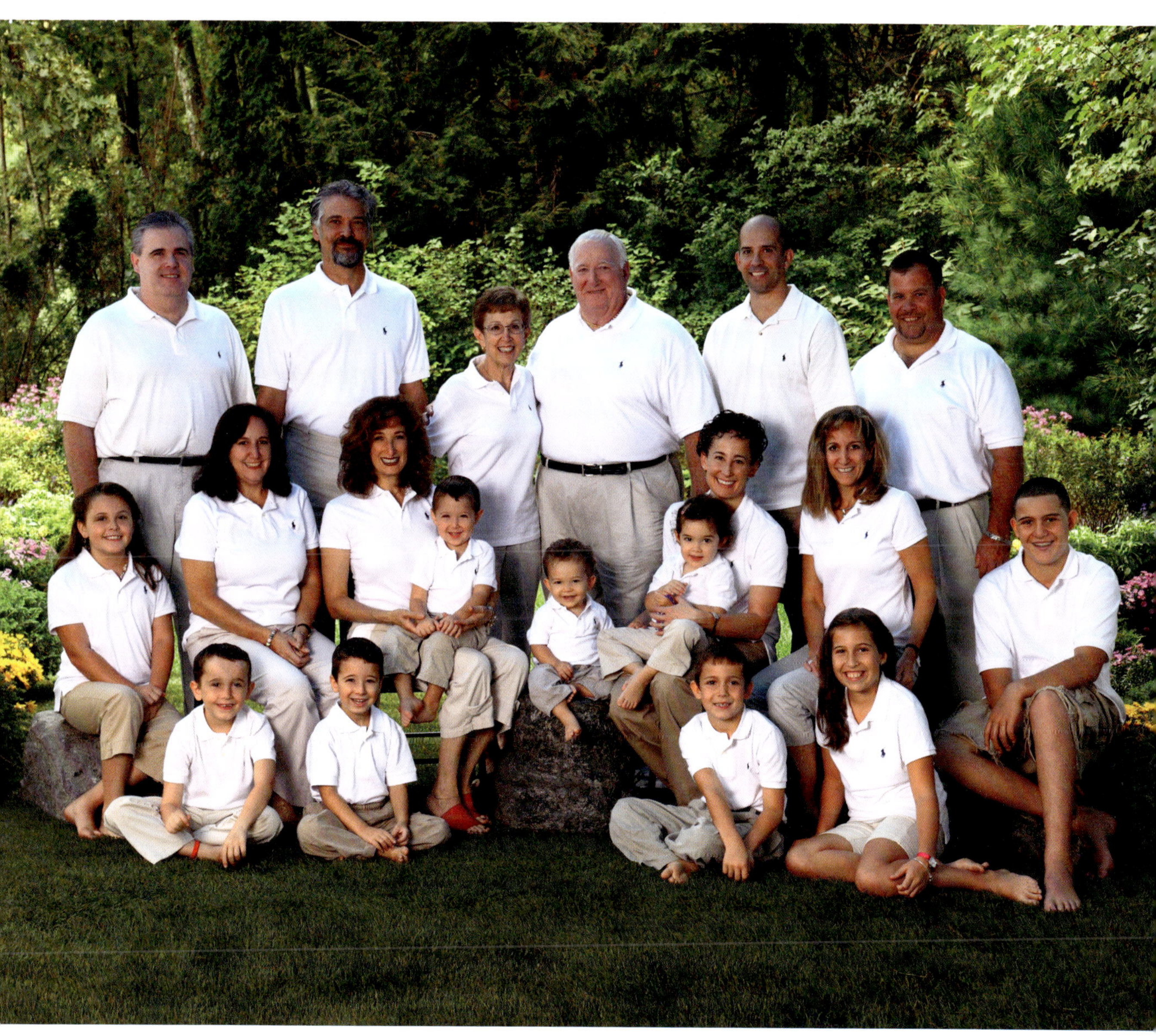

50 The Pedi Family

Purpose

I wanted a family portrait with my father, five brothers, and two sisters. Mom passed away when I was twenty and we have no family portraits with her. Dad was getting on in years and I wanted something nice of all of us with Dad, who has since passed away. I preach about family portraits and wrote this book about family portraits, so it only makes sense to include one of my family here. I would have loved a nice family portrait with Mom and Dad in front of our home. My father was a policeman who worked two jobs, and Mom stayed home and raised eight kids.

Background

It was 1999, and my brothers and sisters were visiting from all over the country. I told them that there would be no excuses; we were going to have a portrait with Dad.

This was when I began to use the plants to cover the edges, and the rocks in this photograph pre-date my custom-designed rocks. We were being photographed in the area that is now the fish pond. I posed everyone and had my brother-in-law sit where I would sit so I could see how it looked and then I changed places with him.

This Is Why I'm a Portrait Photographer. We didn't have a lot of money growing up and could not afford a family portrait; this is one of the reasons I do what I do. I will even photograph a family who might not be able to afford my service and give them a portrait.

Clothing Choices. Clothing choices that are haphazard can make a group of related individuals seem "unrelated." Coordinating the clothing can show that everyone is part of the group.

Coordination of Clothing for Families

We kept it casual with dark, long-sleeved shirts and blue jeans. It is important to select clothing for all individuals in the group in the same tonal range. Although some of the people in this portrait wore different colors, the tonal range of these colors were very similar. Consequently, each person's clothing had a similar value of light or darkness. The result is that no single person sticks out more than the others because their clothing is lighter or brighter.

A Very Important Display

I have a 30x40-inch print of this pose in my studio and it has been displayed there since I opened my studio in 2000. Not only does it feel good to have this portrait where I can see it every day, it also helps when someone inquires as to what a 30x40-inch print looks like and I can show them *my* family portrait.

TECH SPECS > This was photographed with a Mamiya RZ67 and 800 film. My exposure was f/8 at 1/60 second.

We kept it casual with dark, long-sleeved shirts and blue jeans.

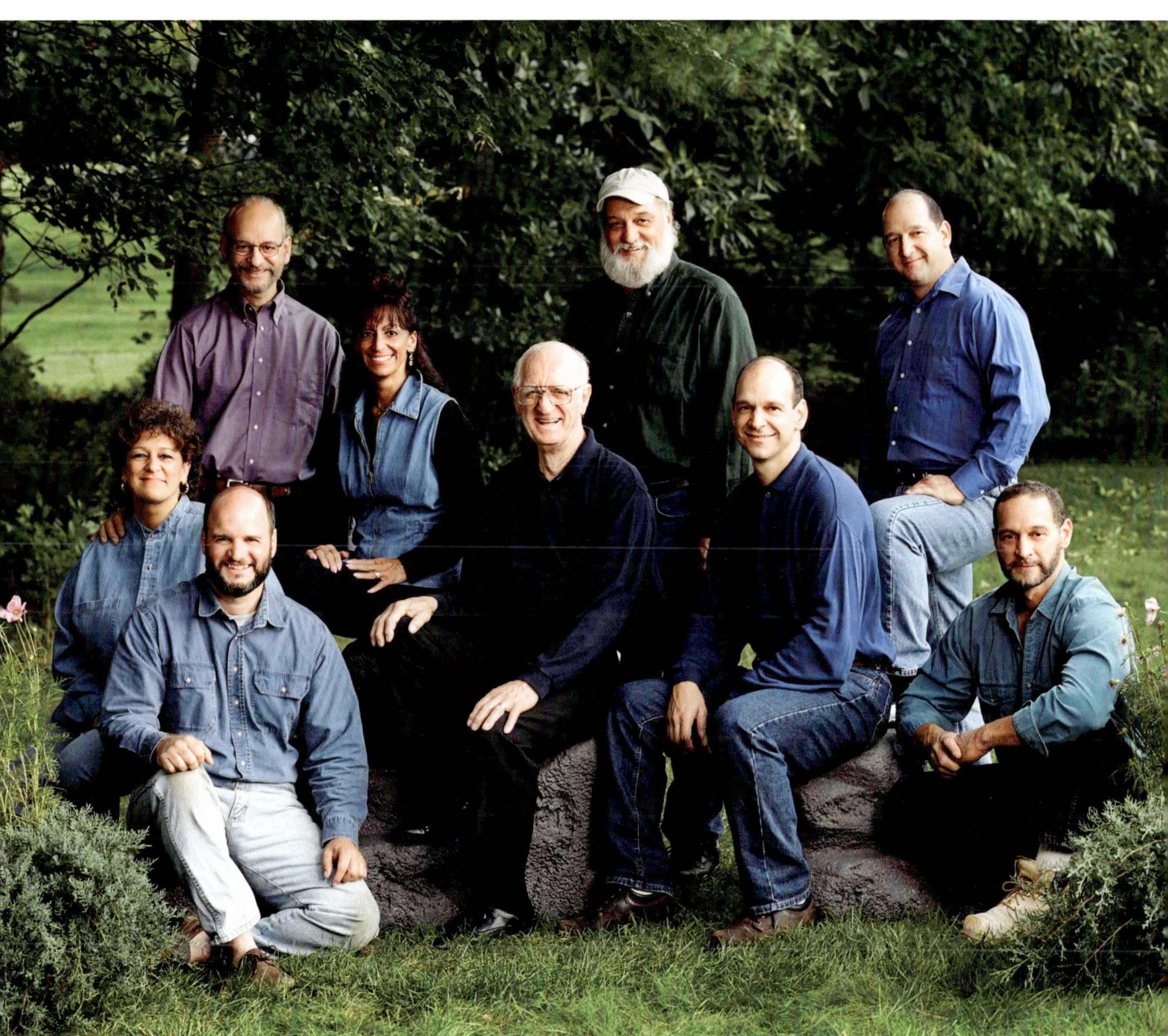

51 Studio Portrait #5: Three Generations

Purpose

This portrait of the grandparents with their daughters and their families was created because the military family on the left was home for Christmas. The man is a service chaplain and he and his wife and son move around the world with the military. The woman on the right is shown with her husband and their three children.

Posing

For compositional balance, I posed the grandparents in the middle, holding onto the hands of their oldest grandson. The moms faced the center, with their children across their laps. The dads stood on the rear left and rear right. I had the boy in the middle stand on a box to bring him to a better height; this helped block the grandmother's midsection.

I photographed the entire group as well as the breakdowns of each family and the children together and separately.

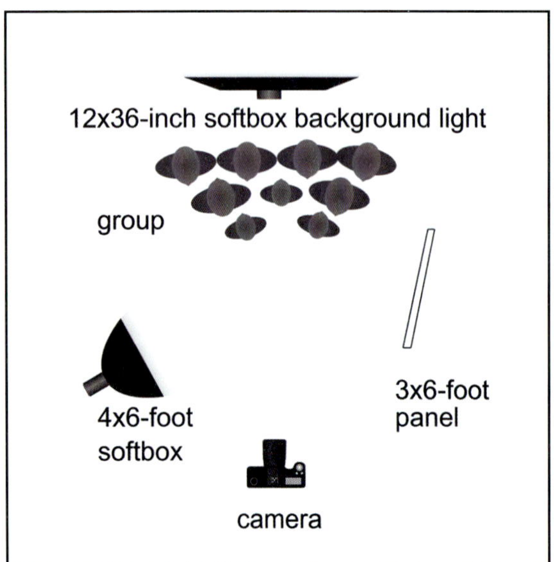

Lighting and Exposure

I photographed them at f/11 because of the distance from the boy in the front to the people in the back; f/11 keeps everyone in focus.

My 4x6-foot horizontal softbox was on the left raised up high to avoid glare in the glasses. The light was skimming the group and there is a 3x6-foot vertical panel in front of the people on a rolling stand on the right throwing fill light back into the faces via reflection.

A Photogenic flash in a 12x36-inch softbox used to light the background was set at f/8 and the hair light was turned off because I was getting a glow on Granddad's head.

TECH SPECS > This was photographed with a Canon 5D Mark II and 24–105mm lens set at 80mm. My exposure was f/11 with a ISO 100.

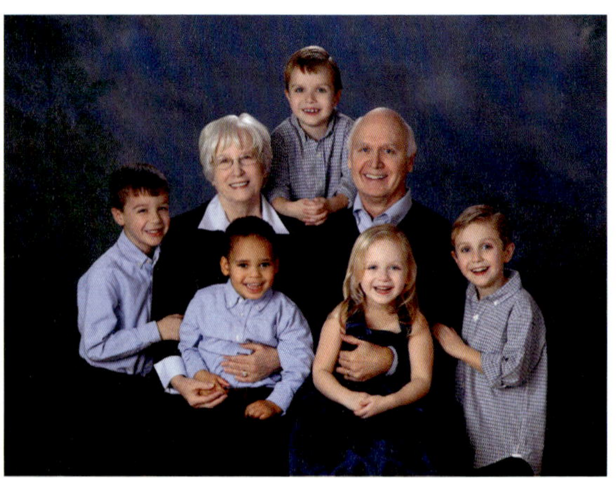

Three Years Later. The portrait (above) of the grandparents with the grandchildren was taken approximately three years later, after the little boy on Grandma's lap was adopted.

For compositional balance, I posed the grandparents in the middle, holding onto the hands of their oldest grandson.

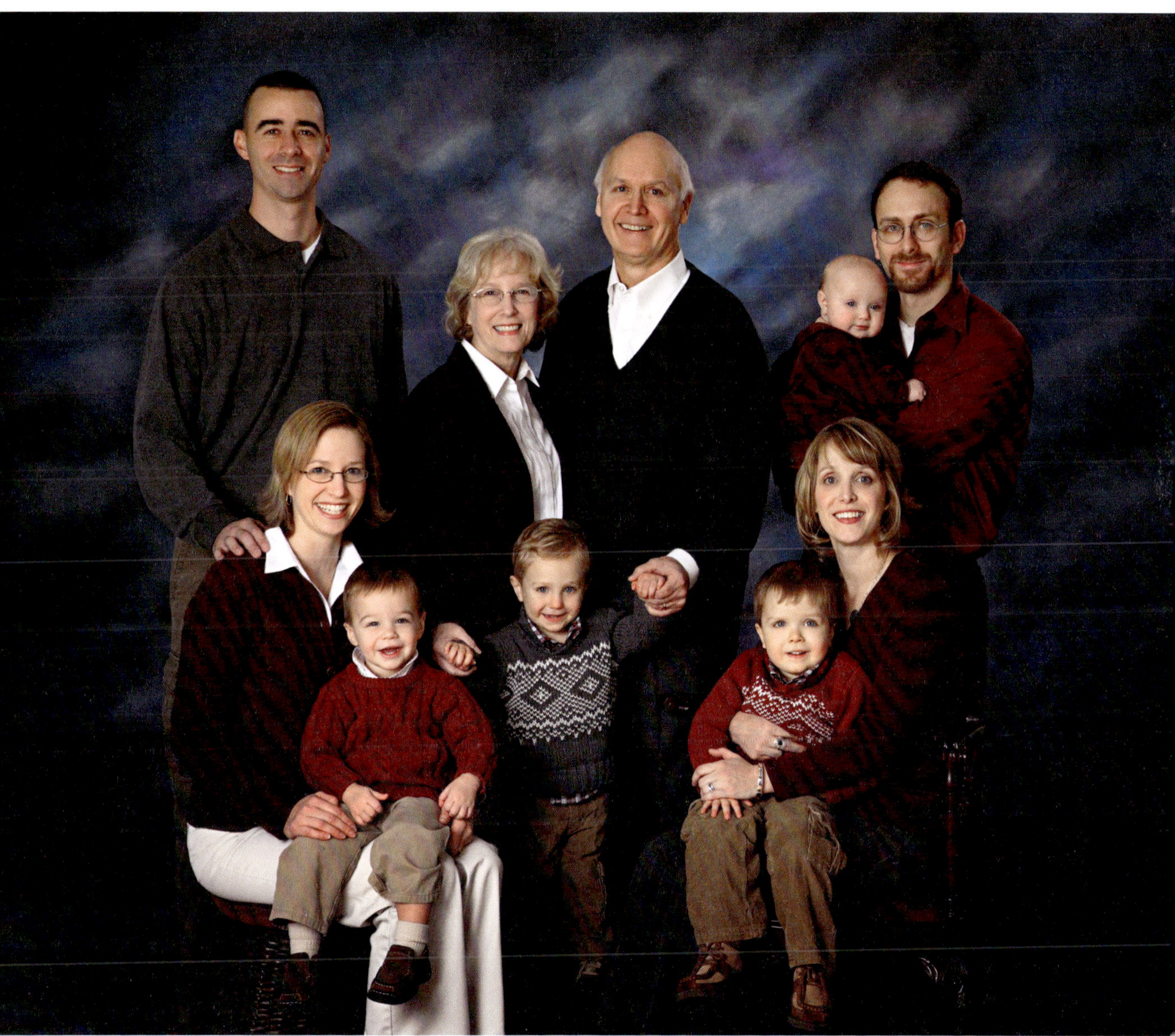

52 Family and Their Yellow House

Setup

The sun was bright and peeking through the trees. My umbrella with a Photogenic flash was to the left of the camera and was plugged into the house with 200 feet of extension cord for a quicker recycle time. The umbrella was raised high so I could get the light at 10 o'clock in their eyes. My 6-foot white reflector panel was on a stand on the right, throwing light back into their faces. My assistant held the 8-foot wind panel on the left to block the sun from hitting the people.

I posed the daughter in the middle between her Mom and Dad, with the sons on either side of their parents.

They were photographed with a 24–105mm lens set at 40mm. I wanted to be in close, so the wide-angle lens was necessary in order to get the five people and the house in the background.

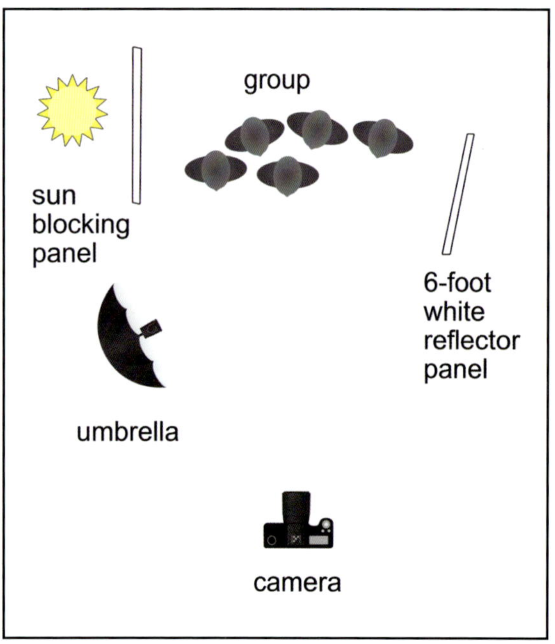

Backstory

They found me through an auction that I participated in at the children's school. Whenever I do an auction, I always have a framed wall portrait on display on a 6-foot easel with a portrait light attached to the easel to make the portrait really pop out. For their convenience, I also have my business cards and brochures showing a variety of my portraits on the table.

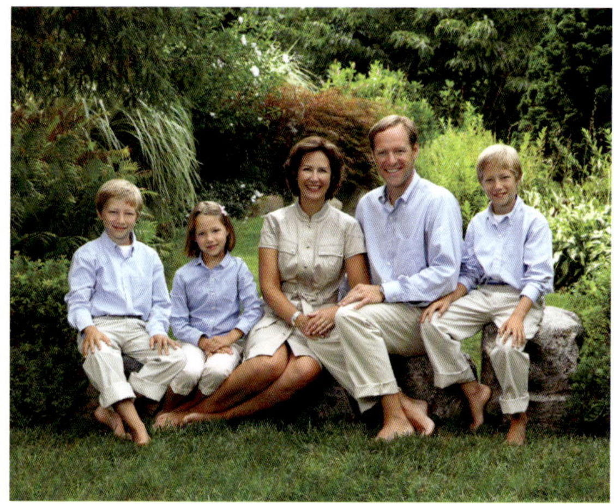

Alternative Portrait. This family was also photographed in their backyard with my rocks and their plantings. This portrait shows the versatility of the rocks; I am able to bring them on location, and it makes the posing much easier.

TECH SPECS > This was photographed with a Canon 5D Mark II and 24–105mm lens set at 40mm. My exposure was f/7.1, 1/60 second, and ISO 600.

The umbrella was raised high so I could get the light at 10 o'clock in their eyes.

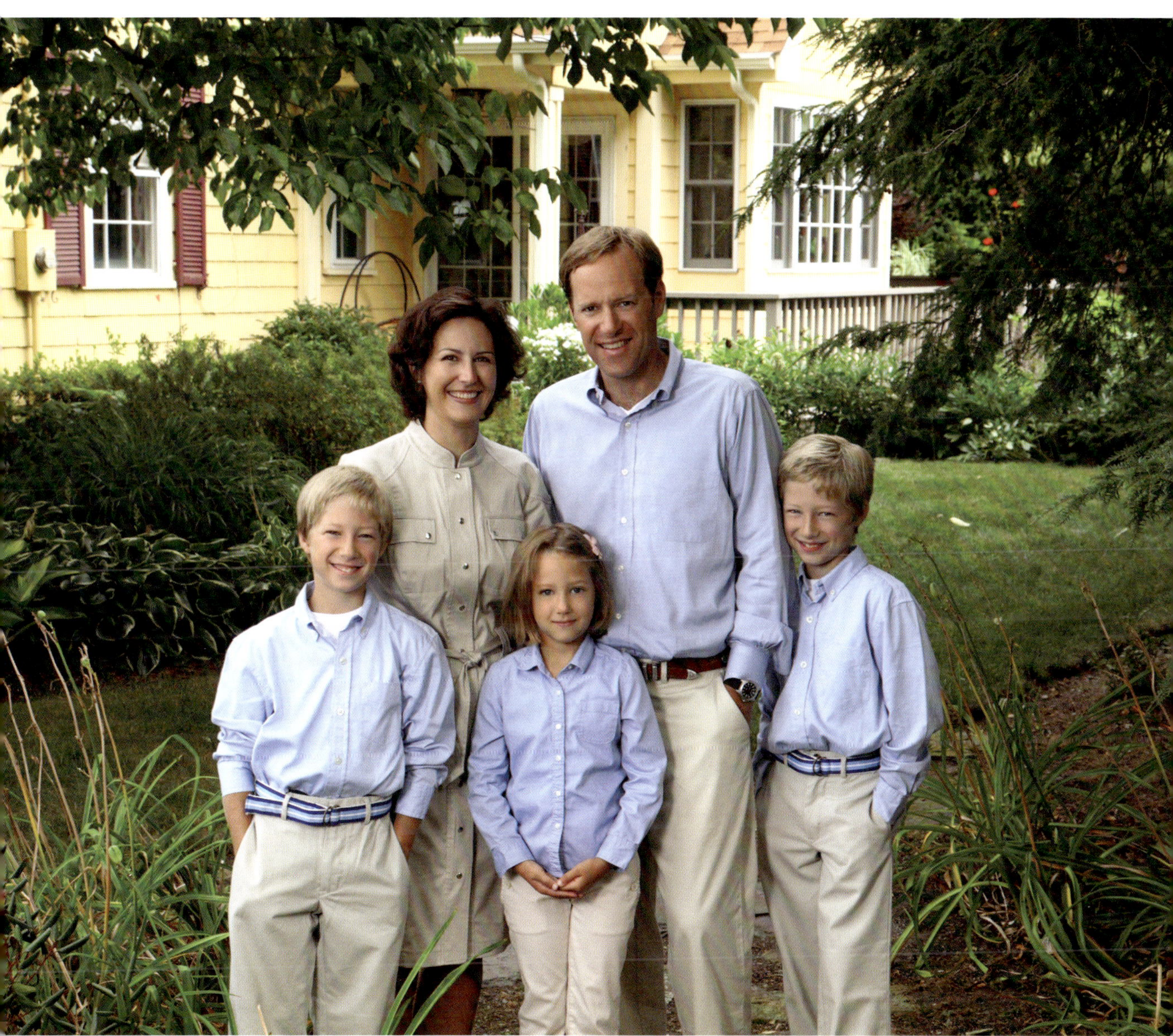

53 Relaxing in the Grass #3

We Have History

This mom was a New England photographer twenty years ago and now lives in Virginia, working in the marketing division of MSNBC. Her husband still has family in Maine and she always contacts me for a family portrait when they make their annual visit to see his parents. I began photographing her family when the older son was just a baby.

Posing

I always try to do something a little different with their portrait. By posing them on the ground I created a triangle with Mom between her two sons and a reverse triangle with Mom and Dad and the younger son between them. They really liked this because they felt that it was unique. I liked the fact that Mom coordinated the outfits, and they wore the same clothing.

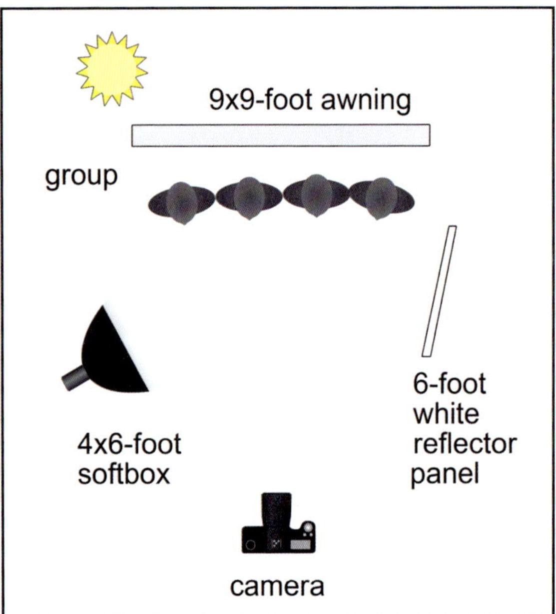

Lighting and Exposure

I used the Canon 5D Mark II with the 70–200mm lens set to the maximum at 200mm, which I could do because the boys were older and I could be farther away from them and still hold their attention. My exposure was f/6.3, 1/60 second, and ISO 800 to brighten the naturally dark background. They were under and to the back of my 9x9x9-foot awning. Their hair was illuminated by the light from the sky coming in behind my awning.

My softbox was very close to the ground on the left side, skimming across from left to right. My white reflector panel was on the right. My camera was also very low to the ground. There are a lot of cool tones with the green shirts and green (artificial) grass, which pulls the viewer into the warm tones of their faces.

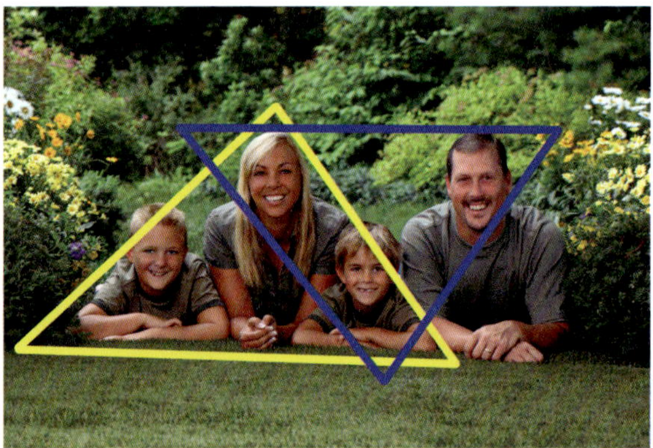

TECH SPECS > This was photographed with a Canon 5D Mark II and 70–200mm lens set at 200mm. My exposure was f/6.3, 1/60 second, and ISO 800.

I created a triangle with Mom between her two sons and a reverse triangle with Mom and Dad and the youngest son between them.

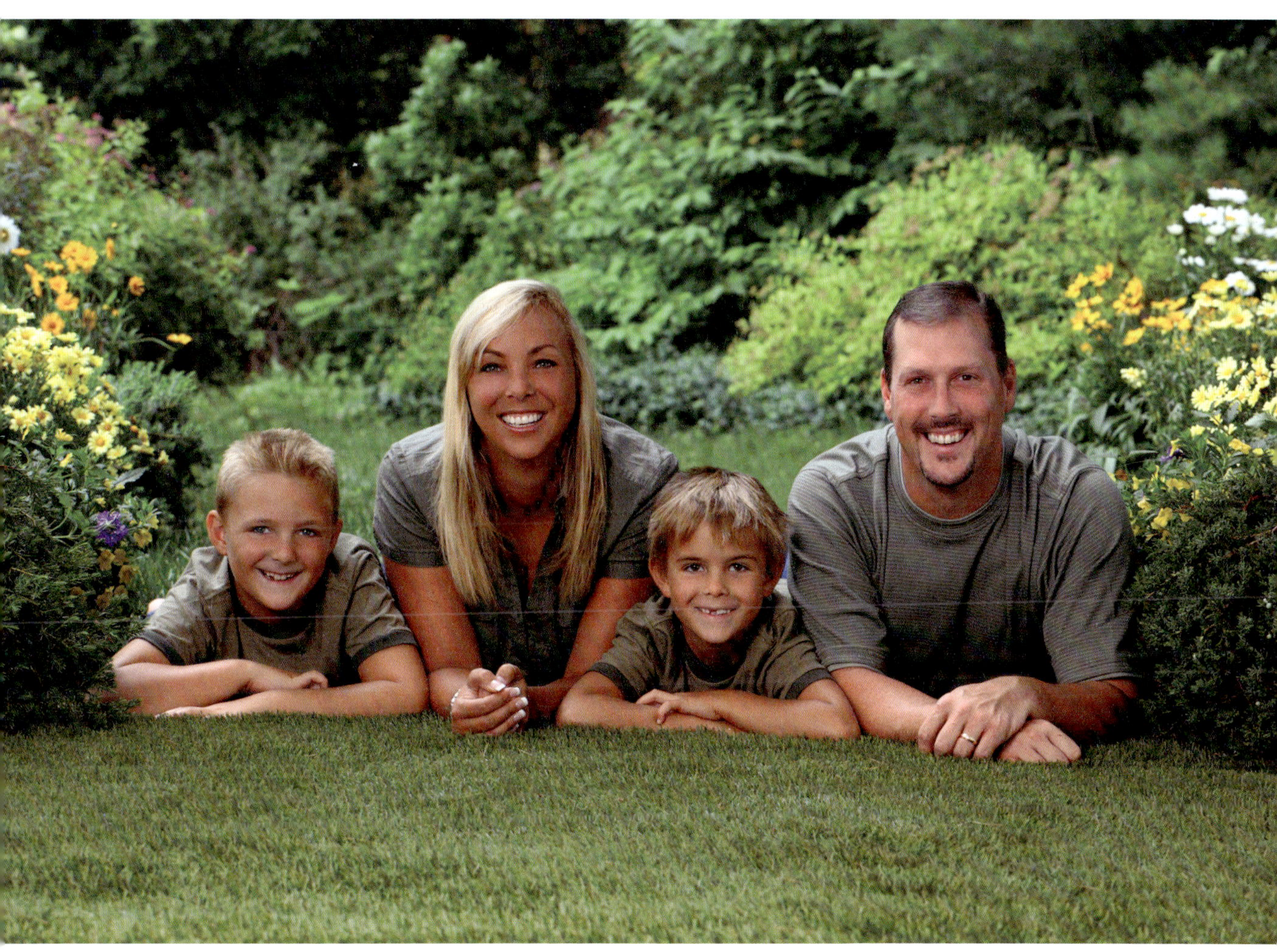

54 Four Generations with Sixteen People

History

This portrait was my first Professional Photographers of America Loan Collection image in 2004. To answer the question I am often asked, yes, this was made with one exposure without Photoshop or head swapping.

Posing

This was taken on the front lawn of the home of the family on the left; they were on the lawn, I was standing in the street. The ninety-three-year-old great-grandparents were sitting in the center, each holding onto a great-grandchild. The grandparents were standing on the right and their family of two daughters and one son were with their respective families. The woman on the far right was visiting with her family from Singapore. Her daughter was with the great grandfather; the little boy with the great-grandmother was part of the family on the left.

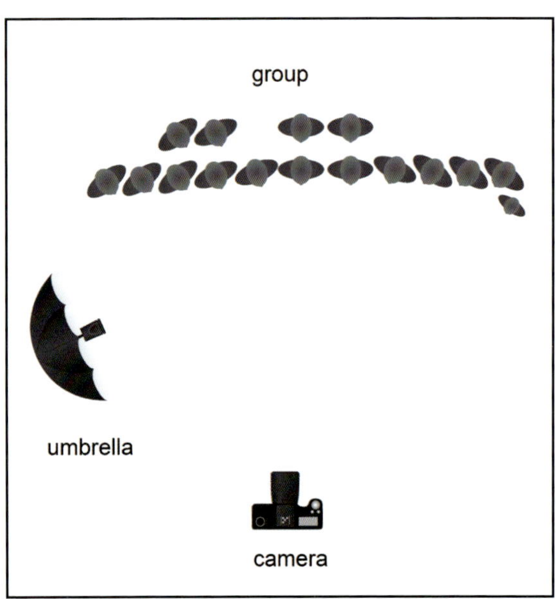

I used my groupings to create triangles and the tree branch to help frame the group. Some of the plants in the photo are theirs, but I brought the juniper plants, the plants on the right, and the black-eyed Susans.

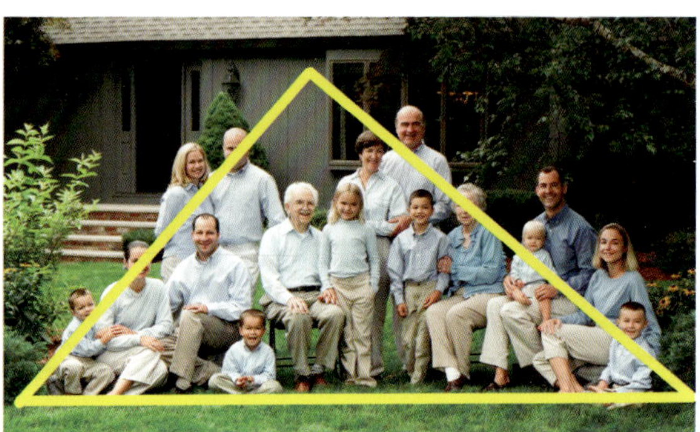

Lighting

I used one umbrella on the left and a lot of light coming from the sky on a cloudy, overcast day. This was photographed at f/11 to keep everyone in focus.

Postscript

I photographed the great-grandfather in his woodwork shop, as he made a lighthouse when he was ninety-eight. This portrait was for me and was done at no charge. A few months later, I was asked to visit him at his home, and he gave me the lighthouse. I have a 24x30-inch print portrait of him making the lighthouse in my studio and the 2½-foot tall lighthouse in the portrait is on the shelf below it.

TECH SPECS > This was photographed with a Mamiya RZ67 and a 127mm lens. My exposure was f/11 and 1/60 second using Kodak 400 film.

I used the tree branch to help frame the group.

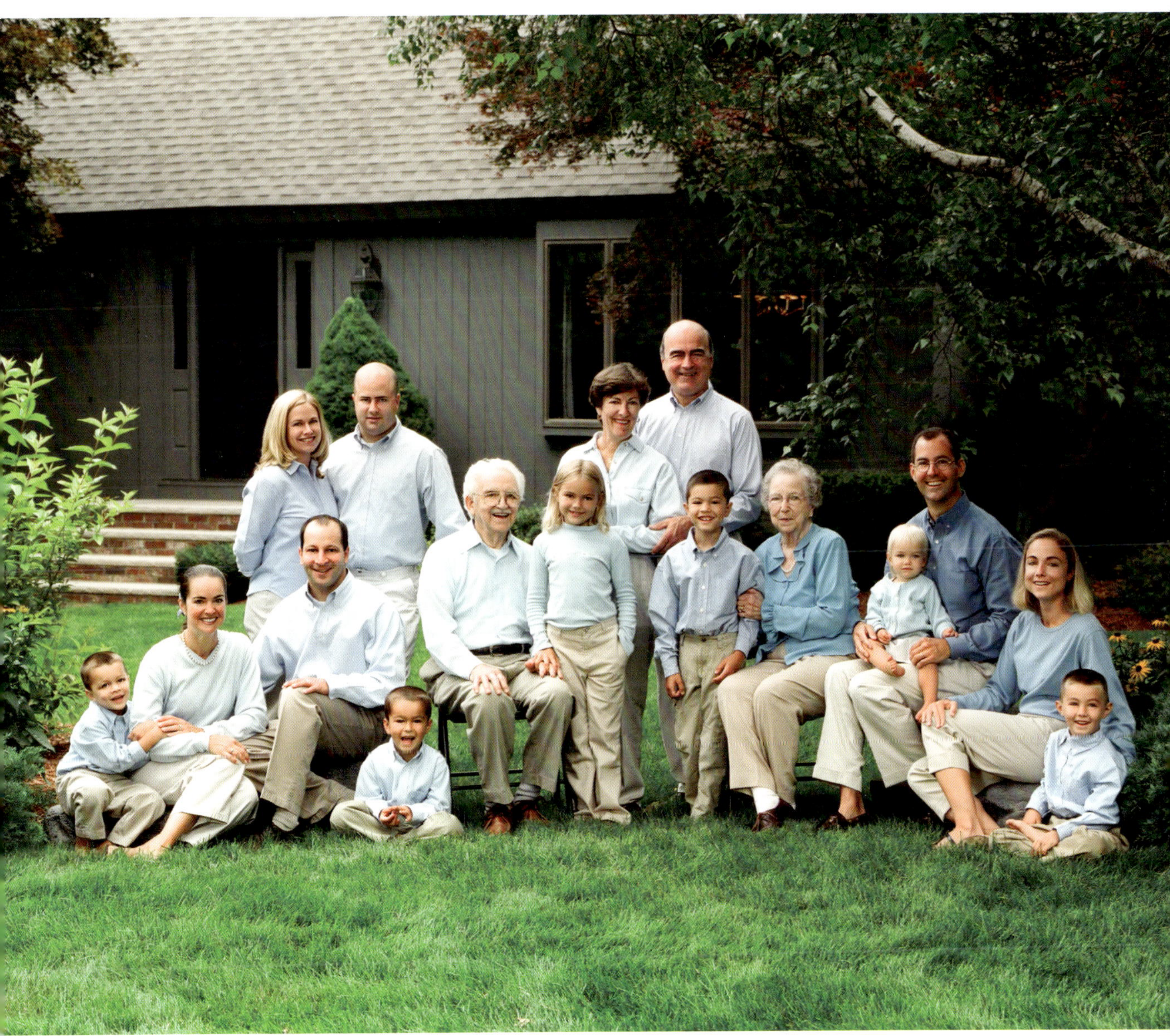

55 Plum Island Beach Portrait #3

Purpose

This family wanted a beach portrait, so we began while the sun was up. We also did a series of breakaways of just the kids together and separately and some of just Mom and Dad together; I wanted to give them as much variety as possible. With any family portrait, and especially a beach portrait where I have to travel forty minutes each way, I want many opportunities to sell portraits as possible. If all I did was take the one photograph that was requested, my options of larger sales would be diminished. By creating a variety of images in different locations, my sales opportunities are greatly increased.

Exposure

This image was created while the sun was still up. I used a Quantum flash with a battery on a light stand to the left of the camera. You can see the shadows are a bit harsher. When the flash is housed in a parabolic, the light is hard, but because of the wind, I could not use a softbox on the beach. I used the Q-flash to bring out the intensity and to bring out the background light. By doing this, I maintain color in the beautiful sky. I exposed for the background and used the flash to light the family. I had my lab print this image to give me good flesh tones and good color in the sky.

I used a Canon 5D Mark II with a 70–200mm lens set at 120mm. Because I wanted to show the bright, colorful sky, I photographed them at 1/60 second at f/8. The ISO was 640 and the flash was set at f/5.6.

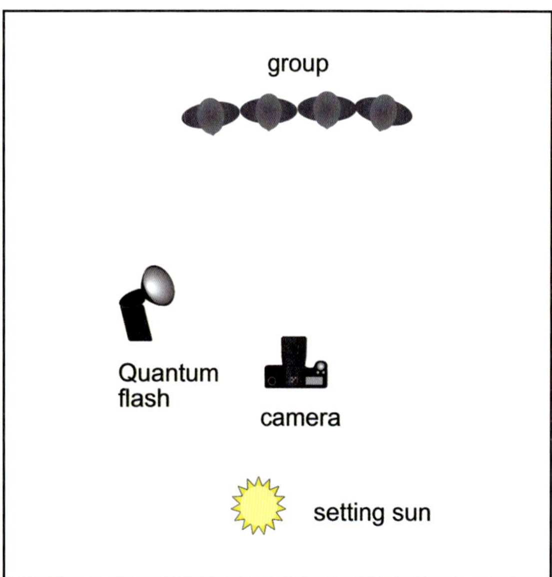

Composition

I liked the composition; I liked the little hill on the left sweeping down and leading the eye into the water and the group. Then when the sun hit the horizon, we moved to do *Plum Island Beach Portrait #4.*

Clothing Choice and Outdoor Settings. Informal clothing complements portraits made in outdoor settings.

TECH SPECS > This was photographed with a Canon 5D Mark II and 70–200mm lens set at 120mm. My exposure was f/8, 1/60 second, and ISO 640.

I exposed for the background and used the flash to light the family.

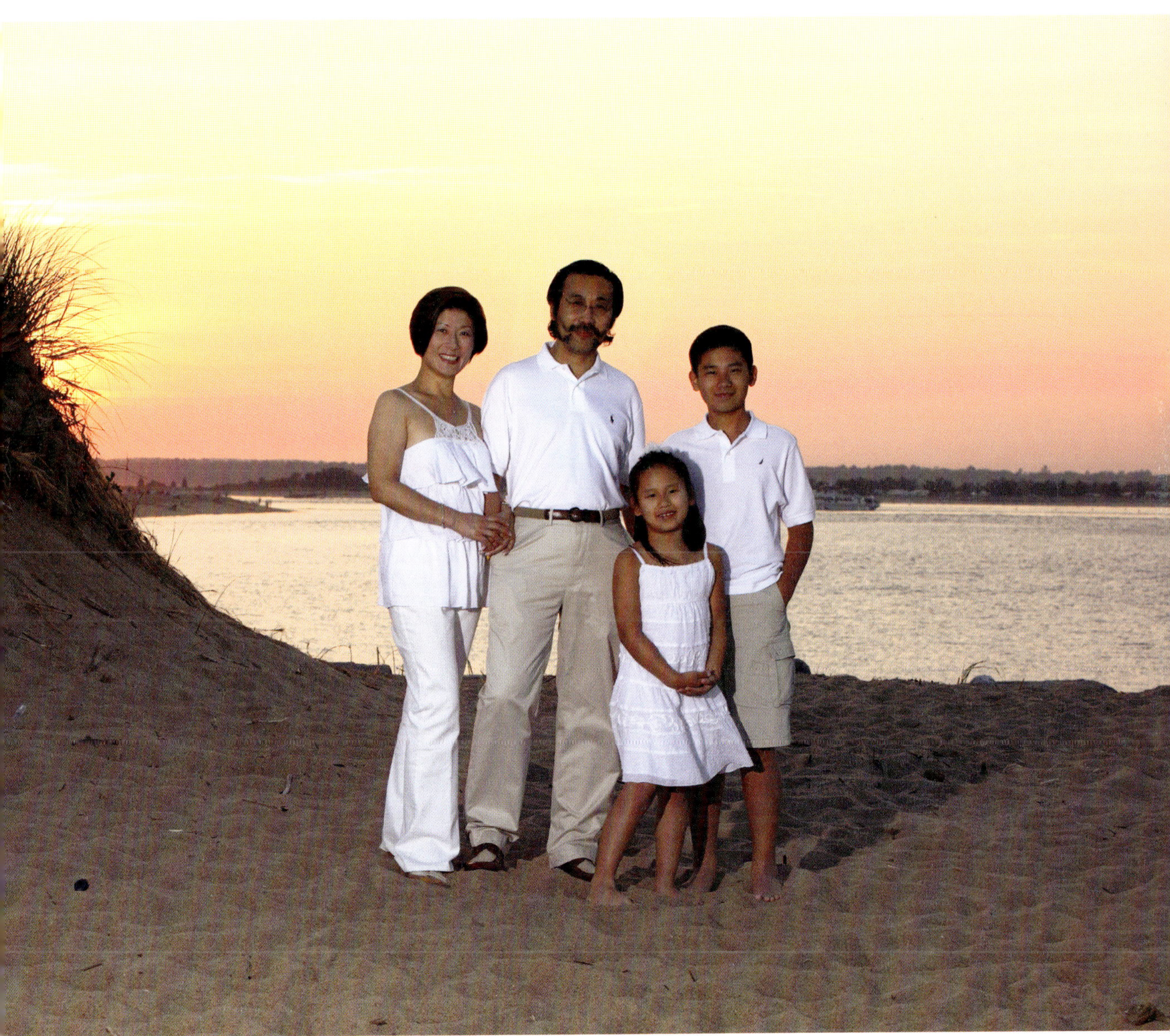

56 Plum Island Beach Portrait #4

Purpose

We moved to a different location for this portrait as the sun was setting. Again, I created a variety of images of the kids separately and together and of the parents without the kids. This portrait earned me a Merit Award from the Professional Photographers of America.

Lighting

For a portrait like this, you have to wait until sunset. This image, I pointed the dome of the meter towards the sun, which was behind me, and I was able to use the end of the day's flat lighting. This image was made using natural sunlight with no reflectors and no additional flash.

Posing

I had Dad on one knee to give a little height. Mom leaned in towards the daughter and put her hand on her daughter's arm. The boy crossed his left leg over his right leg and brought his arm over to cover his crotch. I crossed the little girl's legs. I had Dad's arm on Mom's arm; I always like my subjects touching to show warmth and family togetherness.

I positioned the camera to make sure that the horizon line was nice and straight and not going through anyone's head, and angled the camera to be sure that the heads were clear of distractions.

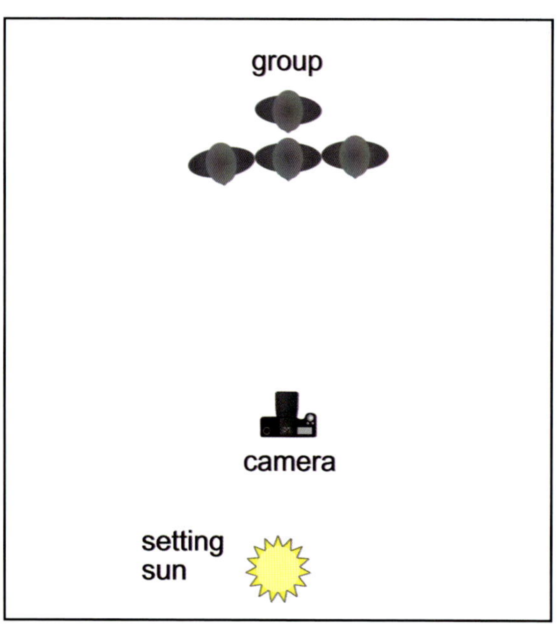

TECH SPECS > This was photographed with a Canon 5D Mark II and 70–200mm lens set at 150mm. My exposure was f/5.6, 1/60 second, and ISO 800.

Estimating the Sun's Descent. For a portrait like this, you have to wait until sunset. To check how long before the sun hits the horizon line, I extend my right arm all the way out towards the sun and bend my fingers to the left. For every finger between the sun and the horizon, I have fifteen minutes, so if all four fingers fit under the sun, it will be one hour until sunset.

For a portrait like this, you have to wait until sunset.

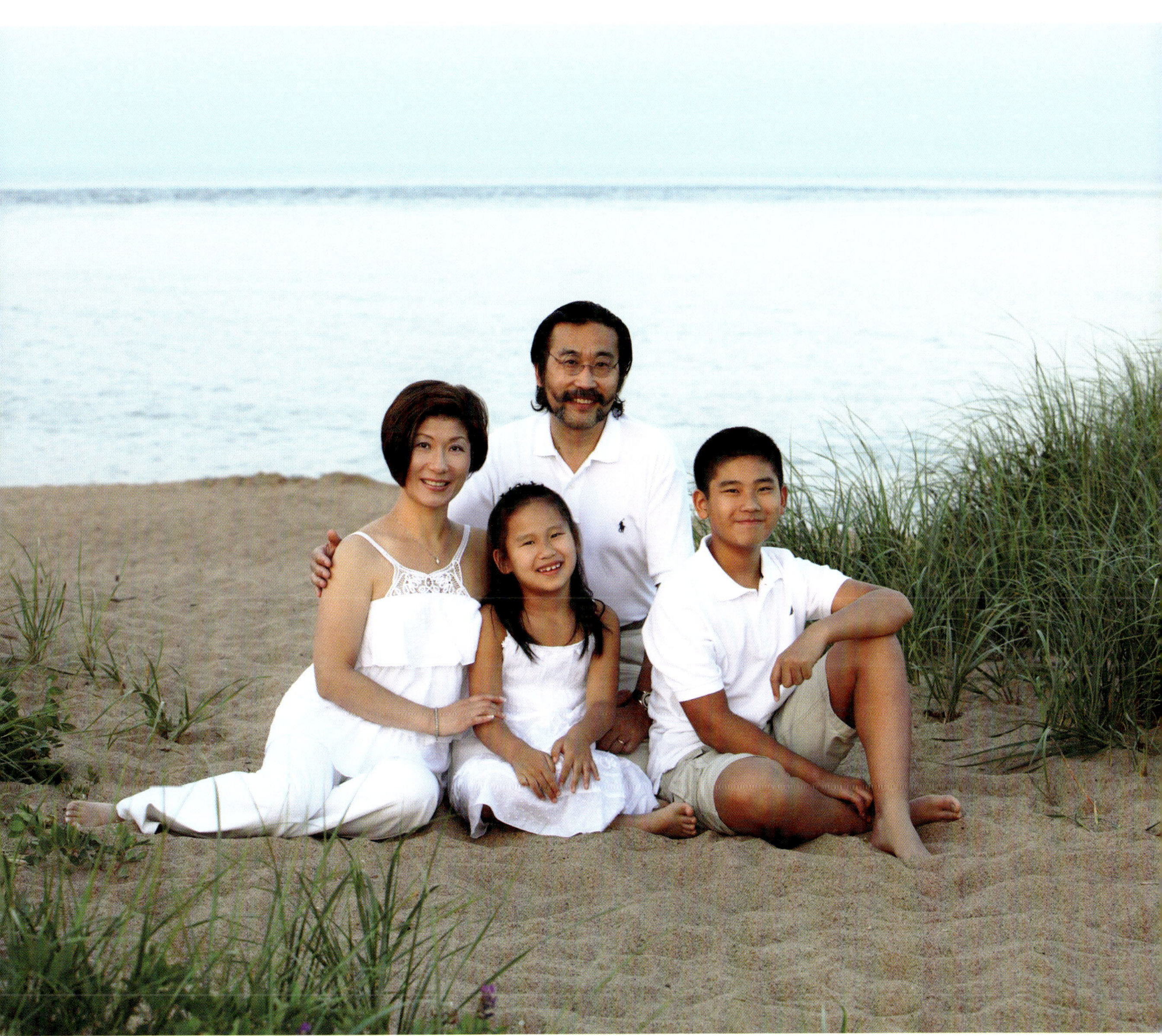

57 Empty Nesters

Purpose

With their children grown and out of the house, this couple wanted a portrait with their newest baby, their dog. They discovered me at a Family Day event similar to Art in the Park, where we display our portraits. The Family Day and Art-in-the-Park events are successful because we always gain new clients.

Posing

They were sitting in my outdoor studio on my custom-made rocks with the dog in her lap; I added flowers to the background for color and balance. I used my squeaker to get the dog's attention as well as to get the husband and wife to smile.

Lighting

My 4x6-foot softbox was to the left of the camera and the 6-foot square white reflective panel was on the right, throwing light back to their faces. My assistant held an 8-foot wind panel on the left to block the sun from bathing them in sunlight. The dog faced towards the light source. This was especially important because his coat was black needing definition and to create catchlights in his eyes.

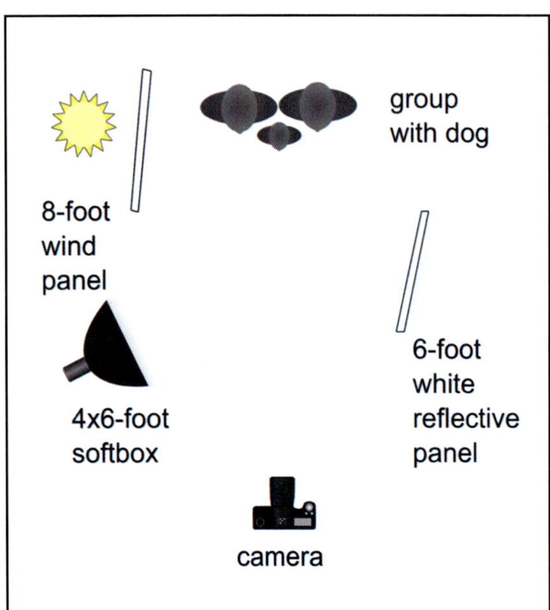

Postproduction

LucisArt was used in postproduction to lighten the fur on the dog to give him separation from the black shirt. LucisArt is not standalone software —it works as a Photoshop plug-in through the Filters menu.

Postscript

They loved this portrait and gave copies to their two sons. A year later, when the sons were in the area, I photographed their family portrait.

Clothing Choices. Simple garments within the same tonal ranges should be chosen. Another thing to keep in mind is how the clothing and background selection will affect the stylistic intent of the portrait.

TECH SPECS > This was photographed with a Canon 5D Mark II and 70–200mm lens set at 180mm. My exposure was f/6.3, 1/60 second, and ISO 800.

LucisArt was used in postproduction to lighten the fur on the dog to bring out details and to give him separation from the black shirt.

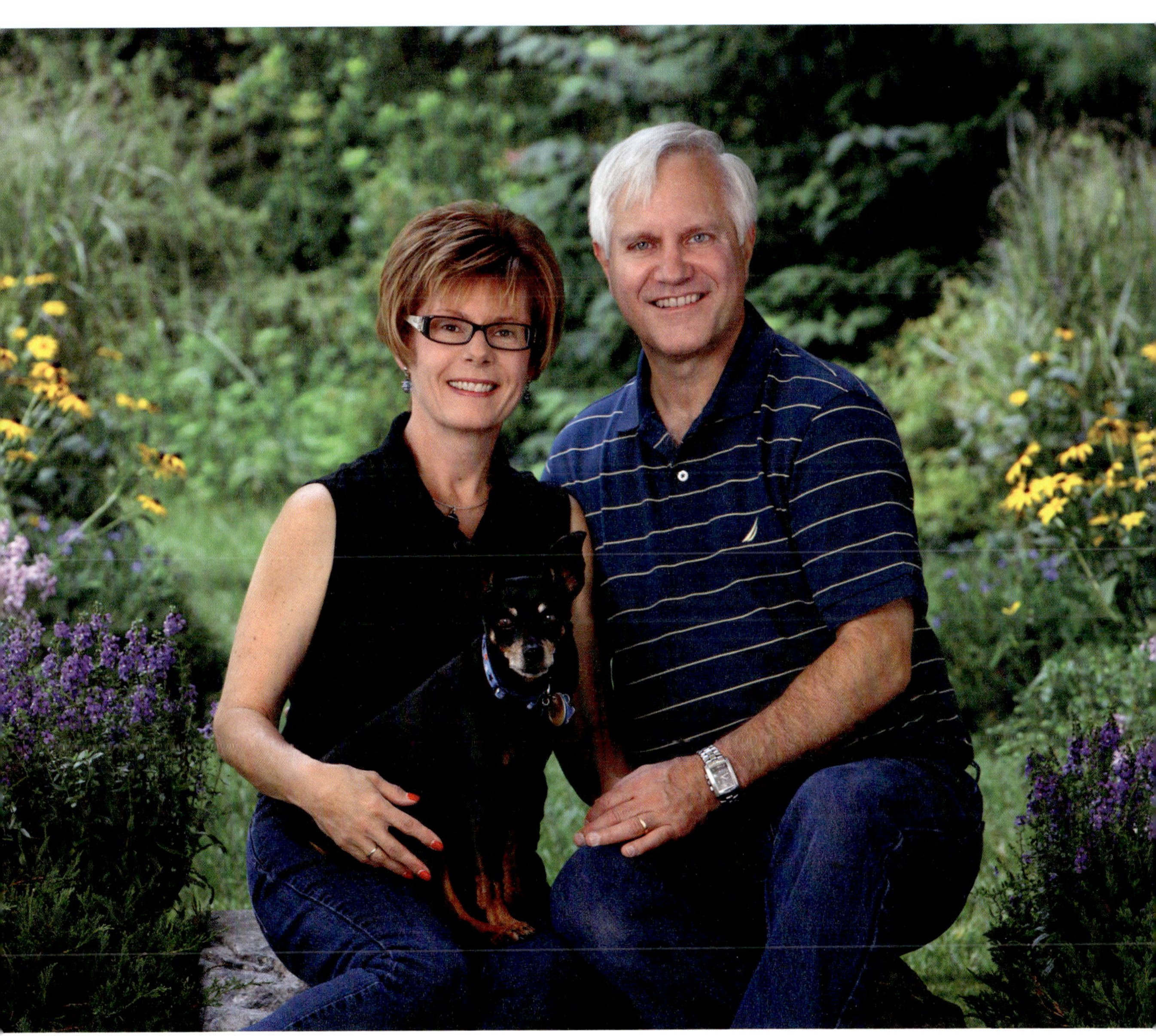

58 1966 Mustang

History and Concept

I had photographed the daughter's First Communion portrait. When the family drove up in this Mustang to pick up their order, I commented on the car and Dad said it was the ride he always wanted, a 1966 Mustang. A year later they contacted me about a family portrait and I suggested photographing them with the car. I also suggested that they wear T-shirts and jeans and I would photograph them on a dirt road in black and white to make it look like 1966. They loved the idea.

Composition and Lighting

I asked Mom to sit in the front seat on the passenger side, the older son in the back seat, the youngest on the trunk, and the daughter standing in front of her dad. With no access to an electrical outlet, I used a Quantum flash with an umbrella on a stand on the left to put a little light in their eyes. We were in the road, so most of the light was coming from the sky. I was on a ladder photographing down because I liked the angle of the road in the background.

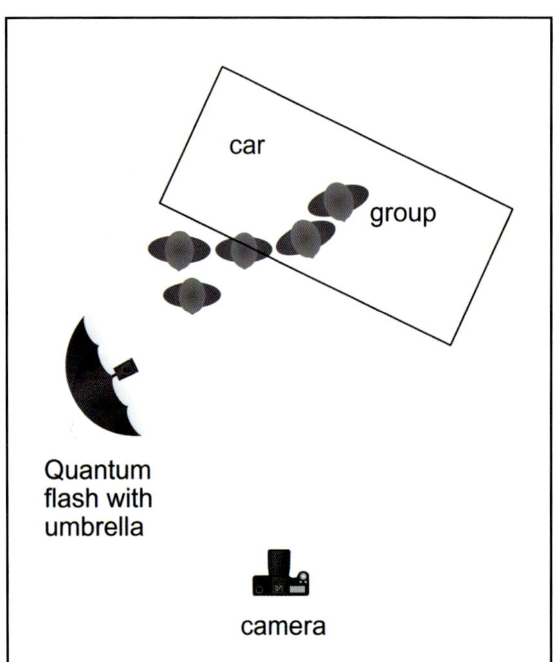

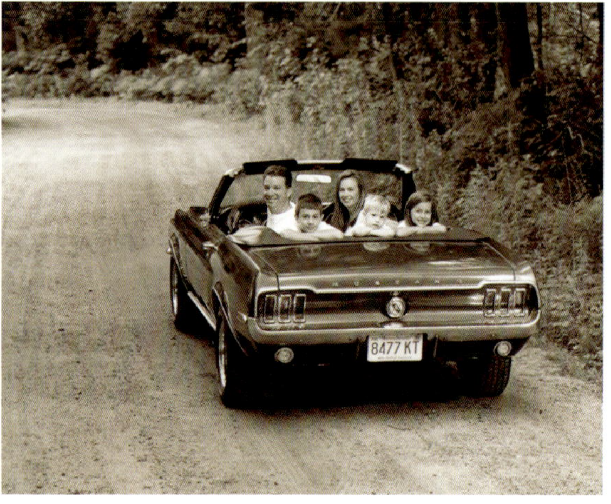

An Alternate Photograph

The second photograph (above) looks like a car commercial to me. I had them face me from the back of the car. I was up on a ladder and had the kids face me, resting their arms and elbows on the car, with Mom and Dad turning around to look at me over their left shoulder as if they were glancing back just before driving away. The camera, lens, and exposure were the same for both shots.

TECH SPECS > This was photographed with a Mamiya RZ67 and a 127mm lens. My exposure was f/8, 1/60 second, and ISO 400.

I was on a ladder photographing down because I liked the angle of the road in the background.

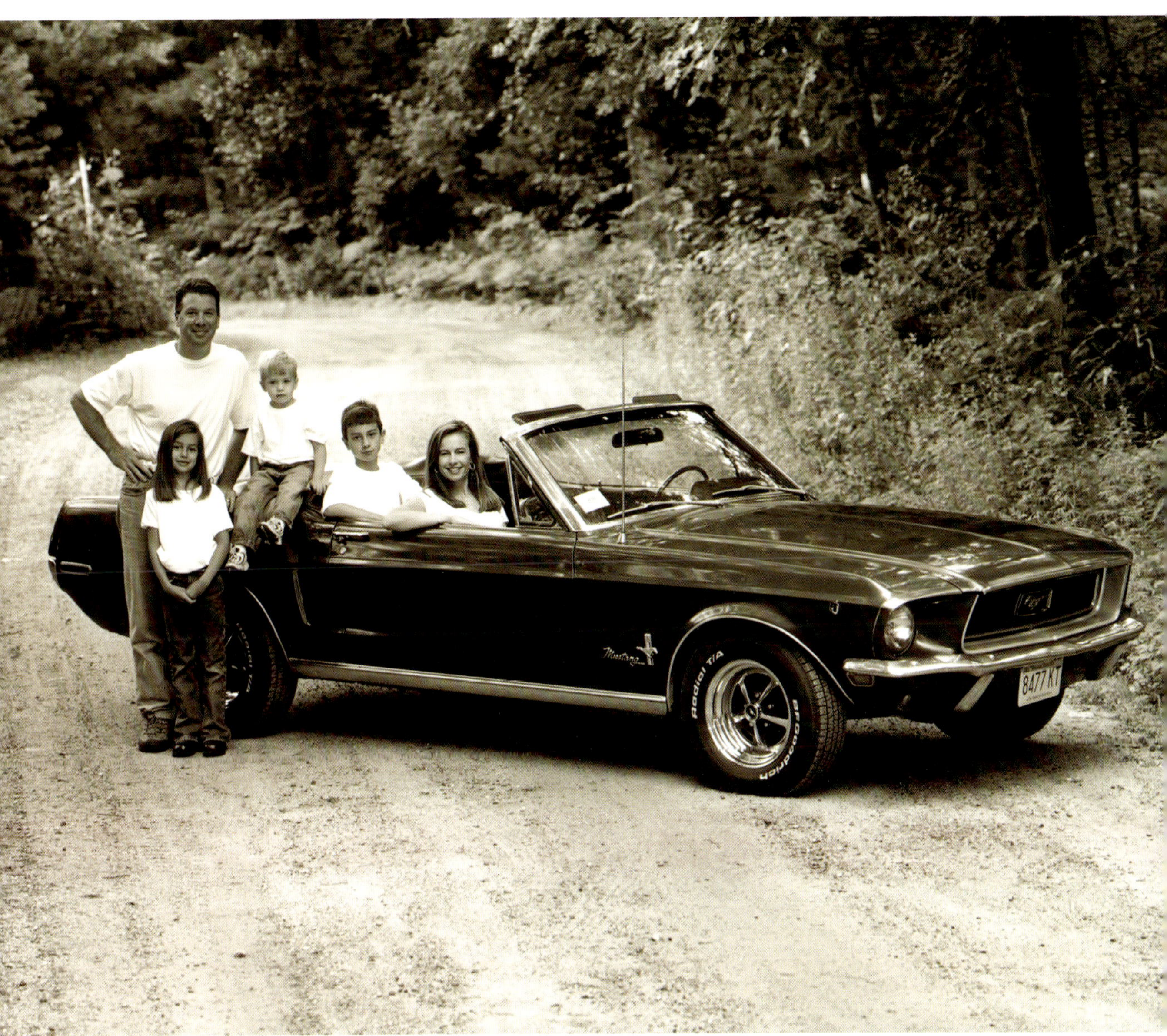

59 Studio Portrait #6

Purpose

Mom and Dad wanted this family portrait because their teenage daughter, a high-school senior, would soon be going off to college.

Lighting

The main light was the 4x6-foot softbox to the left of the camera. The 6-foot white reflective panel was on the right, throwing light back to their faces. My hair light was a Photogenic flash in a Larson 10x36-inch softbox and was set at f/5.0. It cannot be too strong with blond subjects, or it will blow out their hair. My background light was a Photogenic flash in a 12x36-inch softbox, also set at f/5.0.

Posing and Composition

I selected a David Maheu background to match the colors they wore. The diagonal composition of Mom, Dad, and daughter going up from left to right is mimicked by their left arms also flowing left to right.

An Exception to a Rule. While I usually have Dad as the tallest figure in a portrait, the progression of Mom and Dad sitting at different heights to their daughter gave this image a strong appeal and the inference that she would soon flee the nest and embark on her own.

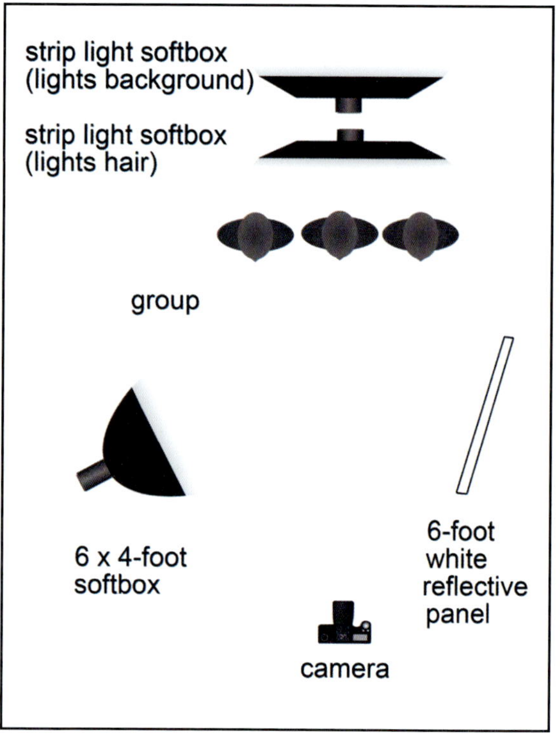

Repetition of elements, such as color, position, or lines, can be pleasing to the eye. It also helps combine the components of the photograph into a pleasing and successful composition.

TECH SPECS > This was photographed with a Canon 5D Mark II and 70–200mm lens set at 150mm. My exposure was f/6.3, 1/125 second with ISO 100.

The diagonal composition of Mom, Dad, and daughter going up from left to right is mimicked by their left arms also flowing left to right.

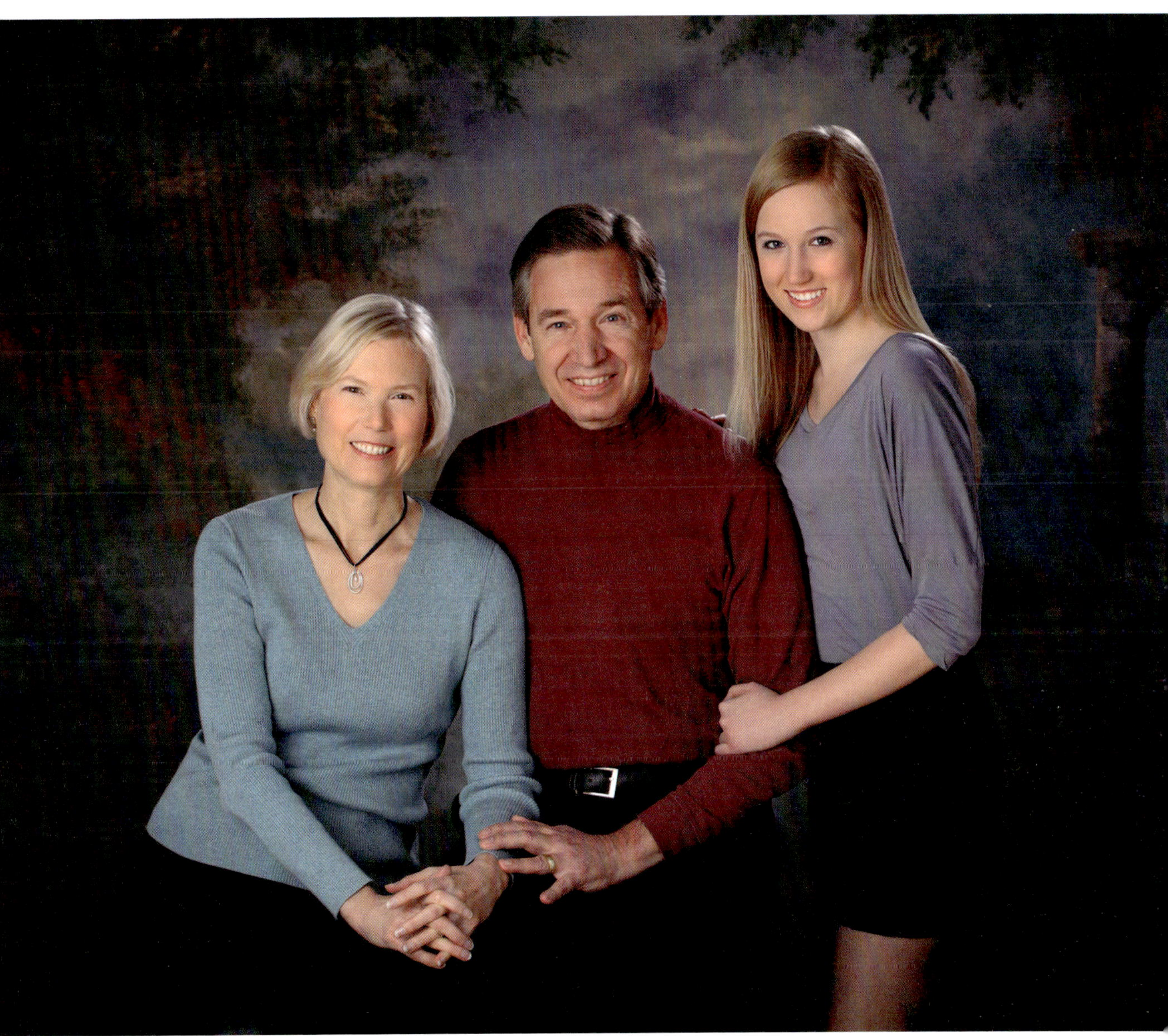

60 Winter Portrait

Purpose

The grandparents seated in the center were visiting their daughter and her family on the left, who wanted a family portrait made in their home. Their other daughter and her family were sitting on the right.

Posing

With their permission, I moved the plants in on the left and right to fill in dead space as well as to balance the composition. If I had not moved the plant on the right, there would have been a large bright area that would have been distracting.

The table was moved closer to the family to take up some of the foreground space, and I placed a plant that was in another part of the room on the table to add a little color.

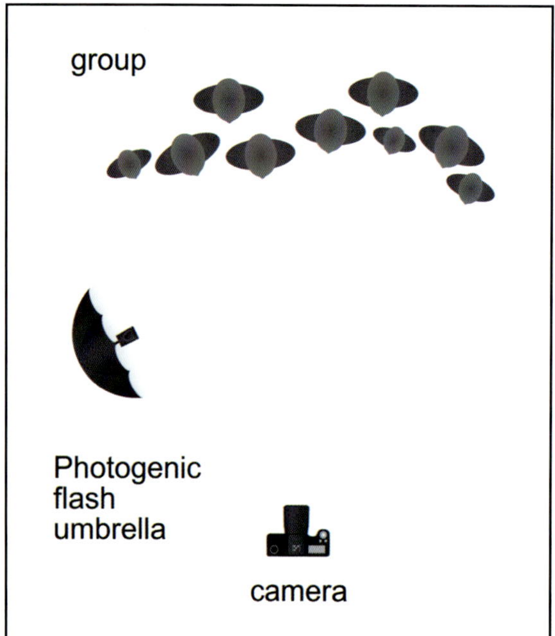

About the Composition

- Notice that the rug, drapery, upholstery, and walls were light neutrals that helped to surround and frame the subjects.
- The three plants placed on each side and in the front keep the viewers' eye moving through the image.
- The image has a nice balance of red and blacks with most of the blacks in the middle, and it is further balanced by the three points of green provided by the plants.

Lighting and Film

An umbrella with a Photogenic flash was on the left, skimming the light across to the right. This image was photographed with film; if it had been captured digitally, it would have been simple to swap the dog's head with another image if he were not looking up. In the days of film, it was not so easy to exchange a blurred or distorted portion of the image with a selection from another image.

TECH SPECS > This was photographed with a Mamiya RZ67 with the 127mm lens using 400 film. My exposure was f/8 at 1/125 second.

I moved the plants in on the left and right to fill in dead space as well as to balance the composition.

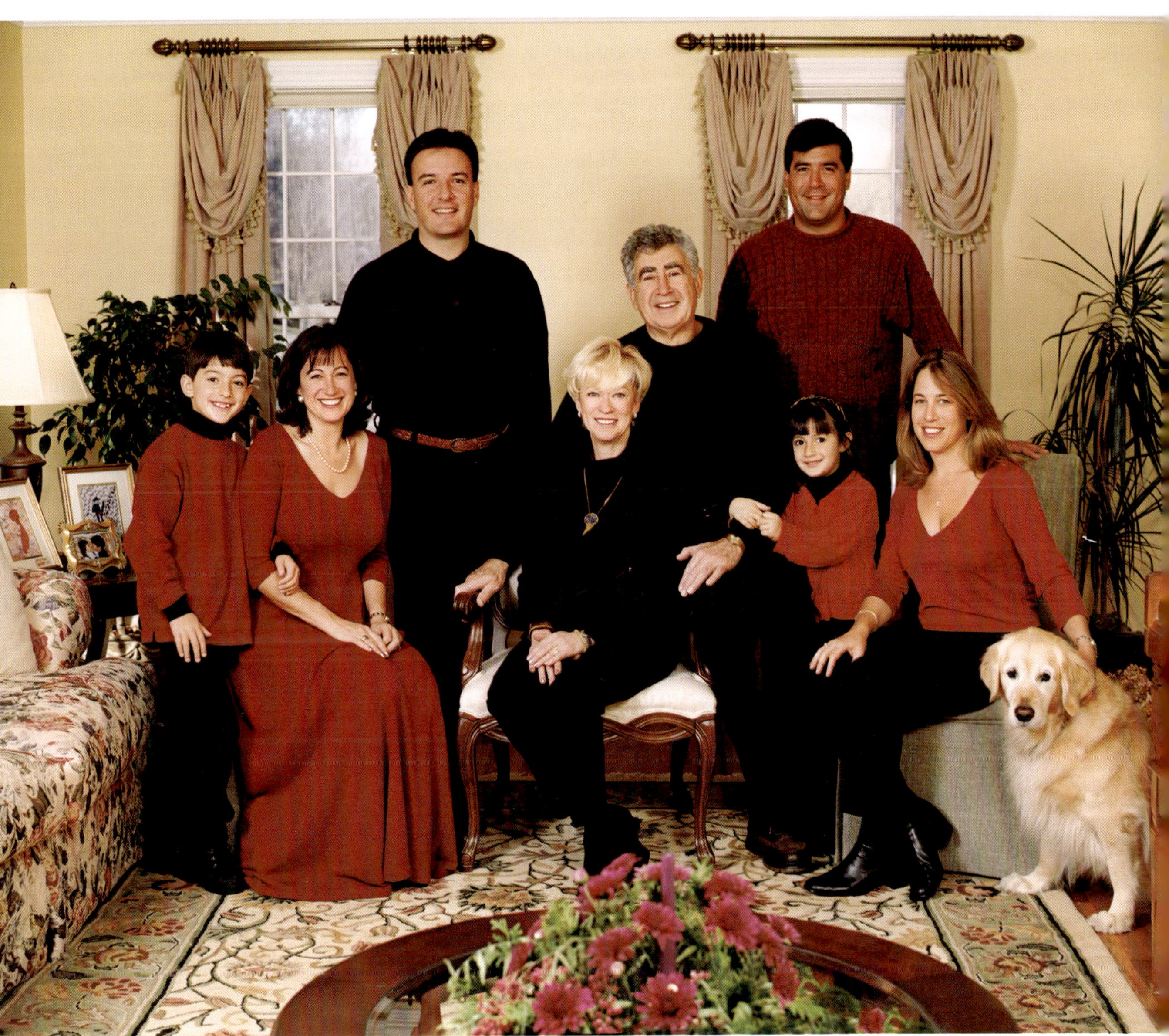

Index

OTHER BOOKS FROM
Amherst Media®

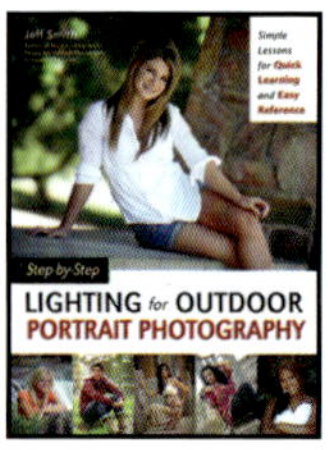

Step-by-Step Lighting for Outdoor Portrait Photography

Jeff Smith brings his no-nonsense approach to outdoor lighting, showing how to produce great portraits all day long. *$27.95 list, 7.5x10, 128p, 275 color images, order no. 2009.*

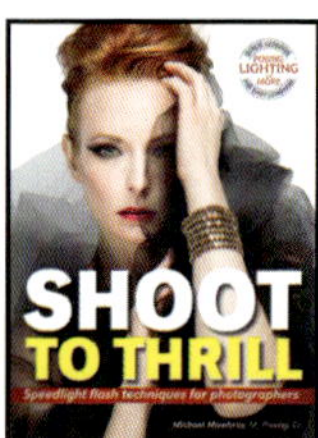

Shoot to Thrill

Acclaimed photographer Michael Mowbray shows how speedlights can rise to any photographic challenge—in the studio or on location. *$27.95 list, 7.5x10, 128p, 220 color images, order no. 2011.*

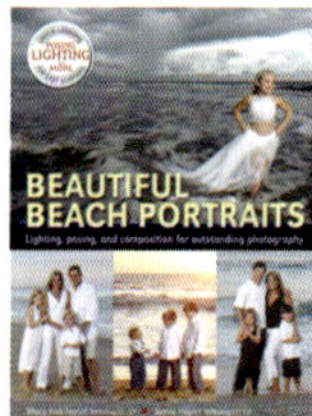

Beautiful Beach Portraits

Mary Fisk-Taylor and Jamie Hayes take you behind the scenes on the creation of their most popular images, showing you how each was conceived and created. *$27.95 list, 7.5x10, 128p, 180 color images, order no. 2025.*

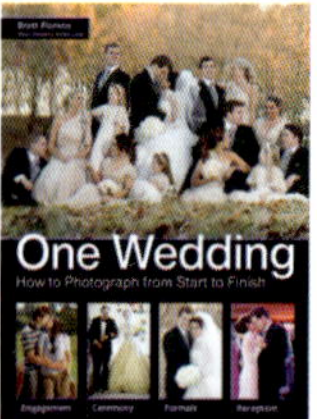

One Wedding

Brett Florens takes you, hour by hour, through the photography process for one entire wedding—from the engagement portraits, to the reception, and beyond! *$27.95 list, 7.5x10, 128p, 375 color images, order no. 2015.*

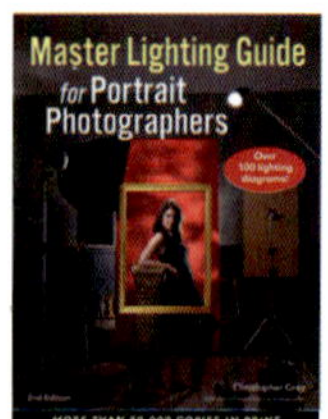

Master Lighting Guide for Portrait Photographers, *2nd ed.*

Christopher Grey shows you how to master traditional lighting styles and use creative modifications to maximize your results. *$27.95 list, 7.5x10, 160p, 350 color images, order no. 1998.*

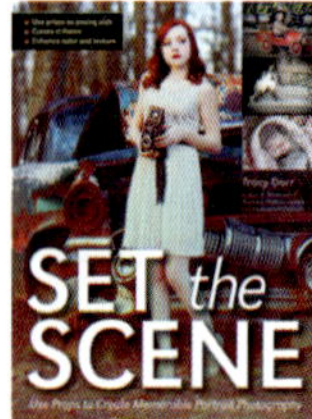

Set the Scene

With techniques and images from nearly a dozen top pros, Tracy Dorr shows you how using props can inspire you to design more creative and customized portraits. *$27.95 list, 7.5x10, 128p, 320 color images, order no. 1999.*

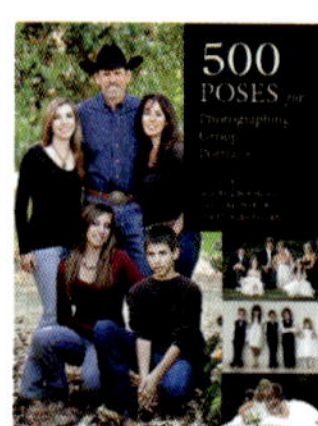

500 Poses for Photographing Groups

Michelle Perkins provides an impressive collection of images that will inspire you to design polished, professional portraits. *$34.95 list, 8.5x11, 128p, 500 color images, order no. 1980.*

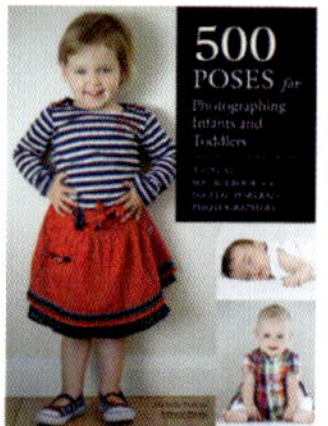

500 Poses for Photographing Infants and Toddlers

Michelle Perkins shares a host of top images from the industry's best to help you conceptualize and deliver the perfect kids' poses. *$34.95 list, 8.5x11, 128p, 500 color images, order no. 1991.*

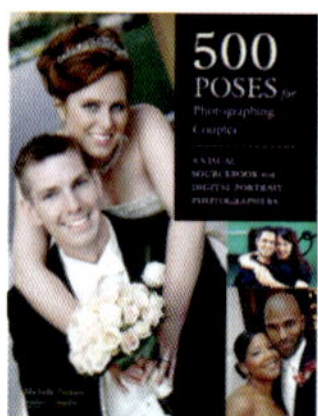

500 Poses for Photographing Couples

Michelle Perkins showcases an array of poses that will give you the creative boost you need to create an evocative, meaningful portrait. *$34.95 list, 8.5x11, 128p, 500 color images, order no. 1943.*

MORE PHOTO BOOKS AVAILABLE

Amherst Media®
PO BOX 586
BUFFALO, NY 14226 USA

Individuals: If possible, purchase books from an Amherst Media retailer. To order directly, visit our web site, or call the toll-free number listed below to place your order. All major credit cards are accepted. *Dealers, distributors & colleges:* Write, call, or fax to place orders. For price information, contact Amherst Media or an Amherst Media sales representative. Net 30 days.

(800) 622-3278 or (716) 874-4450
Fax: (716) 874-4508

All prices, publication dates, and specifications are subject to change without notice. Prices are in U.S. dollars. Payment in U.S. funds only.

WWW.AMHERSTMEDIA.COM
FOR A COMPLETE LIST OF BOOKS AND ADDITIONAL INFORMATION